The Clarendon Press for permission to reprint Milton's *Epitaphium Damonis,* edited by H. W. Garrod, from *The Poetical Works of John Milton* (Oxford, 1955), Vol. II, edited by Helen Darbishire; and pp. 71–88 from F. T. Prince's *The Italian Element in Milton's Verse* (Oxford, 1954).

Columbia University Press for permission to reprint Charles Knapp's translation of the "Argument" to the *Epitaphium Damonis* from Vol. I of *The Works of John Milton,* edited by Frank Patterson (New York, 1931).

Cornell University Press for permission to reprint pp. 170–195 from David Daiches' *A Study of Literature* (Ithaca, N. Y., 1948), as revised in *Milton* (London, 1957), pp. 73–92.

J. M. Dent & Sons (Canada), Limited, for permission to reprint p. 9 from A. S. P. Woodhouse's *Milton the Poet* (Toronto and Vancouver, 1955).

Harcourt, Brace & World, Inc., for permission to reprint "Essays in Analysis: *Lycidas,*" pp. 169–186 from *Poems of Mr. John Milton* by Cleanth Brooks and John Edward Hardy, copyright, 1951, by Harcourt, Brace & World, Inc. and reprinted with their permission.

Harvard University Press for permission to reprint "Theme, Pattern, and Imagery in *Lycidas,*" pp. 73–111 in Rosemond Tuve's *Images and Themes in Five Poems by Milton* (Cambridge, Mass.: Harvard University Press), copyright, 1957, by The President and Fellows of Harvard College.

The Macmillan Company for permission to reprint pp. 79–85 from E. M. W. Tillyard's *Milton* (New York, 1930).

The Modern Language Association of America for permission to reprint three articles from the *Publications of the Modern Language Association:* James H. Hanford, "The Pastoral Elegy and Milton's *Lycidas,*" XXV (1910), 403–447, as revised for this book by the editor; Richard P. Adams, "The Archetypal Pattern of Death and Rebirth in Milton's *Lycidas,*" LXIV (1949), 183–188, as condensed for this book by the author; and Wayne Shumaker, "Flowerets and Sounding Seas: A Study in the Affective Structure of Milton's *Lycidas,*" LXVI (1951), 485–494.

Princeton University Press for permission to reprint "How to Read *Lycidas,*" pp. 184–202 in Paul Elmer More's *On Being Human* (Princeton, N. J., 1936), copyright Princeton University Press; first published in the *American Review,* VII (1936), 140–158.

The University of California Press for permission to reprint, in revised form, pp. 86–90 from Josephine Miles' *The Primary Language of Poetry in the 1640's,* University of California Publications in English, XIX (1948).

University of North Carolina Press for permission to reprint Northrop Frye's "Literature as Context: Milton's *Lycidas,*" from *The Proceedings of the Second Congress of the International Comparative Literature Association,* edited by W. P. Friederich, University of North Carolina Studies in Comparative Literature, XXIII (1959), 44–55.

Helen Waddell for permission, granted through Constable and Company, Ltd., to reprint her translation of *Epitaphium Damonis,* privately printed in 1943 under the title *Lament for Damon.*

Samuel Johnson's observations on *Lycidas* are from his *Life of Milton,* first published in *The Works of the Most Eminent English Poets, with Prefaces, Biographical and Literary* (London, 1779), Vol. II, and later issued separately as *Lives of the Poets.*

Foreword

M. H. Abrams

On the basis of a decade of experiment with almost exactly the materials gathered in this book, I can bear witness that this is a very valuable anthology, remarkably versatile in its possibilities. It will be equally useful for courses in the history or theory of literary criticism and for courses in the introduction to literature, or in Milton, or in English poetry. It will be no less valuable for that person to whose formation all our educational endeavors are in theory directed, whose very existence has often been doubted, but who is now proving his reality by buying excellent paperbacks in enormous quantities —the cultivated reader, who turns to poetry not as an academic duty, but for illumination and delight.

The essays collected here manifest dramatically that criticism really matters. They silently refute the widespread opinion that a critic's theory—his stated principles and method of procedure—is merely a philosophical excursus, happily jettisoned when he gets down to his proper job of explicating and evaluating a text. With equal finality they refute the opinion (often but mistakenly deduced from the modern view that a poem is an "autonomous" object, to be discussed "as poetry and not another thing") that a literary work contains within itself everything needed for its interpretation and will yield its full and unequivocal meaning to any reader who will approach it with a lively sensibility, unimpeded by critical prepossessions or by historical knowledge of poetic kinds and conventions. For here we have fourteen critics, all of them skilled and sensitive readers, who address themselves to the one work and issue with an astonishing diversity of interpretations. The essays impress upon us that a poem, which looks so fixed and determinate on the printed page, is in fact a variable, dependent in a high degree not only on the "taste," but on the rational premises, categories, and criteria of a given critic, as well as on his tact, intelligence, and the range of pertinent historical knowledge he can bring to bear. The student of criticism finds his investigation of critical theories in the abstract come alive in this demonstration of the fascinating play of diverse theories put skillfully to work on a given text. On his side the student of poetry finds himself shocked into taking a fresh, long look at the poem and facing up to the hard but necessary questions (which some of these essayists themselves raise) about how we validate a critical assertion and about the proper role of the text and of its historical context in determining our choice between conflicting interpretations. That is why this mode of working with a classic text as the focus of sharp critical disagreement seems to me the most profitable recent innovation in the teaching of literature.

For such a use, Milton's *Lycidas* is the ideal document. It is short enough to be managed at a single reading, yet long and complex enough to raise all the basic issues and great enough to have attracted a large number of the best critics, whose essays have independent value as distinguished instances of the critical art. But hitherto the teacher has been thwarted by the need for the students to have simultaneous access to a great many books, some of them learned periodicals possessed only by large libraries and none of them in a sufficient number of copies to be practicable for any class larger than a small seminar. Professor Patrides has done us the service of making available to each student the equivalent of a sizable shelf of books, and he has made the collection self-sufficient by adding well-edited texts of Milton's two pastoral elegies as well as an annotated guide to everything important that has been written about *Lycidas*, which may be the greatest, and is at any rate the most often discussed, of all lyric poems.

Preface

"In *Lycidas*," declared Mark Pattison in 1879, "we have reached the high-water mark of English Poesy." If there has been no universal concurrence with this judgment, at least no impartial critic has ever failed to number the poem among the foremost productions of the human mind. Samuel Johnson was persuaded, certainly, that in *Lycidas* "the diction is harsh, the rhymes uncertain, and the numbers unpleasing"; but even then the judgment ran so far counter to the general estimate that William Cowper claimed, as many critics have since, that Dr. Johnson had "no ear for poetical numbers, or that it was stopped by prejudice against the harmony of Milton's."

Yet, as we know only too well, Dr. Johnson was often partly right even where he seems to have been most appallingly mistaken. Thus, while censuring the metaphysical poets, he was still perceptive enough to discern and comment upon the essential peculiarities of their achievement; and, similarly, when he attacked the form of *Lycidas* as "easy, vulgar, and therefore disgusting," he expressed precisely the dissatisfaction still felt by readers who are unfamiliar with the tradition of the pastoral elegy. The present edition, in part at least, hopes to eliminate this fundamental difficulty by making available, together with Milton's two pastoral elegies, Professor Hanford's comprehensive study of the elegiac tradition.

The appreciation of the tradition, however, forms only part of a proper background for the reading of *Lycidas*. Fundamentally, far more significant is our method of approach to the poem as a poem; and here, happily, we may seek the enlightened advice of a number of modern critics, most of them exponents of the remarkably varied theories of criticism advanced thus far in this century, who have concentrated on *Lycidas* as a poem deserving of special consideration. Fourteen such commentaries are made available here, printed in the chronological order of their original composition.

The Latin text of the *Epitaphium Damonis* is accompanied by Miss Helen Waddell's translation—decidedly not a literal translation, but one that captures the emotional intensity of the original to such an extent that it deserves greater attention than it has hitherto received. The first edition of the translation in 1943 was dedicated to "The Memory of George Frederick Waddell Martin, Major R.E., Served in the defence of Tobruk 1941, Killed March 17, 1942, Aged 23; And of the men, his brothers-in-arms, who died young."

Changes have been made only in three of the essays reprinted here. Professor Hanford's study, having appeared for the first time in 1910, necessitated slight changes in the light of subsequent work by other scholars; the revisions, undertaken with the author's permission, are indicated by brackets. Two essayists have been generous enough to revise their own work: Professor R. P. Adams, who has condensed his essay out of sympathy with my concern over the limited space at my disposal; and Professor Josephine Miles, who graciously consented to write an essay for this edition, a drastic revision of the section on *Lycidas* in *The Primary Language of Poetry in the 1640's* (1948). Of this revision Professor Miles writes, "Additional study of Milton's predecessors and successors makes it possible to discriminate the terms characteristic not only of the general mode of *Lycidas* but also of the poem as individual structure. The description of the language made in 1948 is therefore placed in the context of this further knowledge."

It is not to be thought that I was unassisted in my editorial tasks. Indeed, I am deeply obliged to numerous individuals for their concern with this edition, but particularly to Professor M. H. Abrams, who has encouraged me from the very beginning and has given generous advice on numerous aspects of this book; to Professor Wayne Shumaker for his welcomed criticism of the content and style of my work; to Professors Merritt Y. Hughes of the University of Wisconsin, A. S. P. Woodhouse of the University of Toronto, James H. Hanford of Princeton University, Rosemond Tuve of Connecticut College, Thomas P. Harrison of the University of Texas, Robert M. Durling of Cornell University, Eugene Brunelle of Mills College, and Bertrand H. Bronson, Howard Hugo, Alain Renoir, Robert L. McNulty, and Mrs. Dorothee M. Finkelstein of the University of California at Berkeley, for various suggestions; and to a number of editors of *Lycidas,* notably Miss Helen Darbishire and Professors Hughes, Hanford, Coffin, and

Fletcher. Finally, I am deeply grateful to Professor Abrams for permission to publish his essay on *Lycidas* in advance of its appearance in another volume.

This edition is dedicated to the late Charles M. Coffin. Shortly after my arrival from Greece, when good fortune led me to Kenyon College in 1948, the wonders of English literature were revealed to me principally by Professor Coffin. When at length I resolved to devote myself to the study of Milton, the deciding factor was the inspiration I received from Professor Coffin; so that should I in the future write something of value on Milton, it will be only a minor footnote to what he taught me of the Renaissance in general and of Milton in particular. In the meantime, this edition is a very small earthly recompense for his labors, not to be compared with the fairer guerdon he found upon his death on July 20, 1956.

C. A. P.

Berkeley, California
January 3, 1961

Contents

Lycidas

In this Monody the Author bewails a learned Friend, unfortunatly drown'd in his Passage from *Chester* on the *Irish* Seas, 1637. And by occasion foretels the ruine of our corrupted Clergy then in their height.

> Yet once more, O ye Laurels, and once more   *a*
> Ye Myrtles brown, with Ivy never-sear,   *b*
> I com to pluck your Berries harsh and crude, *c*
> And with forc't fingers rude,   *c*
> Shatter your leaves before the mellowing year. *b*   5
> Bitter constraint, and sad occasion dear,   *b*
> Compels me to disturb your season due: *c*

Lycidas, the "learned friend," is Edward King (1612–1637), the youngest of six sons of Sir John King, an Irish administrator. A promising youth distinguished by wide learning and a limited poetic faculty, King entertained thoughts of an ecclesiastical career. Soon he attracted the attention even of Charles I: the mandate of his election to a fellowship at Christ's College, Cambridge, states that His Majesty was "well ascertained both of the present sufficiency and future hopes" of young Edward (*DNB*, XI, 128). Milton, similarly impressed by King's "great Learning and Parts," contracted "a particular Friendship and Intimacy" with him (Edward Phillips, *The Life of Mr. John Milton*, 1694). King's untimely death occurred in August 1637 while he was on a journey to Ireland to visit members of his family. Milton's tribute was the last in a collection of memorial poems published in 1638. The present text is reprinted from the second edition of 1645 (see *infra*, Appendix I).

1–2   *Laurels, Myrtles, Ivy:* evergreens with which the ancient poets were crowned; thus traditional symbols of poetry
2   *never-sear:* never dry or withered
3   *crude:* unripe
6   *dear:* grievous

For *Lycidas* is dead, dead ere his prime,
Young *Lycidas,* and hath not left his peer:
Who would not sing for *Lycidas?* he knew   10
Himself to sing, and build the lofty rhyme.
He must not flote upon his watry bear
Unwept, and welter to the parching wind,
Without the meed of som melodious tear.

   Begin then, Sisters of the sacred well,   15
That from beneath the seat of *Jove* doth spring,
Begin, and somwhat loudly sweep the string.
Hence with denial vain, and coy excuse,
So may som gentle Muse
With lucky words favour my destin'd Urn,   20
And as he passes turn,
And bid fair peace be to my sable shrowd.
For we were nurst upon the self-same hill,
Fed the same flock, by fountain, shade, and rill.

   Together both, ere the high Lawns appear'd   25
Under the opening eye-lids of the morn,
We drove a field, and both together heard
What time the Gray-fly winds her sultry horn,
Batt'ning our flocks with the fresh dews of night,
Oft till the Star that rose, at Ev'ning, bright   30
Toward Heav'ns descent had slop'd his westering wheel.
Mean while the Rural ditties were not mute,
Temper'd to th'Oaten Flute,
Rough *Satyrs* danc'd, and *Fauns* with clov'n heel,
From the glad sound would not be absent long,   35

10–11	*he knew / Himself to sing:* King was the author of a modest number of Latin verses
13	*welter:* toss about
14	*melodious tear:* "tearful melody," mourning song, elegy in general
15	*Sisters:* the nine Muses, daughters of Zeus and Mnemosyne; the *sacred well* is the Pierian Spring, a fountain in ancient Macedonia, one of the earliest seats of their worship
18	*coy:* modest, disdainful
19	*Muse:* i.e., poet
20	*lucky:* auspicious
25	*high Lawns:* meadows, pastures
28	*winds:* blows
29	*Batt'ning:* feeding

And old *Damœtas* lov'd to hear our song.

But O the heavy change, now thou art gon,
Now thou art gon, and never must return!
Thee Shepherd, thee the Woods, and desert Caves,
With wilde Thyme and the gadding Vine o'regrown,   40
And all their echoes mourn.
The Willows, and the Hazle Copses green,
Shall now no more be seen,
Fanning their joyous Leaves to thy soft layes.
As killing as the Canker to the Rose,   45
Or Taint-worm to the weanling Herds that graze,
Or Frost to Flowers, that their gay wardrop wear,
When first the White thorn blows;
Such, *Lycidas*, thy loss to Shepherds ear.

Where were ye Nymphs when the remorseless deep   50
Clos'd o're the head of your lov'd *Lycidas?*
For neither were ye playing on the steep,
Where your old *Bards*, the famous *Druids* ly,
Nor on the shaggy top of *Mona* high,
Nor yet where *Deva* spreads her wisard stream: 55
Ay me, I fondly dream! *foolishly*
Had ye bin there—for what could that have don
What could the Muse her self that *Orpheus* bore,
The Muse her self, for her inchanting son
Whom Universal nature did lament,   60

---

36   *Damœtas:* possibly a tutor at Cambridge (for conjectures con-
      cerning his identity, see the entry under M. H. Nicolson, *infra*,
      p. 244)
40   *gadding:* straying
45   *the Canker:* the cankerworm
48   *the White thorn:* the hawthorne
53   *Druids:* members of a religious order in ancient Gaul, Britain,
      and Ireland
54   *Mona:* the isle of Anglesey, off the northern coast of Wales
55   *Deva:* the river Dee, which passes through Chester (the port from
      which King sailed to Ireland) and empties into the Irish Sea;
      called *wisard* because of its reputed powers of prophecy (cf.
      Druids)
56   *fondly:* foolishly
      the Muse: Calliope, the mother of Orpheus and chief of the nine
      Muses, who presided over eloquence and heroic poetry

When by the rout that made the hideous roar,
His goary visage down the stream was sent,
Down the swift *Hebrus* to the *Lesbian* shore.
  Alas! What boots it with uncessant care
To tend the homely slighted Shepherds trade,   65
And strictly meditate the thankles Muse,
Were it not better don as others use,
To sport with *Amaryllis* in the shade,
Or with the tangles of *Neæra's* hair?
Fame is the spur that the clear spirit doth raise   70
(That last infirmity of Noble mind)
To scorn delights, and live laborious dayes;
But the fair Guerdon when we hope to find,
And think to burst out into sudden blaze,
Comes the blind *Fury* with th'abhorred shears,   75
And slits the thin spun life. But not the praise,
Phœbus repli'ed, and touch'd my trembling ears;
Fame is no plant that grows on mortal soil,
Nor in the glistering foil
Set off to th'world, nor in broad rumour lies,   80
But lives and spreds aloft by those pure eyes,
And perfet witnes of all-judging *Jove*;

wouldn't it be better to have

61–63   Orpheus, traditionally regarded as "the father of song" (Pindar,
        Pythian Odes, IV, 176), is said to have withdrawn to the wilds of
        Rhodope and Haemus after the loss of Eurydice; but some
        Thracian maenads, infuriated because he paid no attention to
        them, dismembered him and cast his severed head into the river
        Hebrus, whence it floated to the island of Lesbos. Cf. Virgil,
        Georgics, IV, 517–527, and Ovid, *Metamorphoses,* XI, 1–60.
64   *boots:* profits
65   *Shepherds trade:* poet's craft
67   *use:* do
70   *clear:* pure
70–84   Cf. *Paradise Regained,* III, 47–70
73   *Guerdon:* reward
75   *the blind Fury:* Atropos, the "inflexible," one of the three fates of
        classical mythology, who cut the thread of life spun by Clotho and
        measured by Lachesis
77   *Phœbus:* Apollo, the god of youth, beauty, poetry and music.
        touch'd my trembling ears: a gesture of disapproval. Thus Apollo
        plucked Virgil's ear in an attempt to curtail his excessive ambition
        (Eclogue VI, 3–5). In part at least, the allusion may be to the
        predicament of Midas, who foolishly refused to acknowledge Apollo
        as the best musician and was punished with a pair of ass's ears
        (Ovid, *Metamorphoses,* XI, 146–179).

fun, do what you want to do.
Question the ask?

As he pronounces lastly on each deed,
Of so much fame in Heav'n expect thy meed.

    O Fountain *Arethuse*, and thou honour'd floud,   85
Smooth-sliding *Mincius*, crown'd with vocall reeds,
That strain I heard was of a higher mood:
But now my Oat proceeds,
And listens to the Herald of the Sea
That came in *Neptune's* plea,   90
He ask'd the Waves, and ask'd the Fellon winds,
What hard mishap hath doom'd this gentle swain?
And question'd every gust of rugged wings
That blows from off each beaked Promontory;
They knew not of his story,   95
And sage *Hippotades* their answer brings,
That not a blast was from his dungeon stray'd,
The Ayr was calm, and on the level brine,
Sleek *Panope* with all her sisters play'd.
It was that fatall and perfidious Bark   100
Built in th'eclipse, and rigg'd with curses dark,
That sunk so low that sacred head of thine.

    Next *Camus*, reverend Sire, went footing slow,
His Mantle hairy, and his Bonnet sedge, *genus of*
Inwrought with figures dim, and on the edge *place of*   105
Like to that sanguine flower inscrib'd with woe. *Cambridge*
Ah! Who hath reft (quoth he) my dearest pledge? *hyacenth*

85	*Arethuse:* a spring in the island of Ortygia at Syracuse near the birthplace of Theocritus; here used as symbolic of Sicilian bucolic poetry (cf. note to l. 132)
86	*Mincius:* Mincio, a river in Lombardy near the birthplace of Virgil; here used as symbolic of Latin pastoral poetry
88	*Oat:* oaten pipe (cf. l. 33)
89	*the Herald of the Sea:* Triton, a sea demigod, son of Poseidon and Amphitrite; the sounding of his trumpet raised or calmed the waves.
96	*Hippotades:* Aeolus, the mythical god of the winds
99	*Panope:* a sea-nymph, one of the numerous daughters of Nereus and Doris who attended upon Poseidon
103	*Camus:* the river Cam at Cambridge, symbolizing the university
106	*that sanguine flower inscrib'd with woe:* the hyacinth; according to legend, a flower sprung from the blood of Hyacinthus, a beautiful Spartan prince unwittingly slain by his lover Apollo, was marked in such a way as to bear the Greek word "alas" (AI). Cf. Apollodorus, *Bibliotheca*, I, iii, 3; Lucian, *Dial. deorum*, XIV; and Ovid, *Metamorphoses*, X, 162–219.

Last came, and last did go,
The Pilot of the *Galilean* lake,
Two massy Keyes he bore of metals twain,   110
(The Golden opes, the Iron shuts amain)
He shook his Miter'd locks, and stern bespake,
How well could I have spar'd for thee young swain.
Anow of such as for their bellies sake,
Creep and intrude, and climb into the fold?   115
Of other care they little reck'ning make,
Then how to scramble at the shearers feast,
And shove away the worthy bidden guest.
Blind mouthes! that scarce themselves know how to hold
A Sheep-hook, or have learn'd ought els the least   120
That to the faithfull Herdmans art belongs!
What recks it them? What need they? They are sped;
And when they list, their lean and flashy songs
Grate on their scrannel Pipes of wretched straw,
The hungry Sheep look up, and are not fed,   125
But swoln with wind, and the rank mist they draw,
Rot inwardly, and foul contagion spread:
Besides what the grim Woolf with privy paw
Daily devours apace, and nothing sed,
But that two-handed engine at the door,   130
Stands ready to smite once, and smite no more.

---

109   *The Pilot of the Galilean lake:* St. Peter, keeper of the keys of
         heaven (Matthew 16:19) and the first bishop of the Church (cf.
         l. 112: *Miter'd locks*)
111   *amain:* with force
114 ff. There are a number of Biblical echoes here, as from John 10:1
         ("He that entereth not by the door into the sheepfold, but climbeth
         up some other way, the same is a thief and a robber") and I Peter
         5:2–4 ("Feed the flock of God which is among you, taking the
         oversight thereof, not by constraint, but willingly; not for filthy
         lucre, but of a ready mind. . . . And when the chief Shepherd
         shall appear, ye shall receive a crown of glory that fadeth not
         away").
119   *Blind mouthes:* see Ruskin's explanatory comment on this double
         metaphor, *infra*, p. 245.
120   *Sheep-hook:* the bishop's pastoral staff
122   *They are sped:* they have prospered
124   *scrannel:* weak, feeble
130–131 For various interpretations of this famous riddle, see *infra*, pp.
         240–241

Return *Alpheus*, the dread voice is past,
That shrunk thy streams; Return *Sicilian* Muse,
And call the Vales, and bid them hither cast
Their Bels, and Flourets of a thousand hues.   135
Ye valleys low where the milde whispers use,
Of shades and wanton winds, and gushing brooks,
On whose fresh lap the swart Star sparely looks,
Throw hither all your quaint enameld eyes,
That on the green terf suck the honied showres,   140
And purple all the ground with vernal flowres.
Bring the rathe Primrose that forsaken dies.
The tufted Crow-toe, and pale Gessamine,
The white Pink, and the Pansie freakt with jeat,
The glowing Violet.   145
The Musk-rose, and the well attir'd Woodbine,
With Cowslips wan that hang the pensive hed,
And every flower that sad embroidery wears:
Bid *Amaranthus* all his beauty shed,
And Daffadillies fill their cups with tears,   150
To strew the Laureat Herse where *Lycid* lies.
For so to interpose a little ease,
Let our thoughts dally with false surmise.
Ay me! Whilst thee the shores, and sounding Seas
Wash far away, where ere thy bones are hurld,   155
Whether beyond the stormy *Hebrides*,

132   *Alpheus:* a river in Arcady; according to legend, after the river
       god Alpheus was enamored of the wood nymph Arethusa, she
       was transformed by Artemis into a subterranean stream which,
       still pursued by Alpheus, rose again in the *Fountain Arethuse*
       (l. 85) on the island of Ortygia at Syracuse. Cf. Pausanias, *De-
       scriptio Graeciae,* V, vii, 2, and Ovid, *Metamorphoses,* V, 865–978.
133   *Sicilian Muse:* i.e., of Theocritus and the Greek bucolic poets in
       general
136   *use:* are wont to reside
138   *the swart Star:* Sirius, the Dog Star, under whose malign influence
       vegetation withers
142   *rathe:* early
144   *freakt:* freckled, spotted
149   *Amaranthus:* literally, "the unfading flower"—an imaginary flower
       reputed never to fade (cf. *Paradise Lost,* III, 353: "Immortal
       Amarant")
156   *Hebrides:* islands off the west coast of Scotland

Where thou perhaps under the whelming tide
Visit'st the bottom of the monstrous world;
Or whether thou to our moist vows deny'd,
Sleep'st by the fable of *Bellerus* old,   160
Where the great vision of the guarded Mount
Looks toward *Namancos* and *Bayona's* hold;
Look homeward Angel now, and melt with ruth,
And, O ye *Dolphins*, waft the haples youth.

　　Weep no more, woful Shepherds weep no more,   165
For *Lycidas* your sorrow is not dead,
Sunk though he be beneath the watry floar,
So sinks the day-star in the Ocean bed,
And yet anon repairs his drooping head,
And tricks his beams, and with new spangled Ore,   170
Flames in the forehead of the morning sky:
So *Lycidas* sunk low, but mounted high,
Through the dear might of him that walk'd the waves;
Where other groves, and other streams along,
With *Nectar* pure his oozy Lock's he laves,   175
And hears the unexpressive nuptiall Song,
In the blest Kingdoms meek of joy and love.
There entertain him all the Saints above,
In solemn troops, and sweet Societies
That sing, and singing in their glory move,   180

158　　　*the monstrous world:* the world of [sea] monsters
159　　　*moist vows:* tearful prayers
160　　　*Bellerus:* a mythical giant, here connected with Bellerium, the
　　　　　Roman name for Land's End in the extreme southeast of Cornwall
161　　　*the guarded Mount:* Mount St. Michael in Cornwall, guarded by
　　　　　the archangel; *the great vision* refers to the *fable* (l. 160) that
　　　　　Michael is often seen at the mountain's summit.
162　　　*Namancos and Bayona's [strong]hold:* districts in Spain; thus *the
　　　　　great vision* is conceived as looking southward.
163　　　*Angel:* i.e., Michael, *the great vision,* to whom the poet is now
　　　　　addressing his plea for mercy (*melt with ruth*)
168　　　*the day-star:* the sun
169　　　*repairs:* renovates
170　　　*tricks:* adorns, decks
173　　　*him that walk'd the waves:* Christ, whom "the disciples saw . . .
　　　　　walking on the sea" (Matthew 14:26)
176　　　*the unexpressive nuptiall Song:* the inexpressible marriage song
　　　　　(cf. Revelation 19:9: "Blessed are they which are called unto the
　　　　　marriage supper of the Lamb"). In using the marriage metaphor
　　　　　at this point, Milton is invoking a tradition extending from the
　　　　　Mosaic era through the great prophets (notably Hosea and Jere-
　　　　　miah) to the Johannine Apocalypse.

And wipe the tears for ever from his eyes.
Now *Lycidas* the Shepherds weep no more;
Henceforth thou art the Genius of the shore,
In thy large recompense, and shalt be good
To all that wander in that perilous flood.
    Thus sang the uncouth Swain to th'Okes and rills,
While the still morn went out with Sandals gray,
He touch'd the tender stops of various Quills,
With eager thought warbling his *Dorick* lay:
And now the Sun had stretch'd out all the hills,   190
And now was dropt into the Western bay;
At last he rose, and twitch'd his Mantle blew:
To morrow to fresh Woods, and Pastures new.

181	As before (ll. 114 ff.), Biblical allusions abound in this section—such as Revelation 7:17 and 21:4 ("God shall wipe away all tears from their eyes").
183	*Genius:* guardian spirit
184	*recompense:* reward
186	*the uncouth Swain:* the unknown or rustic poet—the anonymous singer of the pastoral poem, here concluding the *melodious tear* in regular ottava rima
189	*Dorick:* the dialect of the Greek bucolic poets; hence, "pastoral"

In affect does answer questions in very human forens

what do you do when good die

attacks clergy. Gos back to traditional finding chic neuma.

to joe

abbey busine

after someone die

185

CORRIGENDA

Textual notes are listed *infra*, Appendix I. Here, for the convenience of the reader, are indicated the most significant corrections made by Milton in the course of his composition of *Lycidas*. The corrections are reproduced from the manuscript of the poem presently at Trinity College, Cambridge.

Lines

4-5   ~~before the mellowing yeare~~ and wth forc't fingers rude

      ~~and crop yor young~~ shatter yor leaves before ye mellowing yeare

8   for ~~young~~ Lycidas

10   he well knew

22   and ~~to~~ bid

26   ~~glimmering;~~ *in margin:* opening

30   oft till the ~~ev'n~~ starre ~~bright~~ that rose in Evning bright

31   ~~burnisht;~~ *in margin:* westring

47   ~~buttons weare beare;~~ *in margin:* wardrope weare

51   ~~youn~~ lov'd Lycidas

57-63   ~~had yee~~ bin there, ~~for~~ what could that have don?

      ~~what could the golden hayrd Calliope~~

      for her inchaunting son

      ~~when shee beheld (the gods farre sighted bee)~~

      ~~his goarie scalpe rowle downe the Thracian lee~~

                 *whome universal nature

                   might lament

                 ~~and heaven and hel deplore~~

                 ~~when his divine head downe~~

                   the streame was sent

                   downe the swift Hebrus to

                     the Lesbian shore.

      Re-written thus:

     what could the muse her selfe that Orpheus bore

     the muse her selfe for her inchaunting son.

     ~~for her inchanting son~~

                 did

     whome universal nature ~~might~~ lament

     when by the rout that made the hideous roare

               gorie

*goarie   his ~~divine~~ ∧ visage downe the streame was sent downe the swift Hebrus to ye Lesbian shoare.

69 ~~hid in;~~ *in margin:* or with

85 ~~smooth;~~ *in margin:* fam'd; *then corrected to* honour'd

86 ~~soft;~~ *in margin:* smooth

105 scraul'd ore, *not crossed out; but margin has:* inwraught

129 ~~nothing;~~ *in margin:* little; *but* nothing *restored*

138 ~~sparely;~~ *in margin:* faintly; *but* sparely *restored*

139 ~~bring;~~ *in margin:* throw

142-150 Bring the rathe primrose that unwedded dies

~~collu~~ colouring the pale cheeke of uninjoyd love

and that sad floure that strove

to write his owne woes on the vermeil graine

next adde Narcissus y^t still weeps in vaine

the woodbine and ye pancie freak't wth jet

the glowing violet

the cowslip wan that hangs his pensive head

and every bud that sorrows liverie weares

let Daffadillies fill thire cups ∧^{with} teares

bid Amaranthus all his beautie shed

to strew the laureat herse &c.

Above passage cancelled; then re-written thus:

Bring the rathe primrose that forsaken dies

the tufted crowtoe and pale Gessamin

the white pinke, and ∧^{y^e} pansie freakt wth jet

the glowing violet the well-attir'd woodbine

the muske rose and ~~the garish columbine~~

wth cowslips wan that hang the pensive head

and every flower that sad escutcheon ∧ ~~beares~~ ✗^{weare} imbroidrie ~~beares~~ ✗^{weares}

2 ∧^{&} ~~let~~ daffadillies fill thire cups wth teares

1 bid Amaranthus all his beauties shed

to strew &c.

153 ~~sad;~~ *in margin:* fraile

154 ~~floods;~~ *in margin:* shoars

157 the humming tide

160 ~~Corineus;~~ *in margin:* Bellerus

176 ~~listening;~~ *in margin:* & heares

Epitaphium Damonis
edited by H. W. GARROD

ARGUMENTUM

Thyrsis & Damon ejusdem vinciniæ Pastores, eadem studia
sequuti a pueritiâ amici erant, ut qui plurimùm. Thyrsis animi
causâ profectus peregrè de obitu Damonis nuncium accepit.
Domum postea reversus, & rem ita esse comperto, se, suamque
solitudinem hoc carmine deplorat. Damonis autem sub personâ
hîc intelligitur Carolus Deodatus ex urbe Hetruriæ Luca paterno
genere oriundus, cætera Anglus; ingenio, doctrina, clarissimisque
cæteris virtutibus, dum viveret, juvenis egregius.

Himerides nymphæ (nam vos & Daphnin & Hylan,
Et plorata diu meministis fata Bionis)
Dicite Sicelicum Thamesina per oppida carmen:
Quas miser effudit voces, quæ murmura Thyrsis,
Et quibus assiduis exercuit antra querelis,   5
Fluminaque, fontesque vagos, nemorumque recessus,
Dum sibi præreptum queritur Damona, neque altam
Luctibus exemit noctem loca sola pererrans.
Et jam bis viridi surgebat culmus arista,
Et totidem flavas numerabant horrea messes,   10
Ex quo summa dies tulerat Damona sub umbras,
Nec dum aderat Thyrsis, pastorem scilicet illum
Dulcis amor Musæ Thusca retinebat in urbe.

Ast ubi mens expleta domum, pecorisque relicti
Cura vocat, simul assuetâ sedítque sub ulmo, 15
Tum vero amissum tum denique sentit amicum,
Cœpit & immensum sic exonerare dolorem.
    Ite domum impasti, domino jam non vacat, agni.
Hei mihi! quæ terris, quæ dicam numina cœlo,
Postquam te immiti rapuerunt funere, Damon? 20
Siccine nos linquis, tua sic sine nomine virtus
Ibit, & obscuris numero fociabitur umbris?
At non ille, animas virgâ qui dividit aureâ,
Ista velit, dignumque tui te ducat in agmen,
Ignavumque procul pecus arceat omne silentum. 25
    Ite domum impasti, domino jam non vacat, agni.
Quicquid erit, certè nisi me lupus antè videbit,
Indeplorato non comminuere sepulcro,
Constabitque tuus tibi honos, longúmque vigebit
Inter pastores, illi tibi vota secundo 30
Solvere post Daphnin, post Daphnin dicere laudes
Gaudebunt, dum rura Pales, dum Faunus amabit:
Si quid id est, priscamque fidem coluisse, piúmque,
Palladiásque artes, sociúmque habuisse canorum.
    Ite domum impasti, domino jam non vacat, agni. 35
Hæc tibi certa manent, tibi erunt hæc præmia, Damon,
At mihi quid tandem fiet modò? quis mihi fidus
Hærebit lateri comes, ut tu sæpe solebas
Frigoribus duris, & per loca fœta pruinis,
Aut rapido sub sole, siti morientibus herbis? 40
Sive opus in magnos fuit eminùs ire leones
Aut avidos terrere lupos præsepibus altis;
Quis fando sopire diem, cantuque solebit?
    Ite domum impasti, domino jam non vacat, agni.
Pectora cui credam? quis me lenire docebit 45
Mordaces curas, quis longam fallere noctem
Dulcibus alloquiis, grato cùm sibilat igni
Molle pyrum, & nucibus strepitat focus, at malus auster
Miscet cuncta foris, & desuper intonat ulmo.
    Ite domum impasti, domino jam non vacat, agni. 50
Aut æstate, dies medio dum virtitur axe,
Cum Pan æsculeâ somnum capit abditus umbrâ,
Et repetunt sub aquis sibi nota sedilia nymphæ,

Pastoresque latent, stertit sub sepe colonus,
Quis mihi blanditiásque tuas, quis tum mihi risus,   55
Cecropiosque sales referet, cultosque lepores?
   Ite domum impasti, domino jam non vacat, agni.
At jam solus agros, jam pascua solus oberro,
Sicubi ramosæ densantur vallibus umbræ,
Hic serum expecto, supra caput imber & Eurus   60
Triste sonant, fractæque agitata crepuscula silvæ.
   Ite domum impasti, domino jam non vacat, agni.
Heu quàm culta mihi priùs arva procacibus herbis
Involvuntur, & ipsa situ seges alta fatiscit!
Innuba neglecto marcescit & uva racemo,   65
Nec myrteta juvant; ovium quoque tædet, at illæ
Mœrent, inque suum convertunt ora magistrum.
   Ite domum impasti, domino jam non vacat, agni.
Tityrus ad corylos vocat, Alphesibœus ad ornos,
Ad salices Aegon, ad flumina pulcher Amyntas,   70
Hîc gelidi fontes, hîc illita gramina musco,
Hîc Zephyri, hîc placidas interstrepit arbutus undas;
Ista canunt surdo, frutices ego nactus abibam.
   Ite domum impasti, domino jam non vacat, agni.
Mopsus ad hæc, nam me redeuntem forte notârat   75
(Et callebat avium linguas, & sydera Mopsus)
Thyrsi quid hoc? dixit, quæ te coquit improba bilis?
Aut te perdit amor, aut te malè fascinat astrum,
Saturni grave sæpe fuit pastoribus astrum,
Intimaque obliquo figit præcordia plumbo.   80
   Ite domum impasti, domino jam non vacat, agni.
Mirantur nymphæ, & quid <de> te, Thyrsi, futurum est?
Quid tibi vis? ajunt, non hæc solet esse juventæ
Nubila frons, oculique truces, vultusque severi,
Illa choros, lususque leves, & semper amorem   85
Jure petit, bis ille miser qui serus amavit.
   Ite domum impasti, domino jam non vacat, agni.
Venit Hyas, Dryopéque, & filia Baucidis Aegle
Docta modos, citharæque sciens, sed perdita fastu,
Venit Idumanii Chloris vicina fluénti;   90
Nil me blanditiæ, nil me solantia verba,
Nil me, si quid adest, movet, aut spes ulla futuri.
   Ite domum impasti, domino jam non vacat, agni.

Hei mihi quam similes ludunt per prata juvenci,
Omnes unanimi secum sibi lege sodales,   95
Nec magis hunc alio quisquam secernit amicum
De grege, sic densi veniunt ad pabula thoes,
Inque vicem hirsuti paribus junguntur onagri;
Lex eadem pelagi, deserto in littore Proteus
Agmina Phocarum numerat, vilisque volucrum   100
Passer habet semper quicum sit, & omnia circum
Farra libens volitet, serò sua tecta revisens,
Quem si fors letho objecit, seu milvus adunco
Fata tulit rostro, seu stravit arundine fossor,
Protinus ille alium socio petit inde volatu.   105
Nos durum genus, & diris exercita fatis
Gens homines aliena animis, & pectore discors,
Vix sibi quisque parem de millibus invenit unum,
Aut si sors dederit tandem non aspera votis,
Illum inopina dies quâ non speraveris horâ   110
Surripit, æternum linquens in sæcula damnum.

    Ite domum impasti, domino jam non vacat, agni.
Heu quis me ignotas traxit vagus error in oras
Ire per aëreas rupes, Alpemque nivosam!
Ecquid erat tanti Romam vidisse sepultam,   115
Quamvis illa foret, qualem dum viseret olim,
Tityrus ipse suas & oves & rura reliquit,
Ut te tam dulci possem caruisse sodale,
Possem tot maria alta, tot interponere montes,
Tot sylvas, tot saxa tibi, fluviosque sonantes?   120
Ah certè extremùm licuisset tangere dextram,
Et bene compositos placidè morientis ocellos,
Et dixisse vale, nostri memor ibis ad astra.

    Ite domum impasti, domino jam non vacat, agni.
Quamquam etiam vestri nunquam meminisse pigebit,   125
Pastores Thusci, Musis operata juventus,
Hic Charis, atque Lepos; & Thuscus tu quoque Damon,
Antiquâ genus unde petis Lucumonis ab urbe.
O ego quantus eram, gelidi cum stratus ad Arni
Murmura, populeumque nemus quà mollior herba,   130
Carpere nunc violas, nunc summas carpere myrtos,
Et potui Lycidæ certantem audire Menalcam.
Ipse etiam tentare ausus sum, nec puto multùm

Displicui, nam sunt & apud me munera vestra
Fiscellæ, calathique & cerea vincla cicutæ,   135
Quin & nostra suas docuerunt nomina fagos
Et Datus, & Francinus, erant & vocibus ambo
Et studiis noti, Lydorum sanguinis ambo.
   Ite domum impasti, domino jam non vacat, agni.
Hæc mihi tum læto dictabat roscida luna,   140
Dum solus teneros claudebam cratibus hœdos.
Ah quoties dixi, cùm te cinis ater habebat,
Nunc canit, aut lepori nunc tendit retia Damon,
Vimina nunc texit, varios sibi quod sit in usus;
Et quæ tum facili sperabam mente futura   145
Arripui voto levis, & præsentia finxi,
Heus bone numquid agis? nisi te quid forte retardat,
Imus? & argutâ paulùm recubamus in umbra,
Aut ad aquas Colni, aut ubi jugera Cassibelauni?
Tu mihi percurres medicos, tua gramina, succos,   150
Helleborûmque, humilésque crocos, foliûmque hyacinthi,
Quasque habet ista palus herbas, artesque medentûm.
Ah pereant herbæ, pereant artesque medentûm,
Gramina postquam ipsi nil profecere magistro.
Ipse etiam, nam nescio quid mihi grande sonabat   155
Fistula, ab undecimâ jam lux est altera nocte,
Et tum forte novis admôram labra cicutis,
Dissiluere tamen rupta compage, nec ultra
Ferre graves potuere sonos, dubito quoque ne sim
Turgidulus, tamen & referam, vos cedite silvæ.   160
   Ite domum impasti, domino jam non vacat, agni.
Ipse ego Dardanias Rutupina per æquora puppes
Dicam, & Pandrasidos regnum vetus Inogeniæ,
Brennúmque Arviragúmque duces, priscúmque Belinum,
Et tandem Armoricos Britonum sub lege colonos;   165
Tum gravidam Arturo fatali fraude Jögernen,
Mendaces vultus, assumptáque Gorlöis arma,
Merlini dolus. O mihi tum si vita supersit,
Tu procul annosa pendebis fistula pinu
Multùm oblita mihi, aut patriis mutata camœnis   170
Brittonicum strides, quid enim? omnia non licet uni
Non sperasse uni licet omnia, mi satis ampla
Merces, & mihi grande decus (sim ignotus in ævum

Tum licet, externo penitúsque inglorius orbi)
Si me flava comas legat Usa, & potor Alauni,   175
Vorticibúsque frequens Abra, & nemus omne Treantæ,
Et Thamesis meus ante omnes, & fusca metallis
Tamara, & extremis me discant Orcades undis.
   Ite domum impasti, domino jam non vacat, agni.
Hæc tibi servabam lentâ sub cortice lauri,   180
Hæc, & plura simul, tum quæ mihi pocula Mansus,
Mansus Chalcidicæ non ultima gloria ripæ
Bina dedit, mirum artis opus, mirandus & ipse,
Et circùm gemino cælaverat argumento:
In medio rubri maris unda, & odoriferum ver,   185
Littora longa Arabum, & sudantes balsama silvæ,
Has inter Phœnix divina avis, unica terris
Cæruleùm fulgens diversicoloribus alis
Auroram vitreis surgentem respicit undis.
Parte alia polus omnipatens, & magnus Olympus,   190
Quis putet? hic quoque Amor, pictæque in nube pharetræ,
Arma corusca faces, & spicula tincta pyropo;
Nec tenues animas, pectúsque ignobile vulgi
Hinc ferit, at circùm flammantia lumina torquens
Semper in erectum spargit sua tela per orbes   195
Impiger, & pronos nunquam collimat ad ictus,
Hinc mentes ardere sacræ, formæque deorum.
   Tu quoque in his, nec me fallit spes lubrica, Damon,
Tu quoque in his certè es, nam quò tua dulcis abiret
Sanctáque simplicitas, nam quò tua candida virtus?   200
Nec te Lethæo fas quæsivisse sub orco,
Nec tibi conveniunt lacrymæ, nec flebimus ultrà,
Ite procul lacrymæ, purum colit æthera Damon,
Æthera purus habet, pluvium pede reppulit arcum;
Heroúmque animas inter, divósque perennes,   205
Æthereos haurit latices & gaudia potat
Ore Sacro. Quin tu cœli post jura recepta
Dexter ades, placidúsque fave quicúnque vocaris,
Seu tu noster eris Damon, sive æquior audis
Diodotus, quo te divino nomine cuncti   210
Cœlicolæ norint, sylvísque vocabere Damon.
Quòd tibi purpureus pudor, & sine labe juventus
Grata fuit, quòd nulla tori libata voluptas,

En etiam tibi virginei servantur honores;
Ipse caput nitidum cinctus rutilante corona,　　　　215
Letáque frondentis gestans umbracula palmæ
Æternùm perages immortales hymenæos;
Cantus ubi, choreisque furit lyra mista beatis,
Festa Sionæo bacchantur & Orgia Thyrso.

*L*ament for Damon

translated by HELEN WADDELL

ARGUMENT

Thyrsis and Damon, shepherds of the same neighborhood, devoted to the same pursuits, were friends from boyhood up, friends as close as ever men were. Thyrsis, while on a journey for pleasure's sake, received, in foreign lands, a message telling of his friend's death. Later, after his return home, when he found that the message was true, he bemoaned himself and his loneliness. In this poem, by "Damon" is meant Charles Diodati, descended on his father's side from the Etruscan city of Lucca. In all things else he was an Englishman, a youth, the while he lived, pre-eminent in intellect, in learning, and in all the other brightest and fairest virtues.

> *O nymphs that haunt the old Sicilian stream,*
> *Himera's stream, you that do still remember*
> *Daphnis and Hylas, and the death of Bion*
> *Lamented these long years,*
> *Sing dirge beside these English river towns,*   5
> *Sing by the Thames, as once in Sicily,*
> *The low lament, the ceaseless bitter weeping*
> *That broke the quiet of the caves,*
> *River and forest ride and fleeting water,*
> *Where Thyrsis went, bewailing his lost Damon,*   10
> *Walking at dead of night in the silent places*
> *Uncomforted, alone.*

It is the second year.
Twice has the green corn come to ear,
And twice the barns are filled with golden grain,   15
Since the ending day that took him to the shadows,
And I not there. I was in Tuscany,
Making my verses.
But now, my mind assuaged and the old task calling,
Now that I am come home,   20
Sitting again beneath the familiar elm,
Now, now, I know him gone,
And know how vast my grief.

Away, my lambs, unfed : your shepherd heeds you not.

O grief! what gods are there in heaven or earth   25
That I can cry to, since they've taken thee
In unrelenting death? O Damon, so to leave us,
And all thy valour pass, and no man name thee
In that dim fellowship of shades? Ah no!
Sure He whose golden bough divides men's souls   30
Shall lead thee to thy chosen company
And keep at bay the sluggish silent herd.

Away, my lambs, unfed : your shepherd heeds you not.

What e'er befall—unless the wolf first spy me—
Thou shalt not moulder in an unwept grave.   35
Thy honour shall abide, and have long life
Among the shepherds : thou wilt be remembered
When they remember Daphnis, after Daphnis
They'll fall to praising you, whilst the kind gods
Of field and fold still haunt the countryside :   40
If it be aught to have kept the ancient faith,
And loved the arts, and had a poet friend.

Away, my lambs, unfed : your shepherd heeds you not.

These things are yours, O Damon, they are yours,
And yours for ever :   45
But Damon, Damon, what's to become of me?
Who'll walk with me forever by my side,

As you did, through the frost and through the mire,
In the fierce sun, the thirsting dying grass?
Or face the lion but a spear's cast off, 50
Or scare the hungry wolves from the high folds?
Or talking, singing, lull the day to sleep?

Away, my lambs, unfed : your shepherd heeds you not.

To whom can I speak my heart? To whom shall I go
To learn to master the dark thoughts that tear me, 55
And cheat the night with talking, while the pears
Are hissing on the fire and all the hearth
Crackling with chestnuts, and the wind from the South
Is wrecking all without, and overhead
The elm tree cries and groans? 60

Away, my lambs, unfed : your shepherd heeds you not.

Summer and noon, Pan sleeping under the oak,
The nymphs all fled to their cool haunt under the waters,
The shepherds gone to the shade and the swineherd snoring—
But who will bring me back that smiling enchantment, 65
The Greek salt of your wit, and all your ways?

Away, my lambs, unfed : your shepherd heeds you not.

Alone through the plough lands I go, alone through the pas-
ture,
Down where the branching trees grow thick in the valley,
There do I wait the night : above my head 70
Sadly the west wind sighs and the falling rain,
And sighs the shivering twilight of the trees.

Away, my lambs, unfed : your shepherd heeds you not.

The fields that once I ploughed are tangled with weeds,
Couch grass and bindweed : and the standing corn 75
Bows and rots where it grew : the virgin grape
Is shrivelling where it hangs on the unkempt vine.
I am sick of my sheep and the pitiful creatures bleat,
Crowding reproachful faces around their master.

Away, my lambs, unfed : your shepherd heeds you not. 80

One lad shouts from the hazels, and one from the rowans,
One is among the willows, and one by the river.
"Here's a spring well, and grass that is silky with moss,
A warm west wind and water lapping the branches"—
They cry to a deaf man. There's sanctuary in the forest.   85

Away, my lambs, unfed : your shepherd heeds you not. . . .

O God, if one were a bullock!
All of them moving together roaming the field,
Any steer of the herd as good a friend as another.
The jackals crowd at their feasting, and the wild ass   90
Will rub his shaggy head against his neighbour
Indifferent of choice.
This too is the law of the sea : out on the desolate sands
Proteus calls, and the seals come to him in shoals.
Aye, even the lowly sparrow   95
Has never far to seek for company,
Cheerfully pecking his grain, flickering here and there,
Homing again at dusk to the familiar eaves :
Yet should Fate strike down his comrade,
Spitted on beak of hawk, or limed in a ditch,   100
Straight is he off again, the sociable creature,
To find another mate.
But what of men?
Men, the hard stock, schooled by grim destiny,
Alien, aloof in soul,   105
Discordant in their hearts?
Hardly in thousands may a man find one
That is his fellow.
And if at last Fate hath not proved unkind,
Hath given the heart's desire,   110
Comes stealthily the day you had not looked for,
The hour undreaded,
And snatches him, and leaves loss infinite,
For ever and for ever.

Away, my lambs, unfed : your shepherd heeds you not.   115

O grief! what craze for wandering captured me,
Drew me to unknown shores,

Climbing the sky-flung rocks, the Alps in snow?
Was it so great a thing to look on Rome,
Low in her grave—   120
Even had she been as when the Virgilian shepherd
Left his own flocks and herds to gaze on her—
When for her I must lack thy company
And set between us deep estranging seas,
Mountains and woods and rocks and sounding rivers?   125
O had it but been given me at the last
To touch thy hand in the still hour of dying,
And close those eyes beneath the carven brows,
And say "Farewell : go forth on thy high journey :
And still remember me."   130

Away, my lambs, unfed : your shepherd heeds you not.

God knows I do not grudge the memory
Of you, the men I found in Tuscany,
Poets and shepherds : Grace and Wit are there—
And Damon, Damon was himself a Tuscan,   135
His father's house from Lucca of the kings,
Etruscan kings and priests.
How high my heart was, stretched beside the Arno
Cool-fleeting past me, or in shadow of the poplars,
Where the grass is deeper, and violets to gather,   140
Myrtle to reach high for, listening to my poets
Arguing and versing : and sometimes, greatly daring,
I too made verses, that did not much displease.
Dati, Francini, I still have the gifts you gave me,
Fruit baskets, wine bowls, wax for my shepherd's flute. 145
Still I remember the song you made about us,
Singing under the beeches : lyric poets and scholars,
Both of you famous, both of Etruscan blood.

Away, my lambs, unfed : your shepherd heeds you not.

How I would dream there, at moonrise and dewfall,   150
Solitary, closing in the little tender goats,
How often said—and the earth dark above thee!—
"Damon will be singing now, or out to trap a hare,
Weaving his osiers for all his little contraptions!"

And so light-hearted, so sure was I of to-morrow,   155
I held it in my hand, the time to come.
Here! are you busy? If there is nothing you must do,
Shall we go and lie in the glancing quivering shade
Down by the Colne, or the fields above St. Albans,
And you can recite me all your herbs and simples,   160
Hellebore and iris and the saffron-crocus,
And the herbs in the marshland and all the arts of healing.
—O perish all the herbs, and all the arts of healing,
Perish all the simples that could not save their master!
And I—more than a se'nnight gone—so grand, so grave
     a note   165
Rang from my pipe—I scarce had put my lips to it,
The reeds were new—and yet they leapt asunder,
Broke at the join, and that deep resonance
Could bear no more.
I fear I am too bold : yet let me speak,   170
Speak to the silent woods.

Away, my lambs, unfed : your shepherd heeds you not.

I shall sing of the Trojan prows
Cleaving the seas beneath the cliffs of Kent,
And the old Kingdom that was Imogen's,   175
And Arvirach, was son to Cymbeline,
And Bren and Belin, ancient British captains,
And the Breton coast brought under Britain's law,
And Igraine great with child that shall be Arthur,
And the false face of Uther that begat him,   180
Masking her husband's likeness and his armour,
Through Merlin's guile. O, if I live, yet live,
Thou shalt hang, my shepherd's pipe, on some ancient pine,
Remote, all but forgotten—
Unless thou change thy note   185
From the classic cadence to the harsher speech
Of the English tongue.
And then? What then?
It is not given to one man to have all things,
Or even to hope for all things.   190
Enough, enough for me, and grand the honour—

Although I be unknown in time to come,
Yea, be inglorious in the outer world—
If my own folk will chant me in the meadows
Beside the cowslip Ouse and the springs of Allen   195
And the swirling tides of the Severn, and wooded Trent,
And Thames—above all, my Thames—and Tamar tawny
    with ore,
And the far Orkneys in the furthest seas.

Away, my lambs, unfed : your shepherd heeds you not.

These songs I was keeping for thee, in the bark of the   200
    laurel :
These, and how many more!—and the goblets I was given
By Manso, glory of the Campanian shore,
Two chalices of marvellous workmanship
—Yet the old man no less marvellous than they—
Carved and inlaid with two-fold argument :   205
Here, the Red Sea, the long Arabian coast,
And fragrant-breathing spring and the woods of spice,
And in the midst the Phoenix, the divine,
Sole in the earth, blazing with azure wings
Diversely bright, her eyes upon the dawn   210
That breaks above the green crystalline sea.
Obverse, the vast over-arching of the sky,
Height of Olympus,
And Love, aye, Love himself, against the clouds,
The dazzling bow, the torch, the arrows of fire.   215
No puny soul, no sordid breast his target.
Those burning eyes go seeking through the worlds
For the high heart, the proud undaunted spirit.
These, not the sprawling, are his arrows' mark,
The noblest minds, beauty as of the gods,   220
He kindles, and they burn.

And thou art with them, Damon, thou art there,
This is no cheating hope.
Thou too art there : where else should be
That holy sweet simplicity,   225
That radiant valiancy?

We did thee wrong to seek thee in the mirk
Of Lethe's waters.
No tears, no tears for thee, and no more wailing.
I'll weep no more. He hath his dwelling place 230
In that pure heaven,
He hath the power of the air, himself as pure.
His foot hath spurned the rainbow.
Among the souls of the heroes, the gods everlasting,
He drinks deep draughts of joy. 235

Thou hast the freedom of heaven : be with me now.
Canst hear me, Damon, come unto thy peace?
Art thou our Damon still,
Or do they call thee by thine other name,
The given of God, the name they knew in heaven, 240
But Damon in the woods.
Thine was untarnished youth, the flush of honour
Untouched by wantonness : and now to thee
The glories kept for virgin souls are given.
Upon thy radiant head a glittering crown, 245
And in thy hand the joyous green of the palm,
Thou goest deathless to the immortal feast,
Where the sound of the lyre and the voice of singing
Kindle and quicken the dancing feet,
Where the Bridegroom's feast is toward, 250
And the mystic wine is poured,
The madness and the ecstasy of Heaven.

1. ON THE TRADITION

The Pastoral Elegy and Milton's *Lycidas*

James H. Hanford

I

To most modern readers the pastoral setting of Milton's *Lycidas* is far from being an element of beauty. It is doubtful whether anyone, approaching *Lycidas* for the first time, fails to experience a feeling of strangeness, which must be overcome before the poem can be fully appreciated; and not infrequently the pastoral imagery continues to be felt as a defect, attracting attention to its own absurdities and thereby seriously interfering with the reader's enjoyment of the piece itself. The reason for this attitude lies in the fact that we have today all but forgotten the pastoral tradition and quite lost sympathy with the pastoral mood. The mass of writing to which this artificial yet strangely persistent literary fashion gave rise seems unendurably barren and insipid; to return and traverse the waste, with its dreary repetitions of conventional sentiments and tawdry imagery, is a veritable penance. Yet this, if we are to judge fairly of *Lycidas*, or if we are to remove the hindrances to our full enjoyment of it

From *Publications of the Modern Language Association*, XXV (1910), 403–447; revised by the editor.

as poetry, is what in a measure we must do. For in Milton's eyes the pastoral element in *Lycidas* was neither alien nor artificial. Familiar as he was with poetry of this kind in English, Latin, Italian, and Greek, Milton recognized the pastoral as one of the natural modes of literary expression, sanctioned by classic practice, and recommended by not inconsiderable advantages of its own. The setting of *Lycidas* was to him not merely an ornament, but an essential element in the artistic composition of the poem. It tended to idealize and dignify the expression of his sorrow, and to exalt this tribute to the memory of his friend, by ranging it with a long and not inglorious line of elegiac utterances, from Theocritus and Virgil to Edmund Spenser.

To consider this tradition with reference to *Lycidas* is the object of the present essay. I do not propose to write a history of the pastoral elegy, but simply to indicate the origin of those elements of the elegiac tradition which appear in *Lycidas*, and to show in detail Milton's indebtedness to each of the greater examples of the type. Many of the borrowings are noted in the various editions of Milton's works; some of the identifications are new. The material has never, so far as I know, been collected and used for the present purpose.[1]

II

The trifling and artificial spirit of the pastoral would seem at first thought to render the form utterly inappropriate for serious laments; according to the accepted view the pastoral was in its very origin a sort of toy, a literature of make-believe. The poetry which grew up in the happy school of Greek bards who masqueraded as countrymen on the "pleasant sward" of Cos, and whiled away the hours learning to be poets by imitating the song contests of the Sicilian shepherds, could hardly have been anything but pretty and artificial. We might have supposed that it would be as transitory as the conditions which gave it birth. That this *jeu d'esprit* became a permanent literary form and a mode of expression for serious as well as lighter themes, was due to the superior genius of Theocritus, whose dramatic imagination, aided by his knowledge of the sober realities of Sicilian shepherd life, carried him beyond the imitation of mere

---

[1] [For other studies of the elegiac tradition, most of them written after the appearance of the present essay, see *infra*, pp. 238 ff.—ED.]

externals and led him really to identify himself with the characters which he portrayed. All the charm of rustic manners, all
the fresh beauties of Sicilian scenery were preserved in the idyls
of Theocritus; but these served only as a setting for human
passions.

That the change in point of view, the shift of attention from
the machinery of the pastoral to its essence, did not come to
Theocritus all at once, may be inferred from the idyls themselves.
In the Polyphemus idyls, for example, where the monster Cyclops is represented in the grotesque role of a sentimental lover,
we seem to see the poet barely touching the serious note. The
sixth idyl gets little farther than burlesque; in the eleventh, on
the other hand, the author makes us feel not only the absurdity
of Polyphemus in love, but also, by flashes, the pathos of it:

> Come forth, Galatea, [he cries] and forget as thou comest, even
> as I that sit here have forgotten, the homeward way. . . .
> There is no one that wrongs me but that mother of mine, and her
> do I blame. Never, nay, never once has she spoken a kind word
> for me to thee, and that though day by day she sees me wasting.
> I will tell her that my head and both my feet are throbbing, that
> she may also suffer somewhat, since I too am suffering. O
> Cyclops, Cyclops, whither are thy wits wandering? Ah that
> thou wouldst go, and weave thy wicker-work and gather broken
> boughs to carry to thy lambs; in faith, if thou didst this, far
> wiser wouldst thou be.[2]

The author is still trifling, but his imagination has carried him
into the situation; he seems to be holding two points of view,
that of the Cyclops and that of the unsympathetic world which
is laughing at him. In another lover's lament extravagant sentimentality takes the place of incongruity as an element of humor.
The song is addressed to cruel Amaryllis by her disappointed
lover, who, when he finds himself rejected in spite of presents,
prayers, and harmless threats, gives way to despair. "My head
aches, but thou carest not. I will sing no more, but dead will I
lie where I fall, and here may the wolves devour me." [3] In this
passage the contemplation of death as the result of the thwart-
ing of the shepherd's passion brings us a step nearer to the
elegy. The spirit of the piece is, to be sure, not too serious; this

[2] XI, 63 ff.; trans. Andrew Lang.
[3] III, 53 ff.

lover's "complaint" is the very stuff of which the later sentimental or burlesque pastoral was made. Still there are serious
and even tragic possibilities in the theme; characters and passions originally designed as burlesques may spring into life under
the creative touch of genius, and refuse to remain within the
narrow bounds of parody.

It is in the first and second idyls that Theocritus becomes
fully possessed by his theme. Here the spirit of banter and make-
believe is cast aside for a serious artistic purpose. The subject
of the poems is still disappointed love, but the laments are no
longer mere lovers' rhetoric. They claim and receive our sympathy. The second idyl is not pastoral and does not concern us
here, except as it serves to show the trend of Theocritus's poetic
and dramatic genius. It is the monologue of a ruined and deserted girl, who is trying the forlorn hope of magic to bring
back her faithless lover. She tells the story of her passion with
poignant pathos, murmuring an incantation to the moon the
while, and directing a servant in the magic rites. In Virgil's
imitation of this poem (Eclogue VIII) the incantations prove
successful; in Theocritus no lover comes, and the ending is consistent with the hopeless tone of the whole piece. "But do thou
farewell, and turn thy steeds to Ocean, Lady, and my pain I will
bear, even as till now I have endured it." Virgil is primarily interested in the magic machinery and in the sonorous poetry;
Theocritus, in the truth of the character and the tragic pathos
of the situation.

The greatest of the idyls and by far the most important for
the present discussion is the first. For not only is it in many respects the archetype of the pastoral elegy, but it bears a direct
and particularly significant relation to *Lycidas*. The poem opens
with a pretty scene in which Thyrsis, the sweet singer of the vale,
is urged by a goatherd to make pleasant the noontide hour by
singing the "Affliction of Daphnis." A wondrous ivy bowl, and
the privilege of thrice milking a goat that is mother of twins,
shall be his reward. Thyrsis consents and begins the beautiful
lament. The theme is how Daphnis, the ideal hero of pastoral
song, was subdued by a new love, after his marriage to the fairest
of the nymphs, and chose rather to die than to yield. The singer
first rebukes the nymphs for failing to save their Daphnis, and
tells of the universal lament of nature for his loss; he then de-

scribes the visits of Hermes, Priapus, and Cypris to the afflicted shepherd, the first two with words of consolation, the last with a cruel taunt. To her alone does Daphnis reply, reproaching her and bidding her begone to boast of her success; he bids farewell to his native woods and rivers; bequeaths his pipe to his successor, and dies lamenting his own sad fate. The shepherd-singer concludes and claims the gifts, which the goatherd gladly grants, with praise for his companion's song.

The extent to which this poem moulded the tradition of the pastoral elegy will be clear from our discussion of the later examples of the form. That Milton was familiar with it at first hand and consciously adopted it as one of the classical models for *Lycidas* seems practically certain, notwithstanding the wide divergence of the two poems in setting, spirit, and subject matter. For the general plan of making various beings come one after another to add their part to the lament, Milton had a precedent also in the tenth eclogue of Virgil. It is impossible to say that he was influenced more by the one poet than by the other. It is noteworthy, however, that in the *Epitaphium Damonis*, where Milton uses the same motive, he is clearly following Theocritus I. The poem is twice explicitly referred to, and the name of the mourner in both laments is Thyrsis. In the *Epitaphium* the shepherds and nymphs come, not to mourn for the dead as in *Lycidas*, but, in their mistaken way, to bring comfort to the mourner; the contrast between the affliction of the shepherd and the shallow consolations of his friends serves, as with Theocritus and Virgil, to heighten the effect.

A more detailed borrowing is to be found in the passage in *Lycidas* beginning "Where were ye Nymphs." The lament of Thyrsis opens thus:

> Begin, ye Muses dear, begin the pastoral song.
> Thyrsis of Etna am I, and this is the voice of Thyrsis. Where, ah! where were ye when Daphnis was languishing; ye nymphs where were ye? By Peneus beautiful or by the dells of Pindus? for surely ye dwelt not by the great stream of the river Anapus, nor on the watchtower of Etna, nor by the sacred water of Acis.
> Begin, ye Muses dear, begin the pastoral song.

The familiar lines from *Lycidas* are substantially the same, but they bear the touch of a mightier hand:

> Where were ye Nymphs when the remorseless deep
> Clos'd o're the head of your lov'd *Lycidas?*
> For neither were ye playing on the steep,
> Where your old *Bards,* the famous *Druids* ly,
> Nor on the shaggy top of *Mona* high.[4]

For the use of this motive too Milton had the double precedent of Theocritus and Virgil [5]; that the lines are directly reminiscent of the Greek rather than the Latin poet is clear from the fact that whereas Milton, like Theocritus, mentions places near the region where his shepherd met his fate, Virgil declares that the nymphs were absent, not from Arcady where the scene of his eclogue is laid, but from their accustomed haunts in Sicily.

At the close of the lament in Theocritus i there is a passage which bears a still more essential relation to *Lycidas.* "Nay, spun was all the thread that the fates assigned," the shepherd sings, "and Daphnis went down the stream. The whirling wave closed over (literally 'the eddy washed away') the man whom the muses loved, the man not hated of the nymphs." In view of the circumstances of the death of Edward King, these lines are particularly interesting. That Milton noticed their special applicability to his own subject is clear from the passage already quoted:

> Where were ye Nymphs when the remorseless deep
> Clos'd o're the head of your lov'd *Lycidas?*

May it not be that these lines from Theocritus first suggested to Milton the idea of giving his elegy on the death of his friend a pastoral form? It is quite possible that this passage occurred to Milton when he first learned that King was drowned, thus drawing his attention to Theocritus i and to the pastoral elegy in general as an instrument for the expression of idealized grief. The external circumstances of Daphnis's death would at least lead Milton in a manner to identify his own dead shepherd with this legendary hero of pastoral song, and to regard Theocritus's exquisite lament as the prototype of his own elegy.

The influence of Theocritus on *Lycidas* is by no means limited to the Daphnis idyl. The elegiac pastoral tradition is only a part of the pastoral tradition in general, and the whole

---

[4] *Lycidas,* 50 ff.
[5] Cf. Eclogue x, 9 ff.

body of the poetry of Theocritus, as the ultimate source of this general tradition, must be regarded as contributory to the pastoral elegy. Theocritus was the great storehouse of pastoral material; he was plundered again and again, and his plunderers were plundered in their turn, until the incidents, expressions, and motives used by him became common property among pastoral writers. Of this material a due proportion appears in *Lycidas*, whether borrowed directly from Theocritus or descended from him through many hands.[6]

Of the later bucolic writers of the Alexandrine age, but two are known to us by name: Moschus and the somewhat younger Bion, both of whom flourished in the latter half of the third century B.C. Bion's most famous idyl, the *Lament for Adonis*, is, strictly speaking, not a pastoral at all; Adonis was a hunter, not a shepherd. The poem is associated with the pastoral, however, because of its form and because it is the work of a pastoral poet. Its erotic tone serves also to ally it with pastoral poetry. It is not surprising, therefore, that we find the poem influencing the pastoral elegy. The sober and classic genius of Milton seems to have rejected this decadent elegy; for neither *Lycidas* nor the *Epitaphium Damonis* shows any direct trace of its influence. Other pastoral writers, however, have made liberal use of the poem, and it must rank as one of the great classical models of the pastoral elegy.[7] The poem, moreover, derives a special importance in the development of the tradition from its connection with the *Lament for Bion*.

The latter piece, which is commonly attributed to Moschus but probably belongs to a somewhat younger Italian contemporary, is of the greatest significance in the history of the pastoral elegy. It marks, as we shall see, the full development of the pastoral lament as an independent type, and, notwithstanding its sentimentality and absurd exaggeration of the pathetic fallacy, it was adopted as a model by numerous later writers.[8] The origi-

---

[6] The passages in Milton which are directly and certainly traceable to other idyls of Theocritus are very few. Cf., however, *Idyl* VII, 35, with *Lyc.*, 25–27; *Idyl* I, 16–17, with *Ep. Dam.*, 51–52; and *Idyl* I, 27 ff., with *Ep. Dam.*, 181 ff.

[7] For an extensive account of the influence of this poem in the Renaissance and later, see W. P. Mustard, "Later Echoes of the Greek Bucolic Poets," *American Journal of Philology*, XXX (1909), 275 ff. Shelley's *Adonais* is formally modeled on the *Lament for Adonis*.

[8] *Ibid.*, pp. 279 ff.

nals of the *Lament for Bion* were clearly Bion's own *Lament for Adonis* and Theocritus's first idyl; but the poem differs conspicuously from its predecessors in being a lament for the death of an actual person conceived as a shepherd. Adopting the lyric form of the *Lament for Adonis* and the pastoral setting and many of the motives of Theocritus i, the writer has substituted for the legendary character, whether shepherd or hunter, the person of his own friend. Bion was a writer of pastorals; therefore for poetical purposes Bion was a shepherd. By thus applying the imagery of the pastoral to a real person, the author of the *Lament* had transformed what was previously a *genre* of erotic verse into the more serviceable type of the personal elegy in pastoral form.

The pastoral fiction, once employed in lamenting a pastoral poet, was easily extended to poets who did not touch on pastoral themes, and then to men who were not poets at all. The time was soon to come when as unpastoral a figure as Julius Cæsar could be dubbed Daphnis and made the subject of a shepherd's lament. Poor poet as he was, the author of the *Lament for Bion* has the credit of having established a permanent literary form.

The influence of the *Lament for Bion* extended farther than merely to establish the use of pastoral imagery in elegies on the death of real persons; many of the particular motives and ideas which characterize the later tradition may be traced to this first example of the form. The favorite application of the pastoral treatment continued to be to poets. Thus in later times Sir Philip Sidney, John Keats, Arthur Hugh Clough, and Matthew Arnold have been mourned in pastoral song. Even when the person lamented is not primarily a poet, the writer is prone to adopt the old convention and refer to him as one of the sweet singers of the vale. Edward King was not a poet; but Milton did not forget that he wrote verse:

> Who would not sing for *Lycidas?* he knew
> Himself to sing, and build the lofty rhyme.

This character of the shepherd as a poet gives rise to another common motive: namely, the fiction that the writer of the elegy is himself the poetical successor of the dead shepherd. In the first idyl of Theocritus, Thyrsis, who sings the lament, was, as

Daphnis had been before him, the most famous of the rustic poets. The writer of the *Lament for Bion* professes to be heir to his master's song.[9] This sense of personal relation as a poet to the subject of his song justifies the writer in allowing himself digressions concerning his own poetic achievements and aspirations. In *Lycidas* this tendency appears in the passage about fame (ll. 64 ff.), beginning:

> Alas! What boots it with uncessant care
> To tend the homely slighted Shepherds trade,
> And strictly meditate the thankles Muse.

In the *Epitaphium Damonis* the digression is still more personal and explicit (ll. 161 ff.).

Closely connected with the supposed superiority of the shepherd as a rustic poet is the fiction that he is the particular darling of all the creatures of the vale and that they all lament his death. The first suggestion of this motive was undoubtedly found in Theocritus. Not only were the boys and maidens stricken with grief at the loss of Daphnis, but jackals, lions, bulls, and calves bewailed his death. In the *Lament for Bion* everything worth mentioning in nature adds after its fashion to the universal moan. Indeed, the first third of the poem is wholly given over to the agonies of created things. In *Lycidas* we have the motive employed in a passage which may be a direct echo of the *Lament for Bion*:

> Thee Shepherd, thee the Woods, and desert Caves,
> With wilde Thyme and the gadding Vine o'regrown,
> And all their echoes mourn.
> The Willows, and the Hazle Copses green,
> Shall now no more be seen,
> Fanning their joyous Leaves to thy soft layes.

From this conventional use of the "pathetic fallacy" Milton, it will be observed, gets a very different effect from that of his Greek originals. For he does not dwell on the fiction that the natural objects express grief; he is taken up with the beauty of the things themselves. It is the description that we remember, not the conceit.

[9] "To others didst thou leave thy wealth, to me thy minstrelsy" (l. 97).

That Milton regarded the *Lament for Bion*, together with the first idyl of Theocritus, as a great classical original of the pastoral elegy is clear from the invocation in the *Epitaphium Damonis*:

> *Himerides nymphæ (nam vos & Daphnin & Hylan,*
> *Et plorata diu meministis fata Bionis)*
> *Dicite Sicelicum Thamesina per oppida carmen.*

Traces of direct imitation, on the other hand, are very slight. In addition to the lines quoted above, the flower passage in *Lycidas* has been cited as echoing the opening lines in the *Lament*.[10] The resemblance is a shade closer than to the similar passages in Virgil.

With the *Lament for Bion*, the pastoral elegiac tradition in Greek, at least as far as we can trace it, comes to an end. The pastoral form was on its way toward complete decadence; it seemed on the point of total dissolution when it was revived in a new spirit by Virgil.

III

The ampler strain in which Virgil bids the Muses sing his prophecy of the approaching millenium [11] is the keynote of a change in the style and spirit of the pastoral which is of the greatest importance in the history of the pastoral elegy. The tone of the Virgilian eclogue is determined not by the lightness and delicate urbanity of Theocritus, nor by the decadent beauty of his successors, but by the essentially dignified and noble genius of Virgil himself. With all his literary indebtedness to the Alexandrians, Virgil was thoroughly Roman; he was by nature an epic poet, and even in the bucolics he strikes the epic note. Corresponding to this change in expression, and intimately related to it, there came with Virgil a change in the nature of the tradition. The Roman poet, unlike his master, had never known a shepherd life like that which Theocritus describes; the peculiar conditions of simplicity and happiness which had existed in Sicily two centuries before could hardly have been found among the peasants of northern Italy at the close of the civil wars. Hence if Virgil was to write pastorals at all, he must either change the

---

[10] Mustard, *op. cit.*, pp. 281–282.
[11] Ecl. IV, 1 ff.: *"Sicilides Musae, paulo maiora canamus!"* etc.

setting so as to bring it into accord with the rural life he knew, or he must accept the pastoral setting of his master as a literary convention. But the fiction of a shepherd contest was the very essence of the pastoral as a literary form. Accordingly, Virgil took the latter course, thereby completing the process of which we have seen the beginning in the *Lament for Bion*. From Virgil's time forth, conventionality in setting, adherence to an established literary tradition, is a marked characteristic of the pastoral.

That Virgil should have been willing to accept his pastoral setting ready made is partly explained by the fact that he was not particularly interested in this setting for its own sake. His purpose was first of all stylistic. There is in Virgil no such insight into character and dramatic situation as in the first and second idyls of Theocritus; there is no such variety of pastoral ideas and images. In compensation, the Roman poet has taken infinite pains to secure artistic finish. Each eclogue is a carefully constructed whole, usually beginning with something corresponding to an invocation and progressing to a definite artistic close. The verse is polished almost to a point of overrefinement. But style and form are not by any means Virgil's only interest in the eclogues. The methods of personal reference suggested by the practice of Theocritus and the author of the *Lament for Bion* are extensively employed by Virgil and turned to panegyric purposes. The pastoral was, with Virgil, to a large degree personal and allegorical; indeed, if we take the realistic idyls of Theocritus as the type, the eclogues can hardly be considered as pastorals at all.

This change in the spirit and intention of the pastoral in Virgil's hands was, as I have already remarked, of the greatest importance in the history of the pastoral form. It is not only that Virgil reinstated the pastoral and exemplified it in a language which was to be the literary medium for centuries; he also transformed it into an easy and serviceable instrument for a variety of literary purposes. It was no longer necessary to know anything about country life in order to write good pastorals; it was only necessary to know the pastoral formulas—to be able to manipulate the pastoral machinery. Moreover, the pastoral was henceforth to be a garment that would fit all figures. It was a thin and graceful disguise for personal allusion, and especially for panegyric.

What, then, was Virgil's influence on the pastoral elegy? The form already had, as we have seen, a certain grace and pathos to recommend it; it suffered, at least in its later examples, from pettiness, from exaggeration, from erotic sentimentality. In Virgil's hands it was ennobled and made an instrument really worthy of the highest themes. True it is that there were few who could follow Virgil in raising the pastoral by exalted expression; but for those who could, Virgil had shown the way. Of all his successors in the higher pastoral vein, none had more clearly the spirit of the master than John Milton. He echoes the Roman's very lines in bidding his muse rise to the dignity of a loftier theme:

> Begin then, Sisters of the sacred well,
> That from beneath the seat of *Jove* doth spring
> Begin, and somwhat loudly sweep the string.[12]

If Virgil had never written his eclogues, Milton might yet have sung of the death of King in an epic strain; for such expression was as native to Milton's genius as to Virgil's own; but it is not so likely that he would have chosen the pastoral as the form in which to cast his lament. With this elevation of the tone of the pastoral elegy there comes also an enlargement of its scope. The character of the subjects treated by Virgil, which are in many cases serious and far beyond the narrow range of strictly pastoral interests, brought the pastoral nearer to the elegy proper, in which we naturally expect an element of contemplation and didacticism. It also established a precedent for the introduction into the pastoral elegy of a great variety of miscellaneous material, a practice of which the invective against the clergy in *Lycidas* is a striking example.

Two of the eclogues of Virgil, the fifth and tenth, are deserving of especial consideration. Eclogue x is a love lament in imitation of Theocritus 1; but here the shepherd is no mythical Daphnis but the flesh and blood poet, Cornelius Gallus, whose disappointment in love is presumably an actual fact. The poem is conventional in imagery, but sincere in feeling and elevated in tone. It begins with an invocation of Arethusa. There follows a passage lamenting the absence of the nymphs from their accustomed haunts; then comes the inevitable lament for nature. The

[12] *Lycidas,* 15–17; cf. note 14.

shepherds, Apollo and Pan, come to offer their consolation. At length, as in Theocritus I, Gallus himself bewails his misfortune, struggles for a time against fate, then yields. The poem concludes with eight lines in the regular style of the Virgilian close.

In general outline this poem resembles *Lycidas* much more closely than any other of the poems of Virgil or Theocritus. In both we have an invocation at the beginning but no mention of the shepherd singer until the end; in both the motive of a procession of mourners is employed; both poems close with eight lines, very similar in spirit, referring to the end of day and the departure of the shepherd. In addition to these general resemblances there are a few detailed borrowings.[13]

Virgil's fifth eclogue marks a step in advance in the development of pastoral elegy; for here we have for the first time a lament for a great man who was not a poet and who appears, not in his own person, but disguised under a pastoral name. The Daphnis of the fifth eclogue is in all likelihood Julius Cæsar. Reference is apparently made to his reputed descent from Venus, to his introduction into Rome of the Bacchic rites, and lastly to his apotheosis. The setting is the familiar dialogue of Theocritus I. Two shepherds, Menalcas and Mopsus, meet and sing together the death of Daphnis. Mopsus tells of the sorrows of nature for the shepherd's fate: the nymphs wept; lions, mountains, and forests are said to have uttered groans. Pales and Apollo have left the fields; darnel and oats grow instead of barley, thistles instead of violets. Then the shepherds are invited to scatter flowers over Daphnis's grave and build his tomb, and Menalcas concludes, addressing Daphnis as a god:

> *Candidus insuetum miratur limen Olympi*
> *Sub pedibusque videt nubes et sidera Daphnis.*

The note of joy, thus introduced by Virgil with reference to the deification of the first Cæsar, is henceforth seldom or never absent from the pastoral elegy. In general, the resemblance between this passage and the end of *Lycidas* is not specific. Christianity has lent a new coloring to the consolation in the later poem. With the last three lines, however, where Lycidas is invoked as

---

[13] Cf. Ecl. x, 2–3, 4–5, and 24, with *Lyc.*, 81, 19 ff., and 103–104, respectively. There are several echoes of Eclogue x in the *Ep. Dam.*; cf. Ecl. x, 8, 42, 55–68, 63, with *Ep. Dam.*, 73, 71, 35–43, and 160, respectively.

the "Genius of the shore," the case is different. The conception
contained in them is more pagan than Christian, and it is hard
to believe that they would have appeared in *Lycidas* had not
the idea held an important place in this eclogue of Virgil.

The influence of the bucolics on *Lycidas* is by no means confined to the fifth and tenth eclogues. No edition of *Lycidas* has
ever given anything like an exhaustive list of the passages in
Virgil which Milton either borrowed or imitated. One can never
feel sure that one has got them all; for they extend to the merest
minutiæ, such as the borrowing of a single word. The beautiful
passage in *Lycidas* beginning "Bring the rathe Primrose" bears
only a general resemblance to the similar flower groupings in
the bucolics [14]; Milton is far more imaginative in his description
than Virgil. The Roman poet speaks of "pallid violets," "waxen
prunes," and "quinces with their tender bloom"; the English, of
"Cowslips wan that hang the pensive hed." The reference to
myrtles and laurels at the beginning of *Lycidas*, however, is
clearly reminiscent of line 54 in Eclogue II. In Eclogue III, ll.
26–27, there is a touch of satire which reminds us of *Lycidas*,
l. 124. The moving of natural objects to the song of a shepherd
is twice mentioned in Virgil [15]; so, too, Milton's "smooth-sliding
Mincius, crown'd with vocall reeds," is an echo of Virgil's "*hic
viridis tenera prætexit harundine ripas Mincius.*" [16] The phrase,
"touch'd my trembling ears," used of the admonition of Phœbus,
is borrowed from Eclogue VI. The beginning of the passage on
fame, "Were it not better don as others use, To sport with
Amaryllis in the shade," is evidently modeled on Virgil II, 14–15:
"*Nonne fuit satius tristis Amaryllidis iras Atque superba pati
fastidia.*" [17]

In trying to appraise the relative influence of Theocritus (including the *Lament for Bion*) and Virgil on Milton's pastoral
style, it is necessary to take into account the fact that the Greek
muse, as the first inspirer of pastoral verse, was naturally regarded as the more original and the more authentic. In *Lycidas*
both the Greek and Roman pastoralists are invoked together:

---

[14] Cf. Ecl. IV, 19 ff.; Ecl. V, 35–60; *Aeneid,* VI, 883–884.
[15] Ecl. VI, 27–38 (directly imitated in *Lyc.*, 33–35); and Ecl. VIII, 4.
[16] Ecl. VII, 12–13, and *Lyc.*, 86.
[17] Two further parallels might be given: cf. Ecl. I, 2 and 84, with *Lyc.*, 66
and 190, respectively.

O Fountain *Arethuse,* and thou honour'd floud,
Smooth-sliding *Mincius,* crown'd with vocall reeds.

But *Lycidas* is called a *"Dorick* lay," and after the church digression, Milton bids the "Sicilian Muse" return. So, too, in the *Epitaphium Damonis* it is the *"Himerides nymphæ"* who are invoked. On the other hand, as we have seen, the direct reminiscences of Theocritus in *Lycidas,* are few, while those of Virgil are many. The latter passages, too, have been more completely assimilated; the Virgilian phrases are part and parcel of the style. It seems probable, therefore, that though Milton honored the Sicilian as his original and consciously incorporated some of his motives, he turned to Virgil with greater familiarity. It was the Virgilian rather than the Theocritean phrase which sprang first to his mind when he would express himself in pastoral terms. We may, perhaps, refer the gentler and sweeter passages in *Lycidas* to the flexible and sunny Greek of the author of Daphnis; we must certainly attribute the "higher strain," which is most characteristic of the poem, to the influence of Virgil. It is perhaps significant that Milton, in changing from the harsh tones of invective to strains of pathos and beauty, invokes the presence of the Greek pastoral alone:

Return *Alpheus,* the dread voice is past,
That shrunk thy streams; Return *Sicilian* Muse.

IV

The paramount importance of the classical examples of the pastoral elegy, not only as establishing the type for future ages but also as furnishing Milton with his most important models, has led me to dwell on the subject at considerable length. But these poems are not alone sufficient to account for the form of *Lycidas,* nor are they the only elegies to which Milton is indebted for motives, phrases, and minute turns of style. The pastoral elegy was greatly enlarged in scope by the freer treatment of the Middle Ages and Renaissance; it was to a certain degree changed in essence by its contact with Christianity. It remains, therefore, to examine the chief later modifications of the elegiac tradition, and to consider in particular those poems with which Milton seems to show familiarity.

The later Roman pastoral writers, Calpurnius and Nemesian, had but little influence on the pastoral tradition. Their eclogues reveal the tendency inherent in the pastoral as interpreted by Virgil, to become more and more personal and allegorical. The pastoral writers are no longer content to suggest a personal application of the eclogue as a whole; but, following what they believe to have been the practice of their master, they attempt to give a meaning to each detail, to make each character in the dialogue represent a definite person. The pastorals of Calpurnius contain no elegy; Nemesian I, entitled "Epiphunus Melibœi," is a lament after the style of Virgil v, but containing possible reminiscences of Theocritus. The aged Melibœus is probably a real person, but there is no evidence for his identification. It is interesting to observe that the pastoral consolation does not appear in this elegy. Melibœus is said to be worthy of the councils of the gods, but not to have been made one of their number. In the ordinary pagan eclogue such a passage could find no place. Its occurrence in the fifth eclogue of Virgil was due to a special fact connected with the subject of the lament. With the introduction of Christianity into the elegy, the consolation became essential.

The slender stream of pastoral writing which connects the classical eclogues with the bucolic poetry of the Renaissance need detain us but a moment. The renewed tradition owes little if anything to the Middle Ages, but derives its source directly from the classical originals as interpreted by the allegorical method which had been applied to the works of Virgil almost from the start. The pastoral poetry of the Carolingian Renaissance has, however, an interest of its own, and one elegy belonging to this period deserves consideration here as illustrating the trend of the form in Christian hands, and as anticipating, if it did not suggest, certain important later developments. The poem is a lament for Adalhard, Abbot of old and new Corbeil, and was written by Paschasius Radbertus. Two maidens, Galatea and Fillis, who prove to be personifications of the two monasteries, mourn for their abbot in alternate strains; as usual in the Carolingian eclogue, the writer is interested rather in the content than in the form. The pastoral idea had in it little to attract the writers of the circle of Charles, but fortified as they were with the allegorical interpretation of Virgil, they saw in the

eclogue a convenient form for the expression of a wide variety
of nonpastoral ideas. The pastoral setting tends constantly to
fall away from the skeleton of the dialogue. Radbertus, in the
poem under discussion, has not gone so far as to desert entirely
the Virgilian model, but he has dealt freely with the form, and
by introducing into his poem several new features has taken a
further step in the progressive widening of the scope of the pastoral elegy. Chief among these features are the following: (1)
extended praise of the subject of the lament; (2) abundant
references to his life and work; (3) an invective against death;
(4) a description of the joys of Paradise. The allusions in the
poem to the immortality of the deceased were pretty clearly suggested by Virgil v, but they contain a note of joy and rapture
which is new to the pastoral elegy and reminds us forcibly of
Lycidas. Of particular importance in the history of the pastoral
elegy is the confusion, or rather the direct combination of the
classical pastoral imagery with the Christian figure of the pastor
and his flock, which inevitably took place when the pastoral
came to be treated by religious writers. In a Latin eclogue of
the fourth century by Severus Sanctus, Christ is introduced as
averting a plague from the cattle of a shepherd who worshipped
him. In the poem just discussed, the identification of the two
kinds of "pastor" and the two kinds of "flock" is clearly made.
The connection thus established between the classical pastoral
and the Christian religion served greatly to extend the utility
and scope of the pastoral form. It opened the way, in the eclogue,
for the treatment of matters ecclesiastical, and rendered the
pastoral elegy as appropriate to the death of a member of the
clergy as it was to that of a poet. The significance of these remarks will be clear when we recall the ecclesiastical satire in
Lycidas and remember that Edward King had intended to enter
the church.

It is not to an obscure elegy of the Carolingian Renaissance,
however, that we must trace the direct impulse toward the introduction into the pastoral of ecclesiastical material, which was
so strong in later times, but to the first users of the form in
modern times, Boccaccio and Petrarch. Adopting the allegorical
practices of the Middle Ages and following closely in the supposed footsteps of Virgil, these poets used the pastoral solely
as a means of expressing their political, religious, and moral

ideas. In Eclogues VI and VII of Petrarch an elaborate allegorical satire against the corruptions of the church is introduced. In Eclogue VI Pamphilus, Saint Peter in pastoral guise, rebukes Mitio, Clement V, who was leading a corrupt life at Avignon, for the ill-keeping of his flocks; in Eclogue VII Epy or France conspires with Mitio, whom she has corrupted. In the introduction of ecclesiastical satire into the pastoral, Petrarch led the way for Mantuan and Marot, who were followed in turn by Spenser. It is the latter poet to whom we naturally look as the predecessor in this respect of Milton. Yet the presence of Saint Peter in the satires of both Milton and Petrarch suggests a connection between the two works, and it is quite possible that Milton had read the Latin eclogues.

The freedom with which Petrarch and Boccaccio treated the pastoral form in general is observable in their handling of the pastoral elegy, in so far as they entered that field at all. In the two or three poems of Petrarch's which can be called elegies (Eclogues II, X, XI), the formal lament is subordinate to an elaborate allegorical setting. The classical motives appear, but not in great abundance. Boccaccio's interesting fourteenth eclogue, though it is rather a vision than a lament, is allied to the pastoral elegy by the elaborate description which Olympia, the spirit of Boccaccio's dead daughter, gives of Paradise and her happiness there. I am unable to find traces in any of these poems of direct influence on Milton's *Lycidas*.

The practice of making the eclogue a vehicle for didacticism and personal allegory, thus inaugurated by Petrarch and Boccaccio, characterizes in a varying degree the work of their successors in the pastoral literature of the Renaissance. The typical representative of this didactic tradition is Giovanni Battista, called Mantuan, whose ten eclogues, connected in a kind of series, and entitled *Adulescentia*, were in the sixteenth century regarded not only as an ideal example of pastoral composition but as a goodly moral work, more worthy of being put into the hands of boys than the eclogues of Virgil. They furnished the models for a host of later didactic dialogues, including the crude English pastorals of Barclay, and, in a degree, *The Shepheardes Calender* of Spenser. The influence of this conception of the eclogue on the pastoral elegy was to open the way still further for the introduction of alien materials, personal, philosophic, and didactic. The long personal digressions in the *Epitaphium Damonis* and

Lycidas, while they are hardly to be paralleled in any preceding elegy, are easily explicable when we consider that the pastoral eclogue had been used again and again since Petrarch as a means of expressing in a modest disguise the personal aspirations of its author.[18]

But while poets like Mantuan were handling the classical eclogue in what may be called the medieval spirit, the Renaissance had seized upon the pastoral for purposes of its own. Elaborating the original pastoral motive of simplicity into the fully developed conception of the golden age, the pastoral writers of the Renaissance soon found a wider field for their activity. The new wine of Arcadianism could by no means be contained in the old bottles of the classical eclogue form; and the pastoral idea invaded the realms of the drama and the prose romance. These developments were, to be sure, reserved for the vernacular; but the renewed interest in the pastoral setting for its own sake had its influence, too, on the more conservative Latin eclogue, bringing about a more consistent employment of the pastoral machinery and a closer adherence to the original form. Especially important was the effect of the rediscovery of Theocritus, whose idyls, unlike the bucolics of Virgil, furnished models in which the interest was purely pastoral. It was no longer felt as essential, though it was still common, to conceal an elaborate idea beneath the "cortex" of the eclogue.

From this renewed tendency to seek classical models, the pastoral elegy was not entirely exempt; the laments of the later humanistic writers are generally characterized by excessive conventionality and the absence of real grief. The *Lament for Bion* furnished an abundance of new motives, which were repeated *ad nauseam*. The interest of the pastoral poet was apt to be fully as much in the spectacle of the woeful shepherd and in the propriety of his pastoral language as in the substance of his lament. Nevertheless, the form remained of necessity personal, and might at any time in the hands of an individual poet be expanded to include new elements growing out of special circumstances connected with the subject of the elegy or his personal relation to the writer.

Among the few Latin elegies which are, like the *Epitaphium*

---

[18] Numerous examples of the Latin elegy may be found in the *Carmina Illustrium Poetarum Italorum* (Florence, 1719). [See also the edition by T. P. Harrison, cited *infra*, p. 239.]

Damonis and *Lycidas*, the expression of personal feeling, restrained through artistic combination with the conventional elements of the form, is Castiglione's *Alcon*. The poem is especially interesting for the present discussion because of its emphasis in pastoral terms of the friendship existing between the dead shepherd and the singer of the lament. "We lived together from tender years," the shepherd sings; "we bore together heat and cold, nights and days; we fed our kine together. These flocks of mine were thine also." The resemblance between these lines and the passage in *Lycidas* beginning, "For we were nurst upon the self-same hill," is less striking when we consider how narrow the range of pastoral equivalents for friendship must necessarily be. The possibility of a connection between the poems is strengthened, however, by still another resemblance. Castiglione's shepherd regrets the fact that he was absent when Alcon died; and says he will build an empty tomb, "nostri solatia luctus." So the singer in *Lycidas*, "to interpose a little ease," fancies that he is decking the tomb of Lycidas. There follows in *Alcon* a flower passage like that in *Lycidas*.

The only other Latin elegy of the Renaissance which has, as far as I know, been suggested as having furnished material for *Lycidas*, is Sannazaro's first piscatory eclogue, a lament for the drowned shepherdess Phyllis, put into the mouth of a shepherd named Lycidas. Unlike the majority of the Renaissance elegies this poem is, apparently, pure fiction. It was characteristic of Sannazaro, who wrote the most famous of all the pastoral romances, and made his Latin eclogues an interesting innovation on the old tradition by shifting the scene from the plains of Arcady to the shores of the Bay of Naples, to be interested even when writing an elegy in the pastoral fiction for its own sake. We must look, then, in the poem, not so much for personal feeling as for a beautiful and appropriate handling of the old material. What must have attracted Milton to this poem, if he did indeed know it, is its felicity of style, and the circumstance that the lament is for one who had met death by drowning. The closest parallel to *Lycidas* is to be found in the passage in the Latin work in which the shepherd hails the departed spirit wherever it may be and bids it look towards its former home:

At tu, sive altum felix colis æthera, seu iam
Elysios inter manes cœtusque verendos

Lethæos, sequeris per stagna liquentia pisces;
Seu legis æternos formosa pollice flores,

. . . .

Aspice nos, mitisque veni. Tu numen aquarum
Semper eris; semper lætum piscantibus omen.[19]

In *Lycidas*, it will be remembered, the shepherd after speculating where the body of his friend may be, bids his spirit "look homeward." Later he invokes Lycidas not merely as a protecting spirit, as in Virgil's fifth eclogue, but specifically as the "genius of the shore," and that in words almost identical with those used by Sannazaro:

> Henceforth thou art the Genius of the shore,
> In thy large recompense, and shalt be good
> To all that wander in that perilous flood.

The lines in *Lycidas* following that quoted above,

> Where thou perhaps under the whelming tide
> Visit'st the bottom of the monstrous world,

may perhaps have been suggested by an earlier passage in Sannazaro's poem, in which the shepherd declares that he will wander through and over the sea, amidst its monsters. It is interesting to note, too, that Sannazaro as well as Milton mentions the name of the not very familiar nymph, Panope. These resemblances are too striking to be the result of accident. Sannazaro's eclogues were among the best known of the Latin pastorals of the Renaissance, and it is natural that Milton should have read them.[20]

From the new vernacular developments of the pastoral, the pastoral elegy in the stricter sense remained apart. Lovers' laments exist in the Arcadian literature of the Renaissance in abundance; laments for the death of imaginary shepherds may occasionally be found; but the renewed interest in the pastoral idea for its own sake, which is predominant in the romances of Sannazaro, Montemayor, and Sidney, excluded the lament for a real person. Such belong to the didactic and classical tradition of the eclogue, and when serious elegies came to be written in the vernacular they adhered more closely to the original forms.

[19] *Pisc. Eclogue* I, 91 ff.
[20] The influence of Sannazaro may be traced in England in Phineas Fletcher's *Piscatorie Eclogues,* which were published only four years before *Lycidas.*

Even in the case of the fictitious elegy, the influence of the classical conventions remained strong. Eclogue xi in Sannazaro's *Arcadia*, for example, is an almost slavish imitation of the *Lament for Bion*, with the addition of the inevitable consolation. Eclogue v in the same work is, to be sure, composed in an elaborate lyric stanza rather than in the terza rima, which was the common measure for the didactic eclogue in Italian; but even in this poem there is hardly a motive which is not derived from the *Lament for Bion* or from the fifth eclogue of Virgil.

Of the vernacular elegies which preceded *Lycidas*, other than those in English, very little need be said. In general they conform to the type established by the Latin works and depend in large measure on the classics for their pastoral and elegiac motives. The process of transplanting and naturalizing the elegy was not, however, entirely without its effect. Conformably to the spirit and genius of the Renaissance, and to its freer conception of the pastoral, the elegies of the vernacular are somewhat richer in coloring, somewhat more prone to the use of fanciful ornament, than are the classical representatives of the form. The adoption of rhyme and in some cases of a less regular measure made possible a more effective handling of the music of the dirge with its changing keys. The tendency of the didactic Latin pastoral to make the rustic setting merely perfunctory, as in the case of Mantuan, was somewhat checked; the vernacular elegies have rather more of the pastoral atmosphere and of the original grace of the pastoral imagery. On the other hand, the vernacular elegy was even freer than the Latin in its admission of personal references and digression. Ronsard's elegy on the death of Henry II, though sung by a fictitious shepherd in the the course of an elaborate pastoral contest, contains references to Henry's deeds under the slightest veil of pastoral imagery:

> *La sera ton Janot, qui chantera tes faits,*
> *Tes guerres, tes combats, tes ennemis desfaits,*
> *Et tout ce que ta main d'invincible puissance*
> *Osa pour redresser la houlette de France.*

Deserving of particular mention among the French elegies, as the original of Spenser's November eclogue, is Marot's lament for Louise de Savoy. The poem resembles *Lycidas* in having no one of the great classical elegies as its particular model, but employing motives from them all and handling these motives with unusual freedom. Notwithstanding the fact that Marot takes care in general to preserve the genuine pastoral mood, the poem is filled with personal allusions. We are told, for example, how "Bergère Loyse" used to lecture her shepherdesses (the maids of honor?) on the sin of indolence; and how they would straightway betake themselves, one to her needle, another to planting her garden, another to feeding doves. After a description of the happy state of the blessed spirit, which may have influenced Milton through Spenser, we have a flower passage, interesting as showing how this classical motive was inevitably elaborated and colored in the vernacular. One stanza may be quoted.

> *Passeveloux de pourpre colorez,*
> *Lavande franche, œilletz de coleur vive,*
> *Aubepins blanc, aubepins azurez,*
> *Et toutes fleurs de grand beauté nayfve.*

The influence of the Renaissance pastoral in Italian and French may in a general way be traced in *Lycidas;* but it is improbable that Milton owes a special debt to any one of the Continental writers. He must of course have read the great dramas of Tasso and Guarini and the romance of Sannazaro; he probably knew many of the elegies. It is not surprising, however, if few of the latter impressed themselves upon his memory. Samuel Johnson, in his criticism of *Lycidas*, remarks that Milton owed the peculiar metrical structure of his poem to the Italians. This seems entirely probable.[21] The irregular introduction of short lines and the use of an irregular rhyme scheme are characteristic of the choruses of the *Aminta* and the *Pastor Fido*, and they occur but rarely, if at all, in English poetry before *Lycidas*. But what Milton owes to the specifically Renaissance developments of the pastoral he derived not so much from the Italian and French direct as through the pastoral tradition of his native land.

V

First among the English pastorals in importance, and practically first in time, stands *The Shepheardes Calender* of Spenser,

[21] [See the subsequent work by F. T. Prince, *infra*, pp. 153 ff.]

published anonymously in 1579. The earlier attempts of Barclay and Googe were by that time forgotten, and Spenser regarded himself as a pioneer, setting out deliberately, as "E. K." tells us, "to furnish our tongue with this kind wherein it faulteth." From the publication of this work the stream of pastoral writing in English flows on without interruption until the date of the publication of *Lycidas*.[22] Spenser's poem exhibited a striking divergence from the familiar pastoral tradition, and improvement on it. First of all, it combined in an unusual way the two main tendencies of the Renaissance pastoral, that represented by the Latin eclogue and that represented by the various classes of pastoral writing in the vernacular. Spenser drew without discrimination from the works of Mantuan, Sannazaro (both in his Latin eclogues and in his Italian romance), from the French eclogues of Marot, and from the classics. He added, moreover, to the didactic elements of the eclogue and to the pretty sentiment of the Arcadian pastoral, a freshness of interest in rustic life and a lyric quality which are peculiarly Elizabethan and English. The eclogues of Spenser have little of the epic sweep of Virgil; they have rather the qualities of gentleness, grace, and rustic charm which are characteristic of Theocritus and are more congenial to the true pastoral.

The most important of Spenser's innovations in the pastoral was his introduction of artistic unity into a series of eclogues. Three of the eclogues (January, June, and December) deal with progressive stages in Colin's love, and the moods of the poems change with the changing year. Now the story thus narrated is melancholy, even tragic, and the prevailing tone of the series, notwithstanding the fact that single eclogues are lighthearted or even humorous, is one of gloom. The poems in which Colin gives expression to his grief and despair are particularly mournful; they produce essentially the same effect as the first and second idyls of Theocritus, and are thus closely allied with the pastoral elegy. The series contains, moreover, one formal elegy, a lament "for some maiden of great blood, whom he, the author, calleth Dido." The poem, which is modeled closely on Marot's lament for Louise de Savoy, forms a striking contrast in spirit and style with *Lycidas*. The dominant characteristics of the earlier

---

[22] [But see the subsequent studies by W. B. Austin, H. M. Hall, T. P. Harrison, *et al.*, cited *infra*, pp. 238 ff.]

poet's pastoral style were such as tended to emphasize the very qualities which pastoralism lends to the elegy, a grace and charm which relieve the sad theme and make grief more tolerable by surrounding it with images of beauty. The elaborate lyric stanza in which the poem is written gives an effect far different from the irregular versification of *Lycidas*, which is hardly lyric at all. The fact that Spenser adopts the form of his eclogue with little modification from Marot minimizes the personal element in the elegy.

Less conventional and richer in personal allusion but equally in contrast with *Lycidas* in tone is Spenser's *Astrophel*, one of the numerous pastoral elegies on the death of Sir Philip Sidney. The prevailing note of gentleness is struck in the opening stanza of lament:

> A gentle shepherd borne in Arcady,
> Of gentlest race that ever shepherd bore,
> About the grassie bancks of Hæmony
> Did keep his sheep, his little stock and store.
> Full carefully he kept them day and night,
> In fairest fields; and Astrophel he hight.

The spirit of the closing lines of *Lycidas* has, to be sure, much in common with the above-quoted passage; but in general the later poem strikes a higher note than any heard in Spenser's pastorals. For a parallel in the pastoral to the loftiness of Milton's style we must go not to *The Shepheardes Calender* nor to any English poem, but to the eclogues of Virgil.

Yet Spenser too had his share in supplying the pastoral material of *Lycidas*. Three poems in *The Shepheardes Calender*, the May, July, and September eclogues, contain ecclesiastical satire; and one passage in the first of these bears a marked resemblance to the invective in *Lycidas*.[23] That Milton found in

[23] May, 38 ff:

> Those faytours little regarden their charge,
> While they, letting their sheepe runne at large,
> Passen their time, that should be sparely spent,
> In lustihede and wanton merryment . . .
> But they been hyred for little pay
> Of other, that caren as little as they
> What falleth the flocke, so they han the fleece . . .
> I muse what account both these will make . . .
> When great Pan account of shepherdes shall aske.

Cf. *Lycidas*, 113 ff.

Spenser the best and nearest precedent for the introduction of such material into the elegy can hardly be doubted. He may also have found there a precedent for bringing in allusions to his own poetic aspirations. The October eclogue sets forth "the perfect patern of a poet, which, finding no maintenance of his state and studies, complaineth of the contempt of poetry, and the causes thereof." Cuddie, the disheartened bard, laments thus to his friend Piers:

> The dapper ditties that I wont devise,
> To feede youthes fancie, and the flocking fry,
> Delighten much: what I the bett forthy?
> They han the pleasure, I a sclender prise:
> I beate the bush, the byrdes to them do flye:
> What good thereof to Cuddie can arise?

And Piers replies:

> Cuddie, the prayse is better than the price,
> The glory eke much greater than the gain.[24]

The familiar passage in *Lycidas* about fame is prompted by the same feeling of the uselessness of poetic endeavor, and it contains a very similar turn of thought:

> But not the praise,
> *Phœbus* repli'ed, and touch'd my trembling ears.

The consolation in *Lycidas* resembles the close of the November eclogue to a marked degree; the parallels are, to be sure, little closer than in some of the other Christian elegies; but it is natural to refer the passage particularly to Spenser, from whom, aside from the classics, Milton would have been most likely to derive his conception. It seems probable also that the flower passage in *Lycidas* owes something to the April eclogue, the lines (136 ff.) beginning:

> Bring hether the pincke and purple cullambine,
>   With gelliflowers;
> Bring coronations, and sops in wine,
>   Worne of paramoures.

For Milton, like Spenser, adds to the conventional enumeration a considerable amount of fanciful description:

[24] October, 13 ff.

>Bring the rathe Primrose that forsaken dies.
>The tufted Crow-toe, and pale Gessamine,
>The white Pink, and the Pansie freakt with jeat . . .

The above-mentioned parallels, together with a few detailed reminiscences,[25] are, I believe, sufficient to place Spenser among Milton's direct sources for the pastoral tradition, second only in importance to Virgil.

The vast and multifarious pastoral literature which was written in England between the publication of *The Shepheardes Calender* in 1579 and that of *Lycidas* in 1638, did little or nothing to modify the types established by the classics and by the Arcadian and didactic traditions of the Renaissance. In the eclogues and lyrics, the influence of Spenser continued strong, imparting to the English pastoral a healthier and more genuinely rustic tone than that of the sentimental Italian models which were dominant in the drama and romance. Throughout this literature there was the usual proportion of pastoral elegies on the death of real individuals. A great impulse to this kind of composition was given by the death of Sir Philip Sidney in 1586, an inevitable subject for the pastoral lament. Most important of the tributes to Sidney was the series entitled *Astrophel*, containing the Spenserian elegy already referred to, the *Doleful Lay of Clorinda*, written probably by the Countess of Pembroke, two poems by Lodowick Bryskett, and three nonpastoral laments. The volume contained also a long elegy by Spenser, the *Daphnaïda*, which, though pastoral in imagery and tone, has little relation to the formal elegy, being modeled on Chaucer's *Book of the Duchess*. Among the later elegies, William Browne's poem on the death of Mr. Thomas Manwood, the fourth eclogue in the collection entitled *The Shepheard's Pipe*, published in 1614, is frequently referred to as the source or inspiration of *Lycidas*. It is doubtful, however, if a single undoubted borrowing on Milton's part can be established. The poem, like a dozen others, belongs to the general type of *Lycidas;* it differs from the latter elegy, however, in having the narrative introduction, and in being without digressions. The passages which have been

---

[25] Cf. November, 37–38, with *Lyc.,* 9–10. For a similar repetition, see *Astrophel,* 6–8. The phrase "scorn of homely shepheard's quill" (June, 67) seems to be echoed in Milton's "homely slighted shepherd's trade" (*Lyc.,* 65).

quoted in evidence of a connection between the two poems are of little weight in view of the extreme conventionality of the form.

It is not likely that Milton was much impressed by any of the English elegies beside those of Spenser. Adhering in general to the established tradition, and offering little that was individual in thought or expression, they would, while carrying on the didactic and elegiac tradition to the very date of *Lycidas* and making the eclogue a contemporary type of literature,[26] simply range themselves in his mind with the three or four great examples of the form. Pastoral poetry had a remarkable faculty of holding to the commonplace. It was easy to write pleasingly in the pastoral style; to write in that style a poem that was really great demanded a genius which could triumph over the restrictions imposed upon it by the fact that it must accept much of its poetry ready made. In all the long history of the pastoral before *Lycidas* there are three or four great names. For later writers their works sum up the pastoral tradition. It is to them that the poet will look for direct inspiration. Theocritus, Virgil, and his own Spenser—with these Milton felt a kinship of genius; from them, when he chose to write at all in the most conventional of literary forms, he drew both the conventions themselves and the secret of finding his way beyond them into the realms of lofty and original poetry.

Yet *Lycidas* is to a remarkable degree the result of growth; "it gathers within its compass," says W. W. Greg, "as it were, whole centuries of pastoral tradition." The vast assimilative power of Milton had here its greatest opportunity; for the merit of a pastoral consisted not so much in its originality as in its faithful reproduction of the type. In one important respect Milton does indeed depart from, or rather greatly extend, the traditional practice: in no previous poem of the kind had the author introduced so many allusions to his own poetic career. The opening passage in *Lycidas*, the digression on fame, and the concluding line, are purely personal; in the *Epitaphium Damonis*, fifteen lines are devoted to a description of Milton's Italian journey and over twenty-five to an account of his poetic projects. The introduction of ecclesiastical satire is also new to the pastoral lament. The other characteristics of *Lycidas*

---

[26] *The Shepherd's Oracle* by Francis Quarles, written a few years before *Lycidas* but not published till 1646, contains an abundance of religious satire.

were without exception predetermined by the literary tradition of the pastoral elegy, and even for these Milton had, as we have seen, ample precedent in the pastoral at large.

What, then, shall we say of *Lycidas* as a work of art? Is it the less a perfect whole because it is composite? Does the fact that it is conventional make it any the less original in the highest sense? If we know *Lycidas* well and read it in a fitting mood, we find ourselves forgetting that its pastoral imagery is inherently absurd. The conventions which at first seem so incongruous with the subject, gradually become a matter of course. And when once we have ceased to regard these conventions as anything more than symbols, we find them no longer detracting from the beauty of the poem, but forming an essential element of its classic charm. For the supreme beauty of *Lycidas* lies partly in the very fact of its conventionality. Its grief is not of the kind that cries aloud; it soothes and rests us like calm music. For a moment, indeed, we are aroused by an outburst of terrible indignation, but the dread voice is soon past and we sink back again into the tranquil enjoyment which comes from the contemplation of pure beauty, unmarred by any newness of idea, unclouded by overmastering emotion.

2. ON THE POEM

from *The Life of Milton*

Samuel Johnson

One of the poems on which much praise has been bestowed is *Lycidas,* of which the diction is harsh, the rhymes uncertain, and the numbers unpleasing. What beauty there is we must therefore seek in the sentiments and images. It is not to be considered as the effusion of real passion; for passion runs not after remote allusions and obscure opinions. Passion plucks no berries from the myrtle and ivy, nor calls upon Arethuse and Mincius, nor tells of rough *satyrs* and *fauns with cloven heel.* Where there is leisure for fiction there is little grief.

In this poem there is no nature, for there is nothing new. Its form is that of a pastoral, easy, vulgar, and therefore disgusting; whatever images it can supply are long ago exhausted, and its inherent improbability always forces dissatisfaction on the mind. When Cowley tells of Hervey, that they studied together, it is easy to suppose how much he must miss the companion of his labours, and the partner of his discoveries; but what image of tenderness can be excited by these lines?—

> We drove a field, and both together heard
> What time the grey fly winds her sultry horn,
> Battening our flocks with the fresh dews of night.

First published in *The Works of the Most Eminent English Poets* (London, 1779), Vol. II, and later issued separately as *Lives of the Poets.*

We know that they never drove a field, and that they had no flocks to batten; and though it be allowed that the representation may be allegorical, the true meaning is so uncertain and remote that it is never sought because it cannot be known when it is found.

Among the flocks, and copses, and flowers, appear the heathen deities—Jove and Phœbus, Neptune and Æolus, with a long train of mythological imagery, such as a college easily supplies. Nothing can less display knowledge, or less exercise invention, than to tell how a shepherd has lost his companion, and must now feed his flocks alone, without any judge of his skill in piping; and how one god asks another god what is become of Lycidas, and how neither god can tell. He who thus grieves will excite no sympathy; he who thus praises will confer no honour.

This poem has yet a grosser fault. With these trifling fictions are mingled the most awful and sacred truths, such as ought never to be polluted with such irreverend combinations. The shepherd likewise is now a feeder of sheep, and afterwards an ecclesiastical pastor, a superintendent of a Christian flock. Such equivocations are always unskilful; but here they are indecent, and at least approach to impiety, of which, however, I believe the writer not to have been conscious.

Such is the power of reputation justly acquired, that its blaze drives away the eye from nice examination. Surely no man could have fancied that he read *Lycidas* with pleasure had he not known its author.

from *Milton*

E. M. W. Tillyard

About two months before *Lycidas*, in September 1637, Milton wrote two letters to Diodati. In the first he mentions how exacting and unintermitted his studies have been: the idea that his excursions to London were much relaxation cannot be allowed. He writes:

> Your method of study is such as to admit of frequent interruptions, in which you visit your friends, write letters, or go abroad; but it is my way to suffer no impediment, no love of ease, no avocation whatever, to chill the ardour, to break the continuity, or divert the completion of my literary pursuits.

The second letter gives other and more definite information. First, and this is important as showing the state of mind out of which *Lycidas* grew, he is struck by the longing for immortality. He writes:

> You ask what I am meditating? By the help of Heaven, an immortality of fame. But what am I doing? πτεροφυῶ, I am letting my wings grow and preparing to fly; but my Pegasus has not yet feathers enough to soar aloft in the fields of air.

Of the restlessness or rather mental anguish which *Lycidas* proves to have resulted at times from this longing he indeed states nothing; but he admits that he is tired of Horton and is thinking of a move to London.

London, 1930, pp. 79–85.

I will now tell you seriously what I design: to take chambers in one of the inns of court, where I may have the benefit of a pleasant and shady walk; and where with a few associates I may enjoy more comfort when I choose to stay at home, and have more elegant society when I choose to go abroad. In my present situation you know in what obscurity I am buried, and to what inconveniences I am exposed.

A cause for restlessness, particularly in the mind of one who had nearly finished a long period of preparation for some great work, was that in 1636 and 1637 the plague had been bad in England. In the latter year it spread to Horton, and a number of people there died of it. This is a fact to be remembered in reading *Lycidas*.

Lycidas is the last and greatest English poem of Milton's youth. Though shorter, it is greater than *Comus*, written with newly won but complete mastery and expressing a mental experience both valuable and profound.

Most criticism of *Lycidas* is off the mark, because it fails to distinguish between the nominal and the real subject, what the poem professes to be about and what it is about. It assumes that Edward King is the real, whereas he is but the nominal subject. Fundamentally *Lycidas* concerns Milton himself; King is but the excuse for one of Milton's most personal poems. This cannot be proved: it can only be deduced from the impression the poem leaves. Most readers agree that Milton was not deeply grieved at King's death, as they agree that the poem is great. If it is great, it must contain deep feeling of some sort. What then is this deep feeling all about?

From the circumstances in which *Lycidas* was written and from the two obviously personal passages the question can be answered. When Milton wrote *Lycidas* in 1637 he was twenty-nine years of age, and early in the next year he set out for Italy with perhaps the intention of going on to Greece. Whether the last line of the poem,

> To morrow to fresh Woods, and Pastures new,

refers to this intended journey is doubtful; it may well do so. Anyhow at the time of writing *Lycidas* Milton must have had the Italian and possibly the Greek journey in his mind. When he heard of King's death, and still more when by consenting to write the elegy he had to make his mind dwell on it, he cannot but have felt the analogy between King and himself. Milton and King had been at the same college in the same university. Their careers and interests had been similar there. Milton was a poet, King had written verse too. King had made a voyage on the sea, Milton was about to make voyages. How could Milton have missed the idea that *he* might make the analogy complete by getting drowned, like King, also? At a time when, through plagues and what not, life was less secure than in modern times of peace, Milton, having sacrificed so much to his great ambition, must anyhow, as the time of preparation drew to an end, have dwelt on the thought that it might be all for nothing. Not that he was a coward: but the fear that his ambitions might be ruined at the last moment must have been at times difficult to endure. Those who had experience of the late war must have known the miserable anxiety suffered immediately before going on leave. It was not that people feared to die more then than at other times, but the thought of being baulked by death of their desire for home was peculiarly harrowing. Milton's state of mind must at times have been somewhat similar, and in considering King's fate his fears must have come crowding on him. That he was at least partly thinking of his own possible fate is made clear by the reference in the first paragraph to his own destined urn and sable shroud. As a reason for his singing of Lycidas he writes:

> So may som gentle Muse
> With lucky words favour my destin'd Urn,
> And as he passes turn,
> And bid fair peace be to my sable shrowd,
> For we were nurst upon the self-same hill,
> Fed the same flock, by fountain, shade, and rill.

In other words, "If I die, some one will requite me with a requiem, for in other ways the analogy between us was complete." And much more agonizingly does the thought of premature death start in his mind when he writes of poetic fame and "the blind *Fury* with th' abhorred shears." Why should he have submitted himself to rigorous self-denial, if to no end?

But his fears of premature death, though part of the subject, are not the whole. The real subject is the resolving of those fears

(and of his bitter scorn of the clergy) into an exalted state of
mental calm. The apotheosis of Lycidas in the penultimate paragraph has a deeper meaning: it symbolizes Milton's own balanced
state of mind to which he won after the torments he had been
through. This is the secret of the strength of *Lycidas* and the
reason why it is a greater poem than *Comus:* in the one calm
after struggle, in the other calm of a kind but without the pre-
liminary struggle. To prove that the deepest and most satisfying
calm is that which follows on mental struggle one has only to
point to the greatest tragedies.

If the above idea is accepted, it is possible to see in *Lycidas*
a unity of purpose which cannot be seen in it if the death of
King is taken as the real subject of the poem. In particular the
outburst against the clergy, usually regarded as a glorious excrescence, will be found perfectly in keeping with the profounder
and less elegiac significance of the whole. Let me try to explain
this harmony by describing how the purpose of the poem develops.

Milton begins with characteristic egotism. His first lines do
not concern King but his own reluctance to write a poem before
he is mature. But he must write, for Lycidas died prematurely
—"*Young* Lycidas"—and for a premature death he must be
willing to risk premature poetry. Moreover, if he writes an elegy
for Lycidas, some other poet may reward him when he dies with
an elegy too. The introduction, lines 1 to 24, thus ends on Milton's possible death.

The first section, beginning "Together both, ere the high
Lawns appear'd," consists of lines 25 to 84. It contains a lament
for the death of Lycidas, regret that the Muse could not protect
her son, and leads up to the first great cause of pain in Milton's
own mind: the risk of death before his great work is completed.
What has been the use of all his laborious preparation, his careful chastity (for doubtless he means this by his references to
Amaryllis and Neaera), if fame, for whose sake he has denied
himself, is to escape him, anticipated by death? Earthly fame,
he replies to himself in the person of Phoebus, has nothing to do
with heavenly fame: it depends on deeds, not on what those deeds
effect. So he argues, but one does not get the impression of
emotional conviction yet: the final impression of the first section
is that it would be a cruel shame and a wicked waste, if he were

to die. It should be noted with what consummate skill Milton
in this section works the subject from King to its climax in himself.

In the second section, lines 85 to 131, beginning "O Fountain
Arethuse," he does exactly the same thing. In the elegiac tradition various persons come to visit the body. It is perfectly
natural that St. Peter should come to visit a priest, and equally
natural that he should proceed from lamenting the death of a
good priest to denouncing the bad. But this denunciation reveals
the second great cause of mental pain in Milton: his quarrel
with contemporary Englind, typified by the rottenness of the
clergy. Thus St. Peter's outburst is not an excrescence but
strictly parallel with Milton's earlier outburst about the blind
Fury. One can even see a close connection of ideas between the
two grievances. One grievance is that "the hungry Sheep look
up and are not fed": England has bad or useless teachers;
the other is that he, Milton, whose ambition was to teach by
writing a great epic, to feed the hungry sheep of England, may
easily be cut off before it can be realized. It should be noted
that the second grievance, like the first, is answered at the end
of the second movement. Punishment is waiting; the two-handed
engine stands ready to smite. But even less than at the end of the
first section has mental calm been attained. The end of the second section marks the climax of the poem. Milton has stated
his quarrel with life: we await the conclusion.

Of the third section, lines 132 to 164, beginning "Return
Alpheus," it is more difficult to describe the function. Some
quieter interlude is clearly necessary between St. Peter's bitter
outburst and the heavenly triumph of the final movement. But
it is more than an interlude, it has value as a transition too. The
sudden change from the terror of the two-handed engine to the
incredible beauty of the description of the flowers contains an
implication that somehow the "Dorique delicacy," of which the
description of the flowers is the highest example in Milton, is
not irreconcilable with the sterner mood, and hence is able to
insinuate some comfort. So too from the dallying with a false
surmise, the escape into a region of pure romance

> Where the great vision of the guarded Mount
> Looks toward *Namancos* and *Bayona's* hold,

some comfort is allowed. But these sources of comfort are but minor, leading up to the greater solution.

The fourth section purports to describe the resurrection of Lycidas and his entry into heaven. More truly it solves the whole poem by describing the resurrection into a new kind of life of Milton's hopes, should they be ruined by premature death or by the moral collapse of his country. The loss or possible loss of human fame is made good by fame in heaven, the corrupt clergy are balanced by

> all the Saints above
> In solemn troops and sweet Societies,

and the harsh forebodings of Peter, the pilot of the Galilean lake, are forgotten

> Through the dear might of him who walk'd the waves.

But above all the fourth section describes the renunciation of earthly fame, the abnegation of self by the great egotist, and the spiritual purgation of gaining one's life after losing it.

Some people might call *Lycidas* a religious poem, for Milton appears to found his comfort on his hopes of heaven: others might object that his grounds of comfort are extraordinarily flimsy and that the pessimism of *Paradise Lost* is truer to the facts of life than the optimism of *Lycidas*. But the question of beliefs is unimportant; what matters and what makes *Lycidas* one of the greatest poems in English is that it expresses with success a state of mind whose high value can hardly be limited to a particular religious creed. Milton, by ridding himself of his inhibiting fears, by subordinating the disturbing ambition to have done a thing to the serene intention of doing it as well as possible, had proved his mettle and issued from the ordeal a great man. *Lycidas* expresses a mind of the keenest sensibility and most powerful grasp acutely aware of a number of most moving sensations, but controlling these sensations so that they do not conflict but rather by contrast reinforce one another: a mind calm after struggle but keyed up to perform heroic deeds, should they need to be done.

A Poem Nearly Anonymous

John Crowe Ransom

It was published in 1638, in the darkness preceding our incomparable modernity. Its origins were about as unlikely as they could be, for it was only one of the exhibits in a memorial garland, a common academic sort of volume. It appeared there without a title and signed only by a pair of initials, though now we know it both by a name and by an author. Often we choose to think of it as the work of a famous poet, which it was not; done by an apprentice of nearly thirty, who was still purifying his taste upon an astonishingly arduous diet of literary exercises; the fame which was to shine backwards upon this poem, and to be not very different from the fame which he steadily intended, being as distant as it was great. Unfortunately it is one of the poems which we think we know best. Upon it is imposed the weight of many perfect glosses, respecting its occasion, literary sources, classical and contemporary allusions, exhausting us certainly and exhausting, for a good many persons, the poem. But I am bound to consider that any triteness which comes to mind with mention of the poem is a property of our own registration, and does not affect its freshness, which is perennial. The poem is young, brilliant, insubordinate. In it is an artist who wrestles with an almost insuperable problem, and is kinsman to some tortured modern artists. It has something in common

From *The World's Body* (New York, 1938), pp. 1–28; first published in the *American Review*, IV (1933).

with, for example, *The Waste Land*. In short, the poem is *Lyc-idas*.

A symbol is a great convenience in discussion, and therefore I will find one in the half-way anonymity of the poem; symbolic of the poet's admirable understanding of his art, and symbolic of the tradition that governed the art on the whole in one of its flourishing periods. Anonymity, of some real if not literal sort, is a condition of poetry. A good poem, even if it is signed with a full and well-known name, intends as a work of art to lose the identity of the author; that is, it means to represent him not actualized, like an eyewitness testifying in court and held strictly by zealous counsel to the point at issue, but freed from his juridical or prose self and taking an ideal or fictitious personality; otherwise his evidence amounts the less to poetry. Poets may go to universities and, if they take to education, increase greatly the stock of ideal selves into which they may pass for the purpose of being poetical. If on the other hand they insist too narrowly on their own identity and their own story, inspired by a simple but mistaken theory of art, they find their little poetic fountains drying up within them. Milton set out to write a poem mourning a friend and poet who had died; in order to do it he became a Greek shepherd, mourning another one. It was not that authority attached particularly to the discourse of a Greek shepherd; the Greek shepherd in his own person would have been hopeless; but Milton as a Greek shepherd was delivered from being Milton the scrivener's son, the Master of Arts from Cambridge, the handsome and finicky young man, and that was the point. In proceeding to his Master's degree he had made studies which gave him dramatic insight into many parts foreign to his own personal experience; which was precisely the technical resource he had required the moment he determined to be a poet. Such a training was almost the regular and unremarked procedure with the poets of his time. Today young men and women, as noble as Milton, those in university circles as much as those out of them, try to become poets on another plan, and with rather less success. They write their autobiographies, following perhaps the example of Wordsworth, which on the whole may have been unfortunate for the prosperity of the art; or they write some of their intenser experiences, their loves, pities, griefs, and religious ecstasies; but too literally, faithfully, piously. ingenuously. They seem to want to do without wit and playfulness, dramatic sense, detachment, and it cuts them off from the practice of an art.

Briefly, it was Milton's intention to be always anonymous as a poet, rarely as a writer of prose. The poet must suppress the man, or the man would suppress the poet. What he wanted to say for himself, or for his principles, became eligible for poetry only when it became what the poet, the dramatis persona so to speak, might want to say for himself. The poet could not be directed to express faithfully and pointedly the man; nor was it for the sake of "expression" that the man abdicated in favor of the poet.

Strictly speaking, this may be a half-truth. But if we regard with a reformer's eye the decay, in our time, of poetry, it becomes almost the whole truth we are called to utter. I do not mind putting it flatly; nor drawing the conclusion that poetry appeared to the apprentice Milton, before it could appear anything else, and before it could come into proper existence at all, as a sort of exercise, very difficult, and at first sight rather beside the point. It was of course an exercise in pure linguistic technique, or metrics; it was also an exercise in the technique of what our critics of fiction refer to as "point of view." And probably we shall never find a better locus than *Lycidas* for exhibiting at once the poet and the man, the technique and the personal interest, bound up tightly and contending all but equally; the strain of contraries, the not quite resolvable dualism, that is art.

For we must begin with a remark quite unsuitable for those moderns to whom "expression" seems the essential quality of poetry. *Lycidas* is a literary exercise; and so is almost any other poem earlier than the eighteenth century; the craftsmanship, the formal quality which is written on it, is meant to have high visibility. Take elegy, for example. According to the gentle and extremely masculine tradition which once governed these matters, performance is not rated by the rending of garments, heartbreak, verisimilitude of desolation. After all, an artist is standing before the public, and bears the character of a qualified spokesman, and a male. Let him somewhat loudly sweep the strings, even the tender human ones, but not without being almost military and superficial in his restraint; like the pomp at the funeral of the king, whom everybody mourns publicly and nobody privately. Milton made a great point of observing the proprieties of verse. He had told Diodati, as plainly as Latin elegiacs allowed, that "expression" was not one of the satisfactions which they permitted to the poet: "You want to know in verse how much I love and cherish you; believe me that you will scarcely discover this in verse, for love like ours is not contained within cold measures, it does not come to hobbled feet." As for memorial verse, he had already written, in English or Latin, for the University beadle, the University carrier, the Vice-Chancellor, his niece the Fair Infant Dying of a Cough, the Marchioness of Winchester, the Bishop of Winchester, the Bishop of Ely; he was yet to write for his Diodati, and for Mrs. Katharine Thomason. All these poems are exercises, and some are very playful indeed. There is no great raw grief apparent ever, and sometimes, very likely, no great grief. For Lycidas he mourns with a very technical piety.

Let us go directly to the poem's metre—though this feature may seem a bristling technicality, and the sort of thing the tender reader may think he ought to be spared. I do not wish to be brutal, but I am afraid that metre is fundamental in the problem posed to the artist as poet. During the long apprenticeship Milton was the experimentalist, trying nearly everything. He does not ordinarily, in the Minor Poems, repeat himself metrically; another poem means another metre, and the new metre will scarcely satisfy him any better than the last one did. Evidently Milton never found the metre in which as a highly individual poet he could feel easy, and to which he was prepared to entrust his serious work, until he had taken the ragged blank verse of contemporary drama and had done something to it; tightening it up into a medium which was hard enough to exhibit form, and plastic enough to give him freedom. In other words, it defined the poet as somebody with a clipped, sonorous, figurative manner of speaking; but it also gave a possible if indirect utterance to the natural man. Here let us ask the question always in order against a Milton poem: What was the historic metrical pattern already before him, and what are the liberties he takes with it? For he does not cut patterns out of the whole cloth, but always takes an existing pattern; stretches it dangerously close to the limits that the pattern will permit without ceasing to be a pattern; and never brings himself to the point of defying that restraint which patterns inflict upon him, and composing something

altogether unpatterned. That is to say, he tends habitually towards the formlessness which is modern, without quite caring to
arrive at that destination. It is the principle we are interested
in, not the literal answer to the question, which I will try to get
over briefly.

The answer given by the Milton scholars, those who know
their Italian, might well be that in this poem he made a very
free adaptation of the canzone. This was a stanza of indeter-
minate length, running it might be to twenty lines or so, marked
by some intricate rhyming scheme, and by a small number of
six-syllable lines inserted among the ten-syllable lines which constituted the staple. The poet was free to make up his own stanza
but, once that was given, had to keep it uniform throughout
the poem. Milton employs it with almost destructive freedom, as
we shall see. Yet, on the other hand, the correct stanza materials
are there, and we can at least say that any one of the stanzas
or paragraphs might make a passable canzone. And lest his ir-
regularities be imputed to incompetence, we must observe the
loving exactitude of his line-structure, that fundamental unit
of any prosody, within the stanzas. He counts his syllables, he
takes no liberties there: consisting with our rather fixed impression that he scarcely knew how in all his poetry to admit an imperfect line.

The Milton scholars know their Italian and have me at a dis-
advantage. Milton knew his Italian. But he also knew his Spenser,
and knowing that, it seems unnecessary to inquire whether he
knew his Italian too; for he had only to adapt a famous Spenserian stanza, and his acquaintance with the canzone becomes really
immaterial. I imagine this point has a slight importance. It
would have something to do with the problem of the English
poet who wants to employ an English technique in addressing
himself to an English public which can be expected to know its
English formal tradition. Spenser anticipated Milton by employing the canzone effectively in at least two considerable poems;
they were not elegies, but at least they were marriage hymns. In
1596 he published his *Prothalamion*, upon the occasion of a
noble alliance; the stanzas are exactly uniform, and they com-
pose an admirable exercise in Italian canzoni. But he had published in 1595 his *Epithalamion*, upon the occasion of his own
wedding, which is much more to Milton's purpose, and ours.

Here are ten eighteen-line stanzas, but here are also twelve nine-teen-line stanzas, and one of seventeen lines; and one of the eighteen-line stanzas does not agree in pattern with the others. If these details escape the modern reader, it is not at all certain that they were missed by Spenser's public. I should like to think that the poetical consciousness of the aristocratic literati of that age was a state of mind having metrical form in its fore-ground, and Spenser intended frankly to make use of the situa-tion. Perhaps he calculated that if they would go to the trouble to analyze a poem composed of intricate but regular canzoni, they might go to still greater pains to analyze a poem whose canzoni were subtly irregular. I suppose this was something of a miscalculation, like other of his plans. But if it were a just calculation: then the advantage to be reaped by their going to such pains—it was their advantage as much as his—was the sort of addition to total effect which a labor of love can furnish. A public like Spenser's, if we are to construe it at its best, par-ticipates in the poem as does the author, and it is unfortunate if there lives today some modern Spenser who does not hope for such a reward to his efforts. But probably the sad truth is that a subtle art is unlikely in the first place, whose artist does not reckon upon the background of a severe technical tradition, and the prospect of a substantial public body of appreciation.

The enterprising Spenser prepared the way for the daring Milton, who remarks the liberties which his celebrated exemplar has taken and carries his own liberties further, to a point just this side of anarchy. The eleven stanzas of *Lycidas* occupy 193 lines, but are grossly unequal and unlike. Such stanzas are not in strictness stanzas at all; Milton has all but scrapped the stanza in its proper sense as a formal and binding element. But there is perhaps an even more startling lapse. Within the poem are ten lines which do not rhyme at all, and which technically do not belong therefore in any stanza, nor in the poem.

Now we may well imagine that the unrhymed lines did not escape Milton's notice, and also that he did not mean nor hope that they should escape ours. The opening line of the poem is unrhymed, which is fair warning. The ten unrhymed lines should be conspicuous among the 183 rhymed ones, like so many bache-lors at a picnic of fast-mated families. Let us ask what readers of *Lycidas* have detected them, and we shall see what readers are equipped with the right sensibility for an effect in form. And if the effect in this case is an effect of prose formlessness, and if nevertheless it is deliberate, we had better ask ourselves what Milton wanted with it.

It is tempting to the imperious individualism of the modern reader, especially if he has heard somewhere about the enormous egoism of John Milton, to say that the "expression" in these lines must have seemed to their author "inevitable," and superior to any obligation to the law of the form. Just as we find them, they had leapt out of the tense creative fury of the poet, notable, possibly prophetic; and what higher considerations were there anywhere requiring him in cold blood to alter them? But that does not make sense as an account of the poetic processes of a Milton. The ten lines, as it happens, look at them hard as we like, do not seem more important than ten others, and are not the lines by which he could have set special store. As a matter of fact, he might have altered them easily, tinkering with them as long as necessary in order to bring them within the metre, and they would scarcely have been, by whatever standard, any the worse. So great is the suggestibility of the poet's mind, the associability of ideas, the margin in the meaning of words. It is the inexperienced artist who attributes sanctity to some detail of his inspiration. You may ask him to write a poem which will make sense and make metre at the same time, but in the performance he will sacrifice one or the other; the consequence will be good sense and lame metre, or good metre and nonsense; if he is a man of interests and convictions, the former. But the competent artist is as sure of his second thoughts as of his first ones. In fact, surer, if anything; second thoughts tend to be the richer, for in order to get them he has to break up the obvious trains of association and explore more widely. Milton was not enamored of the ten lines, and they stand out from their context by no peculiar quality of their own but only because they do not belong to it metrically. Therefore I would say that they constitute the gesture of his rebellion against the formalism of his art, but not the rebellion itself. They are defiances, showing the man unwilling to give way to the poet; they are not based upon a special issue but upon surliness, and general principles. It is a fateful moment. At this critical stage in the poet's career, when he has come to the end of the period of Minor Poems, and is turning over in his head the grand subjects out of which he will produce great poems, he is uneasy, sceptical, about the whole foundation of poetry as an art. He has a lordly contempt for its tedious formalities, and is determined to show what he can do with only half trying to attend to them. Or he thinks they are definitely bad, and proposes to see if it is not better to shove them aside.

In this uncertainty he is a modern poet. In the irregular stanzas and the rhymeless lines is registered the ravage of his modernity; it has bit into him as it never did into Spenser. And we imagine him thinking to himself, precisely like some modern poets we know, that he could no longer endure the look of perfect regimentation which sat upon the poor ideas objectified before him upon the page of poetry, as if that carried with it a reflection upon their sincerity. I will go further. It is not merely easy for a technician to write in smooth metres; it is perhaps easier than to write in rough ones, after he has once started; but when he has written smoothly, and contemplates his work, he is capable actually, if he is a modern poet, of going over it laboriously and roughening it. I venture to think that just such a practice, speaking very broadly, obtained in the composition of *Lycidas;* that it was written smooth and rewritten rough; which was treason.

I will make a summary statement which is true to the best of my knowledge. There did not at the time anywhere exist in English, among the poems done by competent technical poets, another poem so wilful and illegal in form as this one.

An art never possesses the "sincerity" that consists in speaking one's mind, that is, in expressing one's first impression before it has time to grow cold. This sincerity is spontaneity, the most characteristic quality in modern poetry. Art is long, and time is fleeting, and we have grown too impatient to relish more than the first motions towards poetic effect. The English and American Imagists exploited and consolidated this temper, which was no longer hospitable to a finished art. In their defence it may be said with justice that the writing of formal poetry, which they interrupted, was becoming a tedious parlor performance in which the poet made much ado about saying nothing of importance, while the man behind him quite escaped acquaintance through sheer lack of force. The verslibrists were determined to be bright, and fresh, and innocent of deep and ulterior designs; but their prose art was an anomaly. It wore out, and strict artistic economy has had a certain recovery; nothing like a complete one, for they left their mark upon our poetry, and I shall certainly not be so dogmatic as to say it has been entirely unfortunate.

It depends ultimately on taste whether we prefer prose to poetry, or prefer even a mixture of prose and poetry. Let us suppose two gentlemen talking a little wildly over their cups, until Mr. *A* insults Mr. *B*. Now if *B* is a modern man, he immediately strikes *A* down, with his knife if it happens to be in in his hand, or his stick, or his fist. He has acted spontaneously, with a right and quick instinct, and he is admired for it. (I do not mean to raise any moral issues with my analogy.) But if the time is about a century or two earlier, *B* steps back and says drily: "My seconds will wait upon you, Sir." The next dawn *A* and *B* repair to the grove, attended by their respective partisans, draw their rapiers, and with great ceremony set in to kill each other. Or apparently they do; but if they are not really prepared to be hurt, nor to hurt each other, but are only passing the time until they are informed that their honors are satisfied, it is a bogus and ineffective action and the serious spectators feel cheated; that represents the sort of art against which the free versifiers revolted. If they fight till *A* puts his steel through the vitals of *B*, or vice versa, the spectators are well rewarded, and the ceremonial has justified itself, though it took time; that stands for the true art. But if they lose their tempers on the field and begin to curse, and kick, and throw stones and clods at each other, they are behaving too spontaneously for a formal occasion. Why were they not spontaneous yesterday if that was their intention? They will have to be recalled to the occasion and come to a conclusion under the terms nominated; and here we have the mixed affair of poetry and prose, a problem in taste; here, I am afraid, we have *Lycidas*.

At any rate Milton thought something of the kind. For he never repeated his bold experiment; and he felt at the time that it was not an altogether successful experiment. The last stanzas become much more patterned, and in the postscript Milton refers to the whole monody as the song of an "uncouth Swain," who has been "with eager thought warbling his *Dorick* lay." That is descriptive and deprecatory.

There is another possibility. Milton had much of the modern

poet's awareness of his public; in this case the awareness of a public not quite capable of his own sustained artistic detachment. What sort of poem would it like? Too perfect an art might look cold and dead; and though an elegy had to be about the dead, it did not want itself to look dead, but to display incessant energy. So he read the formal poem he had written, and deformed it; or he had read other formal poems, like the *Epithalamion*, and remarked that the public, an increasingly mixed lot, thought them a little dull, and he now, as he composed his own poem, remembered to write into it plenty of formlessness. "The formalism," he was thinking, "if unrelieved, will dull the perceptions of my reader, and unprepare him for my surprises, and my tireless fertility. Therefore let him sense an exciting combat between the artist and the man, and let the man interrupt with his prose (comparative prose) the pretty passages of the artist." In that case the artist was only pretending to give way to the man, calculating with the cunning of a psychologist, perhaps of a dramatist, and violating the law of his art entirely for its public effect; a Jesuit of an artist. But the Jesuit, according to the Protestant tradition which reaches me, and which I will trust to the extent of this argument, has an excessive respect for the depravity of the humanity he ministers to, and he needs beyond other priests to be firmly grounded in his principles, lest from fighting the devil with fire he change his own element insensibly, become himself a fallen angel, and bear the reputation of one. The best thing to say for Milton is that his principles were strong, and he did not again so flagrantly betray them.

But if the poem is a literary exercise, it does not consist only in a game of metrical hide-and-seek, played between the long lines and short lines, the rhymed and unrhymed. It is also a poem in a certain literary "type," with conventions of subject-matter and style. Milton set out to make it a pastoral elegy, and felt honor-bound to use the conventions which had developed in the pastoral elegies of the Greeks, of Virgil, of the Italians, of Spenser; possibly of the French. The course of the poem in outline therefore is not highly "creative," but rather commonplace and in order, when the dead shepherd is remembered and his virtues published; when nature is made to lament him, and the streams to dry up in sympathy; when the guardian nymphs are asked why they have not saved him; when the untimeliness of his doom is moralized; when the corrupt church is reproached; when the flowers are gathered for the hearse; and finally when it appears to the mourners that they must cease, since he is not dead, but translated into a higher region, where he lives in bliss of a not definitive sort. In the pastoral elegy at large one of my friends distinguishes eleven different topics of discourse, and points out that Milton, for doubtless the first time in this literature, manages to "drag them all into one poem"; a distinction for him, though perhaps a doubtful one. But in doing so he simply fills up the poem; there are no other topics in it. And where is Milton the individualist, whose metrical departures would seem to have advertised a performance which in some to-be-unfolded manner will be revolutionary?

When we attempt to define the poetic "quality" of this poet's performances, we are forced to confess that it consists largely in pure eclecticism; here is a poet who can simply lay more of his predecessors under tribute than another. This is not to deny that he does a good job of it. He assimilates what he receives, and adapts it infallibly to the business in hand, where scraps fuse into integer, and the awkward articulations cannot be detected. His second-hand effects are not as good as new but better; the features of pastoral elegy are not as pretty in *Lycidas* as they were in Moschus, or Virgil, or Spenser, but prettier; though generically, and even in considerable detail, the same features. We remember after all that Milton intended his effects; and among others, this one of indebtedness to models. He expected that the reader should observe his eclecticism, he was scarcely alarmed lest it be mistaken for plagiarism. It is because of something mean in our modernism, or at least in that of our critics, that we, if we had composed the poem, would have found such an expectancy tainted with such an alarm. Like all the artists of the Renaissance, Milton hankered honestly after "Fame"; but he was not infected with our gross modern concept of "originality." The æsthetic of this point is perfectly rational. If a whole series of artists in turn develop the same subject, it is to the last one's advantage that he may absorb the others, in addition to being in whatever pointed or subtle manner his own specific self. His work becomes the climax of a tradition, and is better than the work of an earlier artist in the series. Unfortunately, there will come perhaps the day when there is no artist prepared to carry on the tradition; or, more simply, when the tradition has gone far enough and is not worth carrying further; that is, when it is worn out as a "heuristic" principle, and confines more than it frees the spirit. (Very few pastoral elegies can have been written since *Lycidas* in our language; very few critics can have deplored this.) On that day the art will need its revolutionist, to start another tradition. It is a bold step for the artist to take, and Milton did not think it needful to take it here. The revolutionist who does not succeed must descend to the rating, for history, of rebel; the fool of a wrong political intuition.

But revolutions, for all that, little and private ones if not big and general ones, come frequently into a healthy literary history, in which variety is a matter of course. The poet may do better with a make-believe of his own than with a time-honored one. There is no theoretical limit upon the variety of literary types, and each good type permits of many explorers, but tends at last to be exhausted. The point of view of Greek shepherds, as romantic innocents and rustics, is excellent, and offers a wide range of poetic discourse concerning friendship, love, nature, and even, a startling innovation of the Italian pastoralists, the "ruin of the clergy." The point of view of the amorous cavalier presenting his compliments and reproaches to his lady is also a good one; it ran through many hundreds of lyrics in the sixteenth and seventeenth centuries, and is still better than no point of view at all, which we find in some very young poet speaking in his own person to his own love. The studied "conceit" of the seventeenth century offered another field of discourse in which poetic exercises took place; logical and academic, but having rich possibilities, and eligible even for religious experiences. The sonnet is primarily a metrical form, but behind it there is an ideal and rather formidable speaker, far from actual, who must get what he has to say into a very small space and, according to the rules, into a very concise style of utterance. The ballad offers a point of view quite alien to the ordinary cultivated poet, because speaking in that form he must divest himself of the impedimenta of learning and go primitive. All these forms lend themselves to individual variations and innovations; call for them, in fact, in the course of time, when the poet can find no fresh experience within the usual thing. It is entirely according to the æsthetic of this art if a poet wants to enter the book of literature with a series of Choctaw incantations, provided he is steeped in Choctaw experience and able to make a substantial exhibit; or with a set of poems from the character of a mere Shropshire lad; or from that of a dry New England countryman. It is important mostly that the poet know his part and speak it fluently.

Of Milton's "style," in the sense of beauty of sound, imagery, syntax and dystax, idiom, I am quite unprepared to be very analytic. It is a grand style; which is to say, I suppose, that it is *the* grand style, or as much a grand style as English poets have known: the style produced out of the poet's remembrance of his classical models, chiefly Virgil. Milton has not been the only English poet to learn from Virgil, but he is doubtless the one who learned the most. Until the nineteenth century Virgil was perhaps the greatest external influence upon English literature. Dryden venerated but could not translate him:

> . . . must confess to my shame, that I have not been able to Translate any part of him so well, as to make him appear wholly like himself. For where the Original is close, no Version can reach it in the same compass. Hannibal Caro's, in the Italian, is the nearest, the most Poetical, and the most Sonorous of any Translation of the Æneid's; yet, though he takes the advantage of blank Verse, he commonly allows two lines for one of Virgil, and does not always hit his sence. . . . Virgil, therefore, being so very sparing of his words, and leaving so much to be imagined by the Reader, can never be translated as he ought, in any modern Tongue. To make him Copious, is to alter his Character; and to translate him Line for Line is impossible; because the Latin is naturally a more succinct Language than either the Italian, Spanish, French, or even than the English (which, by reason of its Monosyllables, is far the most compendious of them). Virgil is much the closest of any Roman Poet, and the Latin Hexameter has more Feet than the English Heroick.

But in spite of the unfitness of an uninflected language like English, poets have occasionally managed a Virgilian style in it. We think at once of Marlowe. Naturally, it was not entirely beyond Shakespeare's powers; but Shakespeare at his highest pitch likes to rely on fury and hyperbole rather than the "smoothness" and "majesty" which Dryden commends in Virgil. Shakespeare writes:

> Rumble thy bellyful! Spit, fire! Spout, rain!

and

> You sulphurous and thought-executing fires,
> Vaunt-couriers of oak-cleaving thunderbolts,
> Singe my white head!

which is in a sublime style but not, if we care to be precise, the grand style. But Milton very nearly commanded this style. And with reason; for he had written Minor Poems in Latin as well as Minor Poems in English, and they were perhaps the more important item in his apprenticeship. This is one of the consequences:

> But now my Oate proceeds,
> And listens to the Herald of the Sea,
> That came in *Neptune's* plea,
> He ask'd the Waves, and ask'd the Fellon winds,
> What hard mishap hath doom'd this gentle swain?
> And question'd every gust of rugged wings
> That blows from off each beaked Promontory,
> They knew not of his story,
> And sage *Hippotades* their answer brings,
> That not a blast was from his dungeon stray'd,
> The Ayr was calm, and on the level brine,
> Sleek *Panope* with all her sisters play'd.
> It was that fatall and perfidious Bark
> Built in th' eclipse, and rigg'd with curses dark,
> That sunk so low that sacred head of thine.

It is probable that no other English poet has this mastery of the Virgilian effect; it is much more Virgilian, too, than the later effect which Milton has in the lines of the *Paradise Lost*, where the great departure from the epical substance of the Virgil makes it needful to depart from the poetic tone. But Milton proves here that he had fairly mastered it. He had simply learned to know it in the Latin—learning by the long way of performance as well as by the short one of observation—and then transferred it to his native English; where it becomes a heightened effect, because this language is not accustomed at once to ease and condensation like this, and there is little competition. The great repute of the Miltonic style—or styles, variants of a style—in our literature is a consequence of the scarcity of Miltons; that is, of poets who have mastered the technique of Latin poetry before they have turned to their own.

But the author of *Lycidas*, attended into his project by so much of the baggage of tradition, cannot, by a universal way of thinking, have felt, exactly, free. I shall risk saying that he was not free. Little chance there for him to express the interests, the causes, which he personally and powerfully was developing; the poem too occasional and too formal for that. Of course the occasion was a fundamental one, it was no less than Death; and there is nobody so aggressive and self-assured but he must come to terms with that occasion. But a philosophy of death seems mostly to nullify, with its irony, the philosophy of life. Milton was yet very much alive, and in fact he regarded himself as having scarcely begun to live. The poem is almost wasted if we are seeking to determine to what extent it permitted Milton to unburden his heart.

But not quite. The passage on mortality is tense; Professor Tillyard finds the man in it. It goes into a passage on the immortality of the just man's Fame, which gives Milton's Platonic version of the ends of Puritanism. More important perhaps is the kind of expressiveness which appears in the speech of Peter. The freedom with which Milton abuses the false shepherds surpasses anything which his predecessors in this vein had indulged. He drops his Latinity for plain speech, where he can express a Milton who is angry, violent, and perhaps a little bit vulgar. It is the first time in his career that we have seen in him a taste for writing at this level. With modern readers it may be greatly to his credit as a natural man that he can feel strongly and hit hard. Later, in the period of his controversial prose, we get more of it, until we have had quite enough of this natural man. In the *Paradise Lost* we will get some "strong" passages again, but they are not Milton's response to his own immediate situation, they are dramatically appropriate, and the persons and scenes of the drama are probably remote enough to bring the passages under the precise head of artistic effect. This may be thought to hold for *Lycidas*, since it is Peter speaking in a pastoral part, and Peter still represents his villains as shepherds; but I feel that Peter sounds like another Puritan zealot, and less than apostolic.

Before I offer some generalizations about the poet and his art, I wish to refer, finally, to a feature of *Lycidas* which critics have rarely mentioned, and which most readers of my acquaintance, I believe, have never noticed, but which is technically astonishing all the same, and ought to initiate an important speculation upon the intentions of this poet. Pastoral elegies are dramatic monologues, giving the words of a single shepherd upon a single occasion; or they are dialogues giving, like so much printed drama, the speeches of several shepherds in a single scene. They may have prologues, perhaps so denominated in the text, and printed in italics, or in a body separate from the elegy proper; and likewise epilogues; the prologues and epilogues being the author's envelope of narrative within which is inserted the elegy. The composition is straightforward and explicitly logical.

Milton's elegy is otherwise. It begins without preamble as a monologue, and continues so through the former and bitterer half of the passage on Fame:

> But the fair Guerdon when we hope to find,
> And think to burst out into sudden blaze,
> Comes the blind *Fury* with th'abhorred shears,
> And slits the thin spun life. . . .

At this point comes an incredible interpolation:

> . . . But not the praise,
> *Phœbus* repli'd, and touch'd my trembling ears . . .

And Phœbus concludes the stanza; after which the shepherd apologizes to his pastoral Muses for the interruption and proceeds with his monologue. But dramatic monologue has turned for a moment into narrative. The narrative breaks the monologue several times more, presenting action sometimes in the present tense, sometimes in the past. And the final stanza gives a pure narrative conclusion in the past, without the typographical separateness of an epilogue; it is the one which contains Milton's apology for the "Dorick" quality of his performance, and promises that the author will yet appear in a serious and mature light as he has scarcely done on this occasion.

Such a breach in the logic of composition would denote, in another work, an amateurism below the level of publication. I do not know whether our failure to notice it is because we have been intoxicated by the wine of the poetry, or dulled by the drum-fire of the scholars' glosses, or intimidated by the sense that the poem is Milton's. Certainly it is Milton's; therefore it was intended; and what could have been in his mind? I have a suggestion. A feature that obeys the canon of logic is only the mere instance of a universal convention, while the one that violates the canon is an indestructibly private thing. The poor "instance" would like so much to attain to the dignity of a particular. If Milton had respected the rule of composition, he must have appeared as any other author of pastoral elegy, whereas in his disrespect of it he can be the person, the John Milton who is different, and dangerous, and very likely to become famous. (It is ironical that the lapse in question celebrates Fame.) The logical difficulties in the work of an artist capable of perfect logic may be the insignia of an individuality which would otherwise have to be left to the goodness of the imagination; and that is a calculation which lies, I think, under much modern art. There are living poets, and writers of fiction, and critics at the service of both, who have a perfect understanding of the principle. The incoherence or "difficulty" in the work is not necessarily to be attributed to the unresourcefulness of the artist, as if he could not have straightened everything out if he had desired, but sometimes to his choice. Under this head comes that licentious typography in which we may find one of the really magnificent manifestations of our modernity. The author is like some gentleman in the world of fashion who is thoroughly initiated, yet takes great pains to break the rule somewhere in order that nobody will make the mistake of not remarking his personality. If there is any force in this way of reasoning, we may believe that Milton's bold play with the forms of discourse constitutes simply one more item in his general insubordinacy. He does not propose to be buried beneath his own elegy. Now he had done a thing somewhat on the order of the present breach in his *L'Allegro* and *Il Penseroso*. There is a comparative simplicity to these pieces amounting almost to obviousness, but they are saved in several ways. For one thing, they are twin poems, and the parallelism or contrast is very intricate. More to our point, there is a certain lack of definition in the substantive detail: long sentences with difficult grammatical references, and uncertainty as to whether the invocation has passed into the action and as to just where we are in the action. That trick was like the present one, indicating that the man is getting ahead of the poet, who is not being allowed to assimilate the matter into his formal style.

More accurately, of course, *they would like to indicate it;* the poet being really a party to the illusion. Therefore he lays himself open to the charge of being too cunning, and of over-reaching himself; the effect is not heroic but mock-heroic. The excited Milton, breathless, and breaking through the logic of composition, is charming at first; but as soon as we are forced to reflect that he counterfeited the excitement, we are pained and let down. The whole poem is properly an illusion, but a deliberate and honest one, to which we consent, and through which we follow the poet because it enables him to do things not possible if he were presenting actuality. At some moments we may grow excited and tempted to forget that it is illusion, as the untrained spectator may forget and hiss the villain at the theatre. But we are quickly reminded of our proper attitude. If the author tends to forget, all the more if he pretends to forget, we would recall him to the situation too. Such license we do not accord to poets and dramatists, but only to novelists, whose art is young. And even these, or the best of these, seem now determined, for the sake of their artistic integrity, to surrender it.

So *Lycidas*, for the most part a work of great art, is sometimes artful and tricky. We are disturbingly conscious of a man behind the artist. But the critic will always find too many and too perfect beauties in it ever to deal with it very harshly.

How to Read *Lycidas*

Paul Elmer More

After passing, as I might say, through the valley of the shadow of death, after months of physical prostration when reading of any sort was beyond the strength of a depleted brain, the poet to whom I turned instinctively with the first renewal of health was Milton. And so I have been reading Milton again and books about him, with the old zest I had as a boy, and with an added joy of almost tremulous excitement such as a miser might feel at the rediscovery of a treasure of gold stolen from him and long buried out of sight. But with this delight have been mingled certain scruples which vexed me a little more than they did in the old days. Again, as many times before, on laying down one of the poems the familiar words of Tennyson would come unbidden to my mind:

> O mighty-mouth'd inventor of harmonies,
> O skill'd to sing of Time or Eternity,
>   God-gifted organ-voice of England,
>   Milton, a name to resound for ages.

Of the mighty harmonies there would be no doubt; God-gifted voice certainly, organ-voice certainly, for those who have ears to hear. If any one in English, Milton had the divine craft of words, the mastery of sonorous speech. His is not Shakespeare's incalculable gift; it lacks the element of magic that captures us

From *On Being Human* (Princeton, N. J., 1936), pp. 184–202; first published in the *American Review*, VII (1936).

in Shakespeare; it is, or soon after his earliest experiments it was, an art that came by reflection, and as we read him we imagine that we might by equal deliberation attain the same perfection—only we never do attain it. And something of this distinction Milton himself seems to have felt when he wrote of Shakespeare:

> For whil'st to th' shame of slow-endeavoring Art
> Thy easie numbers flow.

The same distinction, I think, was present to Irving Babbitt when he spoke, as I have heard him do more than once, of his experience in quoting. It was Babbitt's custom in the first draft of his essays to cite from memory, and then, before printing, to verify the quotation by reference to the text. He would find occasionally that even his retentive memory had slipped and that he had substituted a word of his own for the poet's. And sometimes, he would say, he could not see that the substitution was inferior to the original—except in the case of Shakespeare. He never made a change in Shakespeare's language but some force or charm was lost. That was not so even with Milton. Such a difference exists between the seemingly careless spontaneity and the elaborated art of our two supreme masters of poetical diction; and he would be a rash judge who should say that the advantage was all on one side or the other.

But to return to the question that vexed my mood of acquiescent joy. God-gifted organ-voice Milton possessed in full measure—but "voice of England"? Does he speak for the whole of England, or, that being scarcely possible, does he speak from the heart of England, giving articulate expression to that central quality which has made England what we know and love? And by his influence did he maintain that balance and moderation, that sense of law enveloping the individual, which made of Falkland a true type of the Englishman that was to be? Here the question begins with style, but extends beyond mere style to psychology and to principles of government and life.

Now, if there be any hesitation with me to accept Milton's style as the norm of good English, it is certainly not on the ground of that "dissociation of sensibility" which draws a school of modern critics and poets to repudiate what may be called the Miltonic line of development and to seek their parentage in Shakespeare and Donne and the "Metaphysicals." If I understand what the leader of that Choir means by this rather obscure phrase, it is that Milton by conscious choice and judgement dissociated his mind from one whole range of perceptions, refusing to respond to them emotionally as foreign to his fixed theory of values, and by the same deliberate act of selection created a more or less artificial language; whereas the poets proceeding from Donne held their sensibility open to any and every perception and employed words to convey the sharp immediate impression of each fact of sense and experience without discrimination. The distinction is valid, and it is interesting; for the "modernist" in poetry it is of vital significance. But I am not sure that the "dissociation of sensibility," so taken, has been the source of dead monotony and of verbal unreality in our literature; and I am sure that if Milton failed in national leadership it was not for this reason. Rather I should say that his influence in this respect has made for sanity and form and for limitations which are characteristically English. Rather I should maintain that Milton's failure, so far as he failed, was owing to something essentially un-English, or only partially English, to something belonging to his individual temperament, which passed into his philosophy of life and diverted a noble love of liberty into a morbid and isolating passion. Here too Milton was clear-headed in his application of the law to others, but curiously perverse when his own interests were affected. In the second of the sonnets on the book called *Tetrachordon*, he berates his fellow countrymen as "Owles and Cuckoos, Asses, Apes and Doggs" for the very reason that they have lost the true meaning of liberty, while they

> bawle for freedom in this senceless mood,
> And still revolt when truth would set them free.
> Licence they mean when they cry libertie;
> For who loves that, must first be wise and good;
> But from that mark, how far they roave we see
> For all this wast of wealth, and loss of blood.

That is sound doctrine, but—alas to say it!—Milton did not see how apt would be the retort, *de te fabula;* how easy the reply: License he meant when he cried liberty.

This book called *Tetrachordon*, written by Milton himself, was the second of his treatises on divorce, and is a bitter invective against those who, by opposing the facile freedom of marital separation, enslave the soul under man-made laws, forgetting that which "makes us holiest and likest to God's immortal image," and who, for the law of liberty, set up "that which makes us most conformable and captive to civil and subordinate precepts: . . . although indeed no ordinance, human or from heaven, can bind against the good of man." By "the good of man," as Mr. Tillyard observes in his comment on the passage, Milton means what elsewhere he calls "nature"—damnable word, I add, into which have been distilled all the fallacies of human wit through thousands of years. If you track the word down through its many ambiguities, you will discover that in the end it signifies that which a man temperamentally and personally desires as distinguished from that which is prescribed for him by human rule or divine precept. So it was that Milton, fretted and humiliated because his wife, finding existence with him intolerable, left him and ran away home,—so it was that incontinently he rebelled against the human and divine laws of marriage, and wrote his pleas for freedom of divorce as complying with natural law and the good of man. If ever there was a case of liberty becoming license, it was here. However they may have differed in other respects, in this quality Milton resembled Shelley: they both identified what they desired at any moment with the natural good of man; they both made self-righteousness the law of right.

That was the beginning of Milton's public career and of his prose writings, and it was typical of what ensued. If the bishops in any way interfered with his personal idea of worship, then down with episcopacy and away with the Church; if the monarchical form of government hampered his political independence, then down with monarchy and away with the Constitution. There is no more painful reading in English literature than these apologies for free divorce and regicide which occupied the greatest genius of the age between *Lycidas* and *Paradise Lost*, and the style in which they are written is as heavy and un-English as their spirit is perverse. There are purple patches scattered through these treatises, which are all that most readers know of Milton's prose and which would give the impression that he is as magnificent here as in his verse; but if these passages are examined it will be found that, taken apart from their context, they are expressions of personal ambition, legitimate in itself and magnificent in its devotion to the aim of a poet, while all about them floats and rages a sea of rebellious discontent. I will not endorse Hilaire Belloc's sweeping condemnation of the prose works, but in the mass they do certainly form a repellent body of reading. Following the ideas of the tractates through the surging verbiage, one is reminded of the monsters in the account of creation, "wallowing unweildie" in

> the vast immeasurable Abyss
> Outrageous as a Sea, dark, wasteful, wilde,
> Up from the bottom turn'd by furious windes.

There is something disconcerting in the spectacle of a supreme artist, as Milton was in his verse, so losing his craftsmanship in another medium; what I would insist on is that the very style of his prose has a close relation to the fact that when he passes from imagination to theory his voice is not that of his people but of an exasperated individual. The seventeenth century, with all its greatness, is an age of frustration, filled with fine promises that, except in the field of science, came to no fruition, replete with noble utterance that somehow failed to convince. In the Church, in the State, in society, the one thing needed and not found was a commanding genius that should have been indeed the voice of England. It is the tragedy of the time that he who had the genius so to speak should have wasted his energies in querulous complaints against what was, and in the future was to show itself, the true spirit of the land. In a word that spirit may be described precisely as liberty, not license, as centrality, not dissent.

But I am not concerned to pass judgement on Milton's character and its effect upon his work as a whole; that is a longer theme than I care now to discuss. What I started out to do was to consider one small piece of his output, the *Lycidas*, and to ask myself how it should be read. To this question, at least in its acuter form, I was moved by chancing to take up at the same time Mr. Tillyard's estimation of the poem and Dr. Johnson's. As a whole I should regard Mr. Tillyard's *Milton* as about the best book we have on the man and the poet, a study admirable

for its scholarship and discrimination, and particularly notable
for its treatment of the philosophical problems raised by *Paradise Lost*, such as Milton's conception of the nature of evil and
the cause of man's fall. Now to Mr. Tillyard "*Lycidas* is the
last and greatest English poem of Milton's youth; though
shorter, it is greater than *Comus*, written with newly won but
complete mastery and expressing a mental experience both valuable and profound." That is a sentiment with which my own
judgement is in perfect accord; indeed, I should go further and
hold it to be the greatest short poem of any author in English,
the very criterion and touchstone of poetical taste. Yet with
that opinion I have felt bound to remember the sweeping condemnation of Johnson, to whom "the diction" of the poem "is
harsh, the rhymes uncertain, and the numbers unpleasing." It
is without passion and without art. In part no doubt Johnson's
lack of appreciation can be set down to his known deficiency in
the higher faculty of imagination. His comment on the diction
and rhythm does nothing more than indicate a certain insensi-
tiveness to the finer and more delicate effects of poetry in general.
But one cannot read the whole essay without perceiving that his
hostile criticism of the art of *Lycidas* sprang not so much from
his miscomprehension and æsthetic obtuseness as from hostility
to the poet and to all that Milton as a man stood for. Touching
Milton's plea for looser laws of divorce, the neglect of which by
the ruling Presbyterians turned him against that sect, Johnson
observes, and justly: "He that changes his party by his humour
is not more virtuous than he that changes it by his interest; he
loves himself rather than truth." As for the political tirades,
Johnson in his attack ran true to form: "Milton's republicanism
was . . . founded in an envious hatred of greatness, and a sul-
len desire of independence. . . . He hated monarchs in the State,
and prelates in the Church; for he hated all whom he was required to obey. . . . He felt not so much the love of liberty as
repugnance to authority." Now for myself I do not like Belloc's
summary and contemptuous dismissal of Milton as "a man rotten
with the two worst vices: falsehood and pride"; for somehow
one shrinks from using such language of a very great poet. To
Johnson's charge, on the contrary, I can subscribe without reser-
vation (indeed I have already said much the same thing in weaker
language), and I do not see how the charge, in substance, can

be countered by any impartial student of Milton's life. But to
Johnson the faults of the man were ruinous to the earlier work
of the poet, and he denounced *Lycidas* because he read into it
the author's ecclesiastical and political heresies; whereas I must
reject the maker whilst admiring what he has made. And there
the difficulty lies—or has lain for me: how can one so combine
detestation and love? how can one make so complete a separation
between Milton the destroyer of Church and State, and Milton
the artist? how is one to read *Lycidas?*

That particular difficulty, it will be observed, opens up into
one of the major problems of criticism in general: the relation
between the content of a poem and the art of a poem independent
of its content. In the beginning, when that distinction first presented itself to the Greek mind, it took a very simple form and
indeed was scarcely a question at all: the *Iliad* and the *Odyssey*
were valued primarily, not for their charm and interest, but because in them the statesman, the soldier, the athlete, the man who
desired to live honourably, could find the wisest precepts and the
best models. For later times, and for us of the West, the principle involved was formulated by Horace in his famous saying
that the most successful poet was he who knew how to mix the
utile and the *dulce*. What Horace meant by the *dulce* is clear
enough; it is just that in a poem which gives pleasure to the
reader. And what he meant by the *utile* is equally clear; it is
that in a poem from which we draw instruction. So in one of the
Epistles he tells a friend, held in Rome by the practice of de-
claiming, no doubt about the schools of philosophy, that he is
in the country reading Homer, who is a better teacher than all
the philosophers:

> *Qui, quid sit pulchrum, quid turpe, quid utile, quid non,*
> *Plenius ac melius Chrysippo et Crantore dicit.*

In exactly that form the question reached the Renaissance
critics, with the emphasis still heavily on the *utile*. So Puttenham,
to name a single example, thinks it necessary to preface his
treatise on *The Arte of English Poesie* with a long apology,
wherein is shown how "poets were the first priests, the first
prophets, the first legislators and politicians in the world," as
seen in Homer, Orpheus, Amphion, and the rest. You are back a
thousand years and more, and might be reading one of the an-

cient Greek commentators. But a change came with the advent
of the romantic movement. The *utile* and the *dulce* took on new
significance, and the old division was sharpened to something
like an absolute contrast between two irreconcilable criteria of
excellence. The *utile* was broadened so as to embrace the whole
substance of a poem whether instructive or not, its sense or
meaning. The *dulce* on the other side was refined to a conception
of pure poetry, the quintessence of art, as a sort of abstract
entity which could be felt and judged somehow apart from any
articulate thought or story conveyed; indeed the ideal poem
would be a succession of beautiful words with no meaning at all.
Such a thesis, baldly stated, is manifestly bare nonsense; but
practically the early romantics applied it to criticism by taking
Kubla Khan as the ideal poem, because, while the content was no
more than the shimmering matter of a dream, it reeked of that
mysterious entity called pure poetry. And it was not so long
ago that the theory flared up again in France under the impulse
of the Abbé Bremond's monograph on *La Poésie pure*. The discussion that ensued was confused by the Abbé's association of
æsthetic rapture with a mystical view of the function of prayer.
More illuminating, to me at least, is T. S. Eliot's pursuit and
final rejection of the same ideal of absolute poetry. In his earlier essays, particularly those on Seneca, Shakespeare, and
Dante, you will see him eagerly pursuing this *ignis fatuus* as the
ultimate standard of value. In the first of those studies he ranks
Shakespeare and Dante together as the supreme poets of the
world, and the two are equally great though the Italian has
taken up into the *Commedia* the profoundest wisdom of human
experience as expounded in the Thomistic theology, whereas the
Englishman has no interpretation of life's riddle beyond the
stale platitudes of Seneca. "Perhaps it was Shakespeare's special
role in history to have effected this peculiar union—perhaps it
is a part of his special eminence to have expressed an inferior
philosophy in the greatest poetry." It is true that Mr. Eliot
has his reservations in supporting this romantic dream of pure
poetry which came to him from certain early and, as I think,
unfortunate associations. It is more important to note that in
his latest enunciation he has worked himself quite clear of the
disturbing inheritance. There lies before me now his recently
published volume of *Essays Ancient and Modern*, and in the

opening paragraph of one of the "modern" (that is, hitherto
unprinted) essays I am held by this sentence: "The 'greatness'
of literature cannot be determined solely by literary standards;
though we must remember that whether it is literature or not
can be determined only by literary standards." That I take to
be a complete truth perfectly expressed; and the whole essay
on "Religion and Literature" is á masterly application of this
sentence to modern currents in verse and fiction. It is the critic
come to full maturity after years of probation.

And so, to apply this canon of taste to *Lycidas*, it may be possible for a young man, enamored of the sheer beauty of words
and untroubled as yet by the graver issues of life, to enjoy the
marvelous art of the poem with no thought of what the poem
means if connected with the poet's place in the world of ideas
and action. But such a rupture between the form and the substance of literature cannot long be maintained with the ripen-
ing of experience. Sooner or later we are bound to make up our
account with that law of taste so ably formulated: "The 'greatness' of literature cannot be determined solely by literary standards; though one must remember that whether it is literature or
not can be determined only by literary standards." That *Lycidas*
is literature, poetry and not mere verse, depends on the language,
the images, the form, on that mysterious working of the imagination which we can feel but cannot ultimately analyze or adequately describe; that it is great literature must depend on the
junction of such qualities with nobility of content. And such
nobility is there, in full measure.

The poem is an elegy prompted by the drowning of a college
friend of the author. It has been the complaint of more than
one critic that the expression of grief has little of that warmth
which might be expected from such a subject. Dr. Johnson can
find no "effusion of real passion, for passion runs not after remote allusions and obscure opinions." Against this charge of
frigidity Mr. Tillyard contends with great acumen that the true
theme of the poem is not the death of Edward King at all, but
the possible death of the poet himself. Milton was writing just before he set out on his voyage to Italy, when such an adventure was
more or less perilous and the chance of shipwreck and drowning
might very well have occupied his mind. So taken, the charge of
coldness towards a friend might be changed to one of cowardice

or egotism. But Milton was no coward and, however he may have shown himself elsewhere, the note of egotism is relieved by the artful, though doubtless unconscious transference of anxiety for himself to sorrow for another. And it was not the mere termination of life that made him anxious, but the fear that his one all-absorbing passion might so be. left unfulfilled. To understand his state of mind and the emotion that was impelling him to write, the elegy should be read in the light of those passages of self-dedication scattered through his prose works. These purple patches laid upon the coarse cloth of controversy are too well known to need repeating here. The keynote is given by the words inserted in the gross *Apology for Smectymnuus:*

> He who would not be frustrate of his hope to write well hereafter in laudable things, ought himself to be a true poem; that is, a composition and pattern of the best and honourablest things; not presuming to sing high praises of heroic men, or famous cities, unless he have in himself the experience and the practice of all that which is praiseworthy.

And joined with this personal ambition was the conviction that no loftier or purer service could be rendered to one's country and to the world than such a work as he was preparing himself to produce. Under the spell of a great heroic poem the mind of the people would respond in efforts towards great and heroic living. That was Milton's faith. It was the spirit of the reformer engrafted upon the temperament of the artist. In such a profession, wherein personal glory is identified with public welfare, pride with humility, there lurks, let us admit, a subtle danger; to fall short of brilliant success must leave the professor a monument of ridicule, like the mountains in labor that brought forth only a mouse. But, on the other hand, such a purpose, if carried through valiantly to a successful issue, makes the ordinary ambition of the artist and poet to appear in comparison no more than a cheap display of vanity. And Milton had the courage of conviction and the genius to succeed. In the history of English letters there is nothing like this determination carried through from youth to age, except the solemn dedication of Wordsworth to a similar purpose. All this must be read into *Lycidas*. Under the pretext of grief for the loss of a comrade in hope the poem is in reality as it were the quintessence of those

prose passages through which there speaks a self-confidence as
sublime as it was justified.

It is in the light of this lifelong ambition that we should read
the savage attack on the abuses in Church and State which raises
the note of elegy to the "higher mood" of righteous indignation:

> Last came and last did go,
> The Pilot of the *Galilean* lake. . . .
> He shook his Miter'd locks, and stern bespake,
> How well could I have spar'd for thee, young swain,
> Anow of such as for their bellies sake,
> Creep and intrude, and climb into the fold? . . .
> But that two-handed engine at the door,
> Stands ready to smite once, and smite no more.

And apart from any theory of episcopacy and royalty the abuses
were there and cried out for remedy. Laud knew them as well
as did Baxter, Charles as well as Cromwell; but none but Milton
possessed the "dread voice" which—alas, but for defects of temper!—might have done so much to set them right.

In this light also we should interpret the allegorical symbolism
of the poem:

> The hungry Sheep look up, and are not fed.

To Dr. Johnson all this masquerade of sheep and shepherds
is "easy, vulgar, and therefore disgusting," a cheap device of
images without passion and without art. Johnson had good reason to be suspicious of a genre that has invited so many weak
poets to indulge in flimflam. But he should not have forgotten
how all through the Old Testament, from the call that came to
Amos, "who was among the herdmen of Tekoa," and all through
the New Testament, from the angelic vision that broke upon the
shepherds who were "abiding in the field" about Bethlehem to
the parable that Jesus spake to his disciples, "I am the good
shepherd and know my sheep"—how all through the Bible this
pastoral allegory of the Church runs like the very music of religion.

These were the thoughts that haunted the memory of the poet
when he linked himself with his friend as shepherds:

> Together both, ere the high Lawns appear'd
> Under the opening eye-lids of the morn,
> We drove a field.

Together they were practicing their "rural ditties" in preparation for the louder chant that was to stir the nation from its ignoble lethargy, when one of the twain was washed away by the sounding sea, and his voice forever silenced. And what if a like fate awaited the other, who also was about to start on a voyage? "What boots it with incessant care . . . to meditate the thankless Muse," of what avail to "live laborious dayes," when, just as we

> think to burst out into sudden blaze,
> Comes the blind *Fury* with th' abhorred shears,
> And slits the thin spun life?

"But not the praise," he exclaims; the reward and the outcome are not confined to this world nor are they measured by success "on mortal soil," but in heaven before the "witness of all judging *Jove.*" I do not know how others are affected, but I can never peruse the climax of the poem without a thrill such as scarcely any other verses of the language excite.

> Weep no more, woful Shepherds weep no more,
> For *Lycidas* your sorrow is not dead,
> Sunk though he be beneath the watry floar,
> So sinks the day-star in the Ocean bed,
> And yet anon repairs his drooping head,
> And tricks his beams, and with new spangled Ore,
> Flames in the forehead of the morning sky:
> So *Lycidas* sunk low, but mounted high,
> Through the dear might of him that walk'd the waves
> Where other groves, and other streams along,
> With *Nectar* pure his oozy Lock's he laves,
> And hears the unexpressive nuptiall Song,
> In the blest Kingdoms meek of joy and love.
> There entertain him all the Saints above,
> In solemn troops, and sweet Societies
> That sing, and singing in their glory move,
> And wipe the tears for ever from his eyes.

Milton always rang true when he wrote of the world to come, but never before nor after did he attain quite this elevation, or achieve so realistic an expression of the invisible mysteries wrapt in the future. A few of his contemporaries possessed this power of giving substance to the hopes of eternity—notably Vaughan —but none of them approaches the master. And in later times the art was simply lost. Choose the best of the moderns, Newman for instance in *The Dream of Gerontius*, and they will appear cold and unconvincing beside Milton. Nor did any of the great poets of the earlier ages of faith quite equal him in this field. I would not compare the few lines of an elegy with the mighty structure of Dante's *Paradiso*, but for myself at least there is no single incident in Dante's voyage through the celestial spheres that touches me with the shock of actuality like that which I feel when I read *Lycidas*. I am not competent to explain by what devices, by what choice of words, Milton obtains his sublime effect. It would be easy of course, if it seemed worthwhile, to point to the rich manipulation of vowel sounds in this or that verse, to note the startling obviousness of the allusion to the might of him that walked the waves, but the final alchemy of art escapes such an analysis; indeed I question whether any skill of criticism can penetrate to the heart of that mystery of the word which we call inspiration, and leave at that. But one phase of Milton's method impresses me: the fact that his images are borrowed from the simplest commonplaces of faith— the return of dawn after the sinking of the sun in the ocean stream, the tears wiped away, the heavenly choiring of the blest. A comparison of Newman's attempt to translate the subtler speculations of theology into a poetic account of the soul's awakening after death shows how inevitably right was Milton's choice. There are regions of spiritual experience where the untutored imagination of the people goes deeper into reality than all the groping wisdom of philosophy.

One thing in the end is certain, the "greatness" of *Lycidas* is determined by an intimate marriage of form and matter, expression and substance. He who would read the poem worthily must see this, and must be equally sensitive to the delicacy of its art and to the sublimity of its ideas. This does not mean that he will forget or slur over the disagreeable traits of the poet's character or the repulsiveness of his ecclesiastical and political theories. But for our good fortune what repels us in the man and roused Johnson to a fury of protest is reserved for his prose and is excluded from his poetry—not completely indeed, for, not to mention the more outrageous sonnets, occasionally the bitterness of his disappointed soul breaks out in his later works, yet to such an extent that it is not impossible to keep the poet

and the controversialist apart as two almost separate powers.
That divorce has its unhappy aspect; for one thing it debars
Milton, in his total effect, from being accepted as the voice of
England. But it leaves to him the high credit of having raised
in *Paradise Lost,* to the honor of his native land, the one monu-
mentally successful product of that humanistic culture of the
Renaissance in which originality of genius and faithfulness to
the classical tradition are combined in perfect union. And for
Lycidas there is this further apology, that the elegy was composed before Milton's splendid spirit of liberty was exacerbated
by opposition into petulant license, when his personal pride
flamed with a yet undiverted zeal to make of his own life a true
poem and so to train himself for creating such a work of art as
would lift his people from the ugly slough of faction and greed,
where they were grovelling, into the finer atmosphere where pure
religion and the love of beauty might flourish together.

The Primary Language
of *Lycidas*

Josephine Miles

A study of the primary language of *Lycidas* tells us something of the poem's character. By "primary language," I mean
the words of reference, the nouns, adjectives, and verbs most

From *The Primary Language of Poetry in the 1640s,* University of California
Publications in English, XIX (1948), 86–90; revised for this book by the
author.

repeated throughout the poem; by "character" I mean relation of elements, both internal and external, both in entity and in context.

Repetition is at the heart of poetry; poetry's beats, its measures, its assonances and alliterations, its rhymes and refrains, its repeated structures, all by their recurrence provide its meaningful pattern. Different poems repeat in different ways. In *Lycidas*, just the reference, in addition to sound and structure, takes at least three forms of repetition. It echoes for emphasis, *For Lycidas is dead, dead ere his prime*. It parallels for guidance to main points of view, as in the addresses, *Begin then, Sisters . . . , Where were ye Nymphs . . . , O Fountain Arethuse . . . , Return Alpheus*. It recurs in less emphatic positions, in new contexts, to establish the variation on the themes: *For Lycidas is dead . . . For Lycidas your sorrow is not dead*. Or, *. . . sunk so low that sacred head of thine . . . , Sunk though he be beneath the watry floor . . . , So Lycidas sunk low, but mounted high*. A look at some of these more subtle recurrences will tell us not only of primary substance and shaping structure but of the poem's place in the continuity of poetry.

Most of the repeated terms in *Lycidas* are of common importance for the poets of Milton's day, especially for that certain group which wrote in the line of the "Aureate" poets and Spenser. Such are the terms like *gentle, old, high, sad, come, go, lie, sing, hear, shepherd, flower, muse, power*, in the pastoral tradition, and *eye, tear, dead, weep*, in the elegiac tradition.

Some, on the other hand, were brought into strong use first by Milton, and these particularly help define the singularities of *Lycidas: fresh, new, pure, sacred, green, watry, flood, leaf, morn, hill, shade, shore, stream, star, wind, fame, ask, touch*. What are the particular qualities of these words as a group? They refer primarily to the natural world, in more specific and sensory terms than were usual before Milton's time. They include an unusually large proportion of adjectives, and the adjectives name qualities of intensive value. The verbs are less essential. The nouns establish a physical world of earth and water freshly seen, and emphasized in contrast to star and sun in the more spiritual world of the heavens. Like Satan in *Paradise Lost*, the physical bodily force of earth and water dominates the inventive substance, then to be subdued by the triumph of significant structure, the rising from low to high, from sea and land to heaven, in the sun's motion of renewal. Like Adam and Eve in *Paradise Lost*, the shepherd in *Lycidas* finally takes up life on earth again in the light of his vision of heaven, in the light of hope beyond earth, tomorrow, fresh, and new.

Let us see how this essential motion from low to high, paralleled by that from past to future, takes place through the primary characteristic words of the poem. The opening words *Yet once more I come* become the completing *At last he rose.* The plucked brown leaves of mourning become the twitched blue mantle of hope. The meed of some melodious tear becomes the nectar pure of the blest kingdoms. The singing of Lycidas' own lofty rhymes moves through the lofty meed of fame granted by Jove, to the singing of the nuptial song by the solemn troops and sweet societies of the blest kingdoms in their glory. The memories both pastoral and mythological, of old Damoetas, old Bards, Bellerus old, become the reviews of Camus and St. Peter, of false pastors and even of false pastures—valleys low, shades and wanton winds, sad embroideries—as our frail thoughts "dally with false surmise," until at last, presaged by "those pure eyes and perfet witnes of all-judging *Jove*," the angel looks homeward from the whelming tide, and Lycidas, sunk though he be, rises like the day-star, "through the dear might of Him that walk'd the waves," to preside from above as the good genius of the shore. Even the shepherd, bound to the pastoral earth, looks up and forward, to sun and hills, to the pastures of tomorrow. *Fresh, high, new, pure, sacred,* are the especial terms of value; *pure* and *sacred* both classical and Christian, *pure* marking the two key passages of height, the classical and Christian heavens. The poem tries twice for what it achieves; first in the words of Phoebus and Jove, that fame is no mortal plant; then after a deeper pitch into despair of waters and of earth, more triumphantly in the natural analogy of the sun and the Christian terms of grace.

Two passages in the poem participate less than the rest in the process of cumulative repetition. One is the procession of guardians, Hippotades, Camus, and the Pilot of the Galilean lake, with their special details of reference, especially those for the false shepherd: lean and flashy songs, scrannel Pipes of wretched straw, foul contagion, grim Wolf with privy paw, two-handed engine. The other immediately follows, in ostensible contrast, the details of flowers, "so to interpose a little ease": honied

showers, rathe Primrose, pale Jessamine, Pansy freak'd with jet.
These two passages come between the climactic vision of fame in
the first mourning section and the final vision of recompense and
redemption in the last section. They make up the central portion, less closely patterned than the rest because, as an antis-
trophe, like a fourth act in a drama, they explore the counter-
forms of what the poem has been concerned with, the implications of the pastoral tradition in a world of spirit. Neither false
pastors nor surmised flowers redeem the physical pastoral world
of the human spirit; only as it looks higher is it redeemed and
reconciled.

These amplifying passages lead us to see another strong characteristic of Milton's language, its richness in adjectival quality.
All the way through we have noted repeated nouns, adjectives,
and verbs, but where there is least repetition and most variation
the inventive variation in the adjectives is especially perceptible.
If we try to define actual proportions, in order to corroborate
this impression, we find that the poem uses about twelve adjectives, sixteen nouns, and nine verbs per ten lines; in other words,
more adjectives than verbs, while most poetry in English uses
more verbs than adjectives and proportionately more nouns.
The quantitative power of adjectives in *Lycidas* supports the
qualitative powers we have noted; namely, the use of recurring
adjectives to emphasize structure and theme, the focus on a few
key adjectives to carry the *fresh high pure* values of the poem,
and the use of strong variety in a few passages of amplification.

When we suggest that Milton's use of repetition, especially
his strong repetition of the adjective form, is characteristic not
only because of its integral function in the poem itself but also
because of its unusualness in English poetry, we move into the
realm of comparison. As a unit, *Lycidas* is unique, incomparable,
as is any individual work of art. But in its selection and arrange-
ment of materials it may follow choices like or unlike those in
other poems, and thus provide some basis for comparison, of
elements and patterns if not of wholes. Indeed, comparison by
contrast may heighten our perception of the individuality of
the poem.

By mid-seventeenth century, few poems were so individual in
their use of dominant and repeated language as *Lycidas*. Only
one poet, Phineas Fletcher, out of some forty or fifty preceding

Milton, had emphasized adjectives as Milton did. Of major terms, those most repeated, only about half in *Lycidas* were strongly traditional for poetry: the *dead, dear, old, eye, head, shepherd, power, heaven, flower,* and most of the verbs. Of the rest, a few had been stressed before by a special and limited group: *sad, gentle,* and *new* by Spenser and one or two followers; *sacred* and *muse,* by Sidney, Chapman, and a few other; a few echoes from the "aureate" fifteenth century. This emotional language was poetic language not in the more active traditions of Chaucer, Jonson, and Donne but in the more artful and æsthetic tradition of Spenser and Sidney, the poets most fond of pastoral. A few lines from Spenser's *Astrophel,* the earlier pastoral elegy, will suggest Milton's relation to the tradition.

> A gentle shepherd borne in Arcady,
> Of gentlest race that ever shepherd bore:
> About the grassie bancks of Haemony,
> Did keepe his sheep, his little stock and store.
> Full carefully he kept them day and night,
> In fairest fields, and Astrophel he hight.

The repetitions, of words, of line-lengths, of rhyme-sounds, of alliterations, of phrasal constructions, are tighter than in *Lycidas,* but less related to meaning. The second characteristic term *gentle* has no particular bearing on the first, for example; and the *borne . . . bore* echo is simple word-play; the adjective *grassie* tells us much; but *fair,* little. Note also the later stanza on Astrophel's soul in paradise: like Milton's it relates flowers to immortality, but much more pictorially, less profoundly. Milton's flowers keep their reality and their relative subordination in fancy and on earth, while Spenser's cheerfully bloom in heaven:

> Ah no: it is not dead, ne can it die,
> But lives for aie, in blissful Paradise:
> Where like a new-borne babe it soft doth lie
> In bed of lillies wrapt in tender wise.
> And compast all about with roses sweet,
> And daintie violets from head to feet.

What Milton makes of these two concepts, physical and spiritual, by the widening of the physical and the heightening of the spiritual, is central to the difference between the two poets who in their love of æsthetic sense belong to the same school. Spenser's main repeated terms in *Astrophel* are more frequent, more abundant, and more usual: *dear, fair, gentle, great, good, day, flower, heart, love, shepherd, verse, make, see, hear, sing.* These are specializations within the main line of English poetic vocabulary, upon the sensuous, emotional, and artful. Milton shared more deeply in these specializations than in any other, but took them further, into individual emphasis and interpretation.

One reason that his individual emphases do not sound idiosyncratic to us today is that the language of *Lycidas* has had a powerful effect on English, especially American, poetry. The poem drew on the concrete references, the verbal harmonies, the interwoven and cumulative structures of classical sources, especially Virgil, and turned them to the intense purposes of Protestantism with its sense of the natural scope and magnificence of the universe as God's creation, encompassing the depth of hell and sea, the height of heaven and sky. Thus the special vocabulary of *fresh, high, pure, sacred, new, fountain, hill, leaf, morning, shade, stream, shore, star, wind,* while extremely rare as dominant vocabulary before *Lycidas,* becomes dominant in the mid-eighteenth century, with poets like James Thompson, Collins, Dyer, Blake, and Wordsworth. Especially in America, from Dwight and Trumbull on, the liberal and natural Protestant spirit continued its poetizing in these terms of scope and sacred feeling, one of the most characteristic American poetic adjectives being the *pure* of *Lycidas.* To us today, the integration of sense-imagery with sound-pattern and emotional harmonic structure is natural to poetry. The imagists and symbolists have called for such integration, and we find it in Keats, in Dylan Thomas, in Hart Crane; these are poets in the tradition of *Lycidas.*

To come back, then, from history and tradition to the poem itself: one good way to read it is in its own terms of emphasis, and one of these is its repetition, with variation, of the primary language. Its thematic terms carry the poem's sense of renewal from old past to new future, from deep waters and sad flowers to high heavens, from Jove's fame to Christ's redemption, from westering to rising star. For *Lycidas,* for Milton, for English poetry, this was a fresh beginning.

from *A Study of Literature*

David Daiches

It was not until his former fellow-student at Christ's was drowned in the Irish Sea in August 1637 that Milton was moved to write another English poem. This, too, was wrung from him before he felt himself ready, not this time by the request of an aristocratic family but by "bitter constraint, and sad occasion deare." Edward King does not appear to have been a very intimate friend of Milton's, but he had been a learned and virtuous young man dedicated to a career in the Church, and there must have been some sympathy and fellow feeling between them even though King, unlike Milton, was appointed to a college fellowship by royal mandate and was not "Church-outed by the Prelats." The shock to Milton of seeing a promising and dedicated contemporary cut off in his youth must have been great. Here he was, taking his time in preparing himself to become a poet who would "leave something so written to after-times, as they should not willingly let die," and suddenly the prospect of sudden and premature death was violently brought before him. If he were to die as King had died, what would have been the use, then, of all his laborious self-preparation? The very slowness and deliberation of Milton's progress towards his goal must have increased the shock enormously. He might well have said, as Marvell was to say in another context,

Ithaca, N. Y., 1948, pp. 170–195, as revised in *Milton* (London, 1957), pp. 73–92.

> Had we but World enough, and Time,
> This coyness Lady were no crime.

He had been acting on the assumption that he had world enough and time; and perhaps, after all, he had not. This is not to say that the elegy which Milton wrote for King was not about King but about himself, but it does indicate one of the major streams of feeling that flowed into the poem.

Lycidas, Milton's elegy on King, appeared in a memorial volume which came out in two parts in 1638, the first and larger part containing Latin and Greek poems and the second containing poems in English. *Lycidas* concludes the second part; it is signed "J. M." All but two of the other eleven English elegies are signed with the author's name. It is strange to look at *Lycidas* as it first appeared, tucked away at the end of a collection of poems most of which are uninspired and conventional laments. Henry King's poem begins:

> No Death! I'le not examine Gods decree,
> Nor question providence, in chiding thee:
> Discreet Religion binds us to admire
> The wayes of providence, and not enquire.

Joseph Beaumont's piece began:

> When first this news, rough as the sea
> From whence it came, began to be
> Sigh'd out by fame, and generall tears
> Drown'd him again, my stupid fears
> Would not awake; . . .

Cleveland's opens:

> I like not tears in tune; nor will I prise
> His artificiall grief, that scannes his eyes:
> Mine weep down pious beads: but why should I
> Confine them to the Muses Rosarie?
> I am not Poet here; my pen's the spout
> Where the rain-water of my eyes run out
> In pitie of that name, whose fate we see
> Thus copied out in griefs Hydrographie.

Among this company, Milton's poem stands out at once for its gravity of utterance, its artfully modulated verse, and its formal use of the conventions of the pastoral elegy, as developed in Greek, Latin, and Italian poetry.

The verse of *Lycidas* owes much to Milton's study of Italian poetry. While Milton does not employ the *canzone* (which consists of a complex rhymed verse-paragraph repeated in the same form several times before the concluding *commiato*, which is a shorter stanza), nevertheless his handling of the verse-paragraphs and of varying line-lengths clearly derives from the *canzone*, and the concluding passage of eight lines is his own adaptation of the *commiato*. Mr. F. T. Prince has traced in detail the influence on *Lycidas* of sixteenth-century Italian pastoral poetry, and he has shown how the structure of the *canzone*, as originally explained by Dante in the *De Vulgari Eloquentia*, with its stanza divided into two sections linked by a *chiave*, illuminates the sustained technical discipline shown by Milton in his handling of rhyme-pattern, pauses and transitions in their relation to the movement of thought and emotion.

Lycidas begins with a statement of the occasion which prompted it:

> Yet once more, O ye laurels, and once more,
> Ye myrtles brown, with ivy never-sere,
> I come to pluck your berries harsh and crude,
> And with forc'd fingers rude
> Shatter your leaves before the mellowing yeare.
> Bitter constraint, and sad occasion deare
> Compells me to disturb your season due:
> For Lycidas is dead, dead ere his prime,
> (Young Lycidas!) and hath not left his peere.
> Who would not sing for Lycidas? he knew
> Himself to sing, and build the lofty rhyme.
> He must not flote upon his watery biere
> Unwept, and welter to the parching wind
> Without the meed of some melodious tear.

The very first line introduces Milton in his capacity of young and ambitious poet: he is young because he has to pluck the berries of his art before they are ripe; he has already begun his career as a poet because this is not the first time he has plucked the unripe berries; and he thinks of himself (potentially at least) as a poet in the great classical tradition, as is made clear by his use of such images as laurel, myrtle, and ivy with their traditional associations with triumphant art. The berries may be un-ripe, but they are the true berries of art. He has to interrupt his period of apprenticeship to attempt a mature poem, because the fate of a fellow-poet compels him.

The note of compulsion is urgent. "Yet once more"—in these three opening words, three equally stressed monosyllables which take the reader into the poem suddenly and passionately yet which in themselves are very "ordinary" words with no obvious poetic qualities, we have the first hint of that strongly felt per-sonal concern with himself and his own fate which is to be fully developed later in the poem. Yet that concern is not with his fate simply as man: it is with that aspect of himself which links him with the dead Lycidas and in the light of which Lycidas is himself an impressive subject—they are both poets (or poet-priests: we have seen how the two concepts were linked for Mil-ton).

> Who would not sing for Lycidas? he knew
> Himself to sing, and build the lofty rhyme.

If the subject of the poem is not simply Edward King as man, neither is it (as Tillyard would have it) simply Milton himself. It is man in his creative capacity, as Christian humanist poet-priest. Lycidas has been drowned before he could fulfill his po-tentialities as poet-priest: man is always liable to be cut off be-fore making his contribution; hence the lament, hence the prob-lem, hence the poem. In *Lycidas* Milton circles round the prob-lem, and with each circling he moves nearer the centre (he is spiralling rather than circling), and he reaches the centre only when he has found a solution, or at least an attitude in terms of which the problem can be faced with equanimity.

Of the many points worthy of detailed attention in these open-ing lines, only a few can be selected for brief comment. The image of the unripe berries and such phrases as "season due" and "mellowing yeare" introduce thus early in the poem the richly suggestive notion of the changing seasons with all the emotional implications of seedtime and harvest, of the death of the year being inevitably followed by its rebirth in the spring. These implications (which, it might almost be said, convey a suggestion of comfort even while introducing the cause for la-ment) are not overstressed, but delicately handled by the rhymes and the rhythms. The first sentence of the poem moves up to a climactic autumn image:

> Shatter your leaves before the mellowing yeare.

"Yeare" rhymes with "sere" (dry) at the end of the second line, and the two rhyme words echoing together form a contrast between the withered and the ripe, between death and hope. Thus not only is the theme fully presented in these opening lines; there is also an anticipation of the way in which it is going to be worked out. In the very run of this fifth and just-quoted line there is an implication both of action and of hope, the sharp gesture of "shatter" giving way to the image of "mellowing yeare" as the line slows down, so that the "forced" and "rude" fingers plucking the unripe berries almost become, for a brief moment, harvesting images of active labourers gathering ripe fruit.

The young poet faces the premature death of the unfulfilled fellow-poet. His first reaction is to sing a lament for him:

> He must not flote upon his watery biere
> Unwept, and welter to the parching wind
> Without the meed of some melodious tear.

These three lines bring the first verse-paragraph to an end, on a note which combines resignation with resolve. This quiet close of the introduction not only provides a perfect balance for this opening paragraph, which rests, as it were, on these three lines; it also holds a note of anticipation, and so draws the reader further into the poem.

It is with deliberate awareness of the classical pastoral tradition that Milton begins the actual elegy in the second verse-paragraph:

> Begin then, Sisters of the sacred well . . .

He is invoking the muses with an almost ironic deliberation, the second word of the line, "then," almost suggesting that this is the thing to do, the proper routine. There is an echo of Theocritus' first Idyll in the line, and this adds to the suggestion of routine, of Milton doing his duty. But this is more than a conventional elegy, and its subject is more than Lycidas—or rather, its subject is Lycidas rather than Edward King, for when he

has given his dead friend a classical name, he has elevated him
to the status of fellow-poet and from there the expansion to
creative man can proceed. He does not stay long with these traditional sentiments, but, with a significantly short line, turns the
subject to himself as poet:

> So may some gentle Muse
> With lucky words favour my destin'd urn,
> And as he passes, turn
> And bid fair peace be to my sable shroud.

He will do this for Lycidas so that it will be done in turn for
him; it is what is due to a poet. The death of Lycidas is now
linked to the inevitable death of all men, however talented, however great their promise or achievements; even the present cele-
brator will in his turn become the celebrated. There is a restrained note of self-pity here, conveyed not so much by the
actual words used as by the suggestion given to the words by
rhyme and metre. The short lines in which he breaks off to draw
the parallel with himself are echoed by a later short line which
is pure action or gesture—a striking image of Milton's elegist
turning to invoke peace on *his* remains:

> And as he passes, turn
> And bid fair peace be to my sable shroud.

Nothing could better illustrate the importance of metrical and
semantic context in poetic expression than the first of these two
lines. In itself, it is a wholly "neutral" line, containing no ar-
resting word or phrase, no striking image. But in its context
the very simplicity of the expression, the shortness of the line
(echoing in length the other short line two lines before, but rhyming with the immediately preceding long line), and its effect
purely as sound (three light monosyllables followed by a leaning on the first syllable of "passes" and then on "turn") combine with the purely intellectual meaning to flash forth a significant and moving gesture. Milton has now substituted himself
for Lycidas in the poem, but not before both men have been
identified with a larger and more general conception of man.
Having made the substitution, he again points out why he has
done it:

> For we were nurst upon the self-same hill,
> Fed the same flock, by fountain, shade, and rill; . . .

This is a restatement of the earlier

> Who would not sing for Lycidas? he knew
> Himself to sing, and build the lofty rhyme.

But whereas the first time it was an explanation of why he should sing for Lycidas, the second time it is an explanation of why both Lycidas and himself merit the same consideration. They are both poets: the reason is the same in each case. The description, in the following verse-paragraph, is not so much an account in pastoral imagery of their life together as students in Cambridge; it is an account of their joint self-dedication as poets, and the pastoral imagery is employed in order to link their function as poets with the tradition of Western literature. This continuous linking of the theme with classical mythology is not decorative but functional: it keeps the poem rooted in an elevated conception on the nature, scope, and historical significance of the poet's art.

One notes in this third paragraph a genuine emotion about Nature, which blends effectively with the purely conventional characteristics of the pastoral imagery and which reminds the reader of such earlier images as "mellowing yeare":

> Together both, ere the high lawns appear'd
> Under the glimmering eye-lids of the morn,[1]
> We drove a-field, and both together heard
> What time the gray-fly winds her sultry horn,
> Batt'ning our flocks with the fresh dews of night,
> Oft till the ev'n-starre bright [2]
> Toward heav'ns descent had slop'd his burnisht [3] wheel.
> Meanwhile the rural ditties were not mute
> Temper'd to th'oaten flute:
> Rough Satyres danc'd, and Fauns with cloven heel
> From the glad sound would not be absent long,
> And old Dametas lov'd to heare our song.

[1] This is the reading of the 1638 ed. Milton later changed "glimmering" to "opening."

[2] So 1638. Milton altered the line to "Oft till the Star that rose, at Ev'ning, bright."

[3] So 1638. Later, "westering."

In the first part of this paragraph we get a sense of community
in an elemental activity. Such a phrase as "the opening [*earlier*,
"glimmering"] eye-lids of the morn" (a literal rendering of a
Hebrew phrase used in the third chapter of Job, though also
common in Elizabethan poetry) or the revised line "Oft till the
Star that rose, at Ev'ning, bright" introduces that favourite
attitude to Nature regarded with a sense of the passing of time
already hinted at in the fifth line of the poem and to be used at
the end of the poem in a single great phrase suggesting the dawn
of a new day unobtrusively yet with immense promise:

> To morrow to fresh woods and pastures new.

The two poets are thus described pursuing their activities together against a background of changing nature, which culminates with the rising of the evening star. And so our gaze is
shifted from earth to heaven ("Toward heav'ns descent had
slop'd his burnisht wheel"), and so a whole sense of cosmic implication, before the images suggesting poetry ("rural ditties",
"oaten flute") are introduced. There is almost a suggestion of
dance rhythms about the two lines ending "mute" and "flute",
the second, short line rhyming with the immediately preceeding
longer one. We do not need to speculate on the identity of "old
Dametas" (later spelt "Damætas") in order to see in him a symbol of the approval of the properly constituted judges of poetry
or at least of poetic ambition.

> And old Dametas lov'd to heare our song

ends the paragraph on a note of self-satisfaction: they were
both recognized as promising young poets. They pleased both
those who judge merely by instinct (the rough satyrs and the
fauns with cloven heel) and the cultivated critic. They were, in
fact, both on their way to literary fame.

No sooner has he suggested this than Milton realizes afresh
that one of them is no longer there, that poetic promise is not
enough to guarantee immortality:

> But oh the heavy change, now thou art gone,
> Now thou art gone, and never must return!

The images of Nature which have previously suggested growth
and maturity (i.e., change implying progress and hope) are replaced by images of Nature suggesting decay and death:

> Thee shepherd, thee the woods, and desert caves
> With wild thyme and the gadding vine oregrown,
> And all their echoes mourn.
> The willows and the hasil-copses green
> Shall now no more be seen
> Fanning their joyous leaves to thy soft layes.
> As killing as the canker to the rose,
> Or taint-worm to the weanling herds that graze,
> Or frost to flowers that their gay wardrobe wear,
> When first the white-thorn blowes;
> Such, Lycidas, thy losse to shepherds eare.

One does not need to emphasize the emotional effect of such repetitions as "now thou art gone, and never must return" or "thee shepherd, thee the woods . . ." or the sharpening of the meaning by the inversion in the latter of these. And here again it is Lycidas as poet who is mourned: it is the loss of his song, his loss to shepherd's *ear*, that matters. Even the songster cannot be saved—even the Muses cannot protect their own, as the succeeding verse-paragraph immediately points out:

> Where were ye Nimphs when the remorselesse deep
> Clos'd ore the head of your lov'd Lycidas?

This is the second reference in the poem to the fact that Lycidas had met his death by drowning, and it is introduced here in order that Milton may avail himself of appropriate mythological references. The water nymphs could not save him, nor could the tutelary spirits of that region near which the ship went down:

> For neither were ye playing on the steep,
> Where the old Bards the famous Druids lie,
> Nor on the shaggie top of Mona high,
> Nor yet where Deva spreads her wisard stream:
> Ah me, I fondly dream!
> Had ye been there—for what could that have done?
> What could the Muse her self that Orpheus bore,
> The Muse her self, for her inchanting sonne?
> Whom universall nature did lament,
> When by the rout that made the hideous rore
> His goary visage down the stream was sent,
> Down the swift Hebrus to the Lesbian shore.

King had been drowned off the north coast of Wales, a fact which allows Milton to exploit the old Celtic traditions of England (in which he had always been interested) and enrich the classical pastoral conception of the poet with references to the ancient Druids (who were poet-priests), associated especially with the island of Mona or Anglesey, and to the whole Celtic conception of the bard with its implications. "Deva" is the River Dee, which forms part of the boundary between England and Wales, and is rich in Celtic folk traditions (hence "wisard stream"). Milton has here deftly widened his conception of the poet to include both the classical and the Celtic; and to clinch this paragraph he returns to a classical image, picturing the frightful death of Orpheus, himself the son of Calliope, one of the Muses, and the very embodiment of poetic genius. Orpheus, the founder and symbol of poetry and a son of the Muse, could not be saved from a more frightful death than that which befell Lycidas; and Milton briefly but effectively touches on the gruesome story (told both by Virgil and Ovid) of his being torn to pieces by the frenzied Thracian women, his head being cast into the River Hebrus and carried out to the island of Lesbos. The emotion reaches its height with that final, terrible image:

> His goary visage down the stream was sent,
> Down the swift Hebrus to the Lesbian shore.

This passage is much worked over in the Trinity manuscript, and the sustained power of the final version is the result of several careful revisions. Milton always found the death of Orpheus a peculiarly moving and somehow a very personal story: in the opening of the seventh book of *Paradise Lost* he asks his divine muse to drive far off the royalist revellers whom the restoration of Charles II had brought back to London and compares them to the bacchanalian mob that murdered Orpheus:

> But drive farr off the barbarous dissonance
> Of *Bacchus* and his Revellers, the Race
> Of that wilde Rout that tore the *Thracian* Bard
> In *Rhodope,* where Woods and Rocks had Eares
> To capture, till the savage clamor dround
> Both Harp and Voice; nor could the Muse defend
> Her Son.

"Nor could the Muse defend her Son." "What could the Muse her self that Orpheus bore / The Muse her self, for her inchanting sonne? . . ." To be a poet was no guarantee against sudden death.

The concept of the poet has by now been completely universalized; it is no longer Milton and his friend but the poet in both his classical and Celtic aspects: yet this is the fate he may expect. Why, then, he asks in the paragraph that follows, should one bother to dedicate oneself to a life of preparation for great poetry?

> Alas! what boots it with uncessant care
> To tend the homely slighted shepherds trade,
> And strictly meditate the thanklesse Muse?

Is it worth trying to be a poet? One pursues fame, but before one has won it one is liable to be cut off. This is the theme of this well-known passage in which Milton effectively contrasts images of self-dedication with images of self-indulgence. Can man as Christian humanist achieve anything more than man as mere sensualist? This is one of the main questions posed by the poem and its answer emerges implicitly only at the poem's end. For the moment, the poet finds a tentative answer, but it clearly does not satisfy him any more than it provides a satisfactory conclusion to the poem.

> Fame is no plant that growes on mortall soil,
> Nor in the glistring foil
> Set off to th'world, nor in broad rumour lies;
> But lives, and spreads aloft by those pure eyes
> And perfect witnesse of all-judging Jove:
> As he pronounces lastly on each deed,
> Of so much fame in heav'n expect thy meed.

This reply, given to the poet by Phoebus (Apollo, the god of song and music), is not convincing even in purely formal terms. An explicit reply of this kind would have to be given by a more inclusive representative of poetry than Apollo, for the poem includes nonclassical (e.g., Celtic and Christian) concepts of the poet as well. And the pat aphoristic nature of that final couplet—

> As he pronounces lastly on each deed,
> Of so much fame in heav'n expect thy meed . . .

—could not possibly be a solution to such a complex poem as *Lycidas*. There is almost a note of irony in the copy-book lesson. It is a deliberately false climax, and Milton returns to his pastoral imagery to contemplate his theme again.

In the next verse-paragraph Milton develops his earlier question—What were the responsible authorities doing to allow such a disaster to befall Lycidas?—in traditional pastoral terms. This fact is in itself sufficient indication that he is not satisfied with the solution he has just brought forward. The god of the sea, the god of the winds, and the Nereids are each interrogated or considered, and each is acquitted of having caused Lycidas' death. The poet has here given up for the moment any attempt at a larger solution to the whole problem posed by his friend's death and is trying to find out only who is immediately responsible. But he can find no answer to the question, except the baffling one that it was destiny:

> It was the fatall and perfidious bark,
> Built in th' eclipse, and rigg'd with curses dark,
> That sunk so low that sacred head of thine.

The section thus ends on a note of frustration and even despair. Dark images of superstition and fatalism provide the only response to Milton's questions. This seventh verse-paragraph, which moves from cheerful pastoral imagery to the suggestion of man's helplessness against fate, is worth careful consideration: in structure, movement, and balance it shows a remarkable craftsmanship. Note, for example, the sense of muttering frustration to which the poet is reduced at the end:

> That sunk so low that sacred head of thine.

But with the adjective "sacred" a new thought emerges: Lycidas, like Milton, had been a dedicated man (Edward King had, in fact, been destined for the Church). His university could ill spare such a student and the Church could ill spare such a recruit. The hero as poet is now enlarged to encompass the hero as Christian champion, and as such his loss is deplored both by Cambridge (represented by Camus, the River Cam) and St. Peter. (It is worth noting that Milton uses biographical facts about King only when they help him to expand his meaning at the proper point in the poem; otherwise he ignores or even distorts them.)

The point now becomes not the loss suffered by the poet himself by dying young and being unable to fulfil his potentialities, but the loss to society when the poet (who is now spiritual leader as well as singer) dies before he can serve it. And so we have the famous statement of St. Peter:

> Last came, and last did go,
> The Pilot of the Galilean lake,
> Two massie keyes he bore of metalls twain,
> (The golden opes, the iron shuts amain).
> He shook his mitred locks, and stern bespake,
> How well could I have spar'd for thee, young swain,
> Enough of such as for their bellies sake
> Creep and intrude and climb into the fold?
> Of other care they little reckoning make,
> Then how to scramble at the shearers feast,
> And shove away the worthy bidden guest.
> Blind mouthes! that scarce themselves know how to hold
> A sheephook, or have learn'd ought else the least
> That to the faithfull herdmans art belongs!
> What recks it them? what need they? they are sped;
> And when they list their lean and flashie songs
> Grate on their scrannel pipes of wretched straw,
> The hungry sheep look up, and are not fed,
> But swoln with wind, and the rank mist they draw,
> Rot inwardly, and foul contagion spread:
> Besides what the grimme wolf with privy paw
> Daily devoures apace, and little said.
> But that two-handed engine at the doore,
> Stands ready to smite once, and smite no more.

This passage is, of course, an attack on the Anglican clergy, but it is not the digression that critics have generally assumed it to be. Milton has been developing the theme that the good are destroyed while the bad remain—a theme which in turn emerges from his earlier point that there is no sense in choosing a life of self-dedication to great art if the dedicated man is given no preferential treatment by fate over that accorded to mere sensualists and opportunists. Not only is the potential poet-priest no more likely to survive and fulfil his promise, he seems actually less likely to survive than the evil men who do harm to society where the poet-priest would have done good. Granted that the poet must take his chance of survival along with everybody else, is it fair to *society* to cut him off and let the drones and the parasites remain? The theme of *Lycidas* is the fate of the poet-priest in all his aspects, both as individual and as social figure.

Even this bitter passage retains the pastoral imagery. The shepherd as the symbol of the spiritual leader is of course an old Christian usage, and goes right back to the Bible. But in the classical tradition the shepherd also sings and pipes. So by combining Christian and classical pastoral traditions Milton can use the shepherd as a symbol for the combination of priest and poet which was such an important concept to him. (With reference to the Biblical element in the imagery of this passage, it is worth noting that the first verse of the twenty-third psalm in the English Psalter of 1530 reads: "The lorde is my pastore and feader: wherfore I shal not wante.") The association of classical and Biblical imagery in the passage is further emphasized in the lines

> Of other care they little reckoning make,
> Then how to scramble at the shearers feast,
> And shove away the worthy bidden guest,

with the reference to the parable in the twenty-second chapter of Matthew.

The technical devices employed in this passage to indicate the poet's contempt for those he is attacking have often been noted and scarcely need elaboration here. Once again we have the gesture, the clearly seen movement, presented in terms which associate it with an attitude of contempt:

> Creep and intrude and climb into the fold.

This is a very precise line, with three verbs each possessing an exact, different but complementary meaning. One might note also the effect in their contexts of such phrases as "shove away", "scramble" and "swoln with wind". And one need hardly catalogue the effective qualities of such lines as:

> What recks it them? what need they? they are sped;
> And when they list their lean and flashie songs
> Grate on their scrannel pipes of wretched straw.

Mr. Prince sees in these lines an echo of "rustic raillery" found in the Italian pastorals of Sannazaro, where, in humorous passages with double rhyme, he presents exchanges of abuse between two rival shepherds. But, though Milton might have learned something technically from this sort of Italian verse, the tone here is his own and far from humorous.

The conclusion of St. Peter's outburst suggests, with deliberate and effective vagueness, that something will be done about those who abuse society's trust:

> But that two-handed engine at the doore,
> Stands ready to smite once, and smite no more.

There is no need to follow generations of editors in their speculations on what Milton really meant by the "two-handed engine": all that is really necessary for an understanding of the poem is to note that retribution is certain through a device which suggests purposive activity on the part of society. The implication of "two-handed" is that men will use it with their own two hands, and this suggestion of purposive activity anticipates and prepares the way for the final resolution of the problem posed by the poem—which is that man as poet and moralist should, so long as he remains alive, keep on working and striving, continuing to proceed from task to task until he is no longer able. Thus, though the poem opens on a note of regret that the poet is forced once again to write before his talent is mature, it ends by his turning with renewed zeal to fresh poetic activity:

> To morrow to fresh woods and pastures new.

Having suggested the lines on which the resolution of the poem is to be achieved, Milton returns to the dead Lycidas, aware of the fact that the only answer to the problem posed by his premature death is for those who survive to carry on more zealously than ever. Such an answer implies an abandonment of sorrow and a leaving behind of thoughts of the dead potential poet, and before he can bring himself to do this he must try to transmute the dead Lycidas into something beautiful and fragrant. And so, as a sort of apology to Lycidas before leaving him for ever, he turns passionately to his dead body and attempts to smother it with flowers:

> Bring the rathe primrose that forsaken dies,
> The tufted crow-toe, and pale gessamine,
> The white pink, and the pansie freakt with jeat,
> The glowing violet, . . .
> To strew the laureat herse where Lycid lies.

Milton apparently added this passage later; the Trinity manuscript shows it as an insertion, in two versions, the first longer
and more elaborate than the one finally worked out. Perhaps the
idea of making some sort of amends to Lycidas, as it were, for
having to forsake him at the last, occurred to Milton on reading
over a first draft of the poem, and he therefore inserted the
passage as a transition from the attack on the clergy to the
picture of Lycidas' body washed out to sea. Yet he is still reluc-
tant to leave him:

> Ay me! whil'st thee the shores and sounding seas
> Wash farre away, where ere thy bones are hurl'd,
> Whether beyond the stormy Hebrides,
> Where thou perhaps under the humming tide [4]
> Visit'st the bottom of the monstrous world;
> Or whether thou to our moist vowes deni'd,
> Sleep'st by the fable of Bellerus old,
> Where the great vision of the guarded mount
> Looks toward Namancos and Bayona's hold;
> Look homeward Angel now, and melt with ruth,
> And, O ye dolphins, waft the haplesse youth.

The body of the dead Lycidas refuses to be smothered with
flowers, refuses to allow the poet to "interpose a little ease" and
"dally with false surmise." He is indeed drowned—but no sooner
has Milton accepted this fact anew than, with a deliberate echo
of the references to Mona and Deva in the fifth verse-paragraph,
he exploits geography with tremendous effect. Lycidas lies
drowned off the coast of Wales. Perhaps his body has been
washed northwards up to the romantic Hebrides; perhaps he is
exploring the monstrous depths of the ocean; perhaps—and here
the emotion rises—he has made his peace with the great Celtic
guardians of pre-Anglo-Saxon Britain (Celtic Britain always
had an immense fascination for Milton) and sleeps with "the
fable of Bellerus old," i.e., with the fabled Cornish giant from
whose name the Roman name for Land's End, Bellerium, was

[4] So 1638. Later changed by Milton to "whelming tide."

supposed to have been derived. Milton here suddenly projects an image of the southwest corner of England (Wales and Cornwall, with their associations with the Celtic heritage of Britain) and infuses into this projection a passionate sense of English history and English patriotism. "The guarded mount" is St. Michael's Mount, near Penzance. Following the imagined drifting of Lycidas' body, Milton is led to associate it with that part of England, so rich in history and folklore, which projects into the sea and looks towards Spain (Nemancos and Bayona's hold, i.e., stronghold, were districts in northern Spain, so marked in several seventeenth-century maps; Nemancos was misspelled "Namancos" in Ojea's map of Galicia and in subsequent maps, including Mercator's atlas). England looking towards Spain suggests the whole challenge of Anglo-Spanish relations of the late sixteenth century, culminating in the defeat of the Spanish Armada in 1588. Catholic Spain remained the enemy for the very Protestant Milton, and this passage has its links with the earlier reference to the "grimme wolf with privy paw," which refers to the proselytizing Roman Catholic Church. To see Lycidas in this context is to see him in conjunction with English history and with the guardian angel of England, St. Michael, who looks out over the sea towards the long-since-defeated Spanish enemy. He has thus at last managed to associate Lycidas with a sense of triumph, and he can now afford to leave the dead for a moment and interpose a great cry for his country:

> Look homeward Angel now, and melt with ruth,
> And, O ye dolphins, waft the haplesse youth.

He seems to be saying here: "Look no more out towards Spain, but look instead homeward towards Lycidas." But surely there is a strong implication here of a plea that England's guardian angel should cease to look away from home but look homeward at the state of the country, ministered to by a clergy whose corruption and inefficiency he has already so vividly described. "Look homeward Angel now" rings out like a passionate cry for his country and for himself. The dolphins can take care of the dead man; England and England's potential great poet John Milton require your present aid.

Lycidas can now be disposed of conventionally. The problem has moved beyond him, so Milton can let himself picture his reception in Heaven with all the triumphant resources of Christian imagery. And that is the function of the penultimate verse-paragraph beginning:

> Weep no more, wofull shepherds, weep no more.

There is a content here, a restrained passion, a controlled happiness. Milton has prepared the way for the emergence of the attitude in the light of which the question posed by the poem can be answered—What shall the Christian humanist do in the face of imminent death, what shall man the creator do in the prospect of extinction?—and having done so he can at last accept the conventional Christian answer to the question of Lycidas' own fate. The note of acquiescence emerges clearly here, as it did not in the answer provided earlier by Phoebus. Yet the picture of Lycidas' triumph in Heaven is not altogether conventionally Christian. Lycidas hears "the unexpressive nuptiall song," and this is another echo of Milton's passionate belief in the special reward waiting in Heaven for those who kept themselves chaste on earth. We have seen how that belief combines Pythagorean, Platonic, and Christian elements and is related both to his view of the music of the spheres and his interpretation of the first five verses of the fourteenth chapter of Revelation. He is more explicit and detailed about the mystic joys of heavenly nuptials reserved for those who were chaste on earth in the conclusion of another elegy, the Latin *Epitaphium Damonis* he was to write two years later for his friend Diodati.

But this cannot be the end of the poem, as it should have been if Milton were writing a conventional Christian elegy. He has to return to himself, to man as poet and creator, and give his final statement on the question posed by the poem. What shall the creator do when he knows he may die at any time? The answer, already prepared for in several passages, emerges at the end firmly and with conviction. We return to Milton, to the poet who has been mourning his dead friend. And as we return to him, a new day dawns, and he sets out on new tasks. The answer is not dissimilar to that given in the sonnets on his twenty-third birthday and on his blindness: man can only do what in him lies as best he can.

> Thus sang the uncouth swain to th' oaks and rills,
> While the still morn went out with sandals gray;
> He touch'd the tender stops of various quills,
> With eager thought warbling his Dorick lay:
> And now the sunne had stretch'd out all the hills,
> And now was dropt into the western bay;
> At last he rose, and twitch'd his mantle blew,
> To morrow to fresh woods and pastures new.

He returns at the end to those pastoral images most suggestive of the poet. He pays his respects to the Greek pastoral poets ("Dorick lay") and to the Latin (the fifth line is Virgil's *Majoresque cadunt altis de montibus umbrae*) and thus associates himself firmly with the Western literary tradition. And the last line suggests a determination to proceed to yet greater poetic achievements. Lycidas is forgotten: the world remains in the hands of the living and is shaped by their purposes. Keats, in his sonnet "When I have fears that I may cease to be," faced the same problem Milton faced in *Lycidas*. Suppose he died "before my pen has gleaned my teeming brain"? Keats' answer was to lose himself in a mood of sad-sweet contemplation:

> then on the shore
> Of the wide world I stand alone, and think
> Till love and fame to nothingness do sink.

Milton's answer is very different. His poem ends by his stepping out of himself, as it were, instead of losing himself in introspection. He sees himself humbly, as an "uncouth swain" singing as a new dawn comes up and brings new work to do.

The Archetypal Pattern
of Death and Rebirth
in *Lycidas*

Richard P. Adams

It has been made increasingly evident by critics in recent
years that the drowning of Edward King was the occasion,
rather than the subject, of *Lycidas*. Milton's concern was generally with the life, death, and resurrection of the dedicated
poet, and specifically with his own situation at the time. From
this premise it follows that there are no digressions in the poem
and that the form and traditions of pastoral elegy are entirely
appropriate to its intentions.

Every serious poet must at some time come to an emotional
realization of the length of art and the shortness of life. He,
more than most men, desires immortality, which he tries to
achieve in his works, to leave, as Milton said, "something so
written to aftertimes, as they should not willingly let it die." It
is an appalling thought that he may die himself before his work is
done, and this thought may be most sharply imposed upon him
by the death of a friend or acquaintance who is also a poet of
some worth or promise. Such an event is likely to be felt as an
impelling occasion to find some way of reconciling the desire
for immortality with the certainty of death. Many poets, from

From *Publications of the Modern Language Association,* LXIV (1949), 183–
188; condensed for this book by the author.

Moschus (or whoever wrote the *Lament for Bion*) to Matthew Arnold, have used for this purpose the conventions of pastoral elegy as established by Theocritus in his *Lament for Daphnis*. They have made additions and modifications, but the continuity of the traditional form remains unbroken. Milton chose it because he considered it an appropriate vehicle for the expression of his feelings. The result renders any apology absurd.

The conventions of pastoral elegy were appropriate because they had been hammered out over the centuries by poets concerned, as Milton was, with the problem and the mystery of death. In the cultural medium of their origin, the Hellenistic world of the third century B.C., the most popular solutions of the problem of death were expressed in the rituals of various fertility cults. It is therefore not surprising to find that Adonis appeared in the Fifteenth and Thirtieth Idylls of Theocritus and that Bion's pastoral elegy was a *Lament for Adonis*. Similarly, in the *Lament for Bion*, a long list of mourners was capped by the statement that "Cypris loves thee far more than the kiss wherewith she kissed the dying Adonis." Analogies between the conventions of fertility ritual and those of pastoral elegy are numerous and obvious, and some of them at least were clearly seen by Milton, who used them to reinforce the imagery of *Lycidas*.[1] He also used appropriate Christian materials and some references to mediæval history and legend where they matched his pattern.

The result is a remarkably tight amalgam of death-and-rebirth imagery, drawn from a more than catholic variety of sources. It is far from being merely eclectic, however. Each individual image and reference has its immediate purpose and its relevancy to the form of the whole.

The emotional pattern of the poem consists of a twofold movement. First it goes from the announcement of the friend's death downward through various expressions of sorrow to de-

---

[1] Milton's general familiarity with the fertility cults is attested by his references to Ashtaroth, Thammuz, Isis, and Osiris in the *Nativity Ode* (200–213) and to Adonis and "th' Assyrian *Queen*" in *Comus* (998–1001). His immediate source for all these might have been John Selden's *De Diis Syriis* (London, 1617), *Syn.* II, *Cap.* X, but Lucian's *De Dea Syrea* and Plutarch's *Of Osiris* would have been good collateral sources. The material was also scattered plentifully through Hesiod's *Theogony*, the *Praeparatio Evangelica* of Eusebius, and the other early church fathers and the classical historians whose works Milton studied during the Horton period.

spair; then comfort is offered, and the sequence reverses itself until the conclusion is reached in heavenly joy. It is the conventional pattern of pastoral elegy, at least from the time of Virgil, and it is at the same time the pattern of Milton's feeling about death at the time he wrote *Lycidas*. There is no mystery or contradiction in the facts that *Lycidas* is one of the most richly traditional and conventional of all pastoral elegies, and that it is at the same time one of the most intensely personal in its expression of the poet's emotion. The two things do not conflict; they work together and reinforce each other. This effect can be demonstrated by an examination of individual images in relation to the over-all pattern.

The opening invocation exposes a vein of death-and-rebirth imagery concerned with various forms of vegetation. The laurel, the myrtle, and the ivy are evergreens. Besides being emblems of poetry they are symbols of immortality generally, in contrast to deciduous plants. All of them have been held sacred to fertility gods and demigods. Adonis, in one version of the myth, was born out of a myrtle tree.[2] The laurel was supposed to have been a sweetheart of Apollo transformed into a tree to escape his pursuit. The ivy was sacred to Dionysus.

The transformation by some deity of a mortal into a plant or flower was a favorite symbol of immortality in the classical myths. It is recalled in Milton's reference to "that sanguine flower inscrib'd with woe" (l. 106); that is, the hyacinth, which sprang from the blood of a young prince of Amyclae beloved and accidentally killed by Apollo, just as the rose (l. 45) was said to have sprung from the blood of Adonis and the violet (l. 145) from that of Attis, the fertility demigod of Phrygia.[3] The amaranth (*Amaranthus*, l. 149) was also a symbol of immortality; its Greek root, coined for the purpose, meant "unfading."

These specific references are of course in addition to the general applications of the annual cycle of blighted and reviving vegetation. The ritual observances in the fertility cults were designed partly to assist in the completion of the cycle, the revival of the demigod being accompanied by a sympathetic revival of fertility in plants and animals. In this connection the

[2] Ovid, *Metamorphoses*, X, 512.
[3] J. G. Frazer, *The Golden Bough: Adonis Attis Osiris* (London, 1922), I, 313.

pathetic fallacy, one of the most persistent of the conventions
of pastoral elegy, is no fallacy at all but a perfectly logical
aspect of the ritual. In pastoral elegy, however, the application
is often reversed, as it is in *Lycidas*, so that flowers, and vegetation generally, symbolize the promise of rebirth for the poet's
friend as well as the mourning for his death.

The fact that King died by drowning perhaps fortuitously
but nonetheless effectively opened up to Milton a much larger
range of death-and-rebirth imagery, which he exploited with
his usual thoroughness. Several references involving water are
specifically to themes of death and rebirth, one of the most
definite being the legend of Alpheus and Arethusa (ll. 132–133),
to which Milton had referred in *Arcades:*

> Divine *Alpheus,* who by secret sluse,
> Stole under Seas to meet his *Arethuse.* . . . [30–31]

The nymph herself, transformed into a fountain, is a symbol of
immortality in much the same sense as the rose, the violet, and
the hyacinth. Milton's personification of Cambridge University
as the River Cam (*Camus,* l. 103) is in harmony, and St. Peter
as "The Pilot of the *Galilean* lake" (l. 109) is nearly related.

Milton goes to some length to show that water, the principle
of life, is not responsible for the death of Lycidas. Triton ("the
Herald of the Sea," l. 96) testifies that the winds were at home
and that the Nereids ("Sleek *Panope* with all her sisters," l. 99)
were attending to their duty as protectresses of ships and
sailors. The blame is put finally on the man-made ship which, in
defiance of the powers of nature, had been "Built in th' eclipse,
and rigg'd with curses dark" (l. 101).

The descent into and re-emergence from water is specifically
related by Milton to the setting and rising of the sun as a symbol
of death and rebirth (ll. 165–173). Besides respecifying and
reinforcing the reference to St. Peter's adventure (l. 109) this
passage coordinates two accounts of the sun's journey from
rising to setting. The first of these represents in parallel the life
of the two friends at Cambridge (ll. 25–31), and the second
represents the life of the surviving poet (ll. 186–193). These
passages render in a very striking way the pattern of life, death,
and rebirth with which the poem as a whole is concerned.

Milton was expressing his own feelings in *Lycidas*, and not any abstract or general or public sorrow. The personal note established in the first five lines is maintained throughout. It is struck again in the passage where he puts himself in the dead man's place (ll. 19–22), hoping that "some gentle Muse" will turn aside to confer on him the immortality which he is giving King. He deliberately takes to himself here the emotional experience of death and, at least by implication, of rebirth.

The nadir of the movement from life through death to resurrection follows logically by way of the reference to Orpheus, in which death is presented as final. The reference expands in at least three directions, two of which are exploited. Orpheus's descent into the underworld and not-quite-successful effort to rescue Eurydice is the most obvious, and perhaps for that reason the one that Milton neglects. The death of Orpheus at the hands of the Bacchanals, his dismemberment, and the journey of his head to Lesbos are the things that occupy Milton's attention first. The parallels between this event and the deaths of Adonis, Attis, Osiris, and other fertility demigods have been pointed out by modern scholars.[4] The facts that he was a singer, i.e., a poet, that he died a violent death, that his head was thrown into the water, and that his mother Calliope, the muse of epic poetry, mourned his death made him sufficiently adaptable to the general pattern of pastoral elegy and to Milton's treatment. The third direction gives Milton, in the "digression" on fame, most scope for the expression of his personal feelings, both of despair and of hope. Identifying himself with Orpheus as before with King, he asks what is the use of casting his pearls before the swine by whom the god is killed, to whom he had paid his respects in *Comus* and whom he is about to attack in the passage on the corrupt clergy. Then Phoebus, the patron of Orpheus, representing Milton's patron Christ, promises him his final reward in Heaven.

Such are the means by which Milton in *Lycidas* interrelated elements from the fertility cults, the tradition of pastoral elegy, the Christian religion, and his own past with the purpose and

---

[4] *Ibid.*, II, 99. Milton was undoubtedly familiar with the custom of throwing a vase woven of papyrus, with letters inside, into the sea at Alexandria, whence it floated to Byblos. There the women, who had been mourning the death of Adonis, received it with rejoicing as the reborn demigod. This ritual is described by Lucian and cited from him by Selden, who particularly emphasizes the fact that the vase was called "a papyrus head."

most richly the effect of rendering his present emotion. Such, by the same token, is the meaning of the phrase "With eager thought," and such again is the promise of "fresh Woods, and Pastures new."

Flowerets and Sounding Seas: A Study in the Affective Structure of *Lycidas*

Wayne Shumaker

More insistently, perhaps, than any other poem in English, *Lycidas* raises the purely æsthetic problem of how the emotions may be stirred by lines which at first are much less than perspicuous to the intellect and even after many readings remain obscure at two or three points. Johnson's attack to one side, *Lycidas* has received all but universal praise, couched often in language so high-pitched that it absorbs easily adjectives like "exquisite," "thrilling," "tremendous," and "supreme." Why is the emotional impact so powerful? A reply must be sought (I think) in the affective connotations of words, phrases, and images in formal combination; and it is worth finding because if in one of its aspects literature is history, in another, and not unimportant, aspect it is immediate experience.

In the present paper I shall attempt to make only a small contribution to the complete explanation. I propose, specifically,

From *Publications of the Modern Language Association*, LXVI (1951), 485–494.

to extract two of a large number of formal strands and discuss them as musical themes which blend into a total emotional harmony both massive enough and piercing enough to be overpowering.

I must begin by discussing the place of the two strands in the large structure. Three movements are enclosed within a pastoral introduction and conclusion, each movement in turn depending to some extent on pastoral machinery for its organization. I cannot improve on a summary given by Arthur Barker.

> The first movement laments Lycidas the poet-shepherd; its problem, the possible frustration of disciplined poetic ambition by early death, is resolved by the assurance, "Of so much fame in heaven expect thy meed." The second laments Lycidas as priest-shepherd; its problem, the frustration of a sincere shepherd in a corrupt church, is resolved by St. Peter's reference to the "two-handed engine" of divine retribution. The third concludes with the apotheosis, a convention introduced by Virgil in *Eclogue* V but significantly handled by Milton. He sees the poet-priest-shepherd worshipping the Lamb with those saints "in solemn troops" who sing the "unexpressive nuptial song" of the fourteenth chapter of Revelation. The apotheosis thus not only provides the final reassurance but unites the themes of the preceding movements in the ultimate reward of the true poet-priest.

Barker is almost certainly right in assigning a large part of the poem's impressiveness to the "three successive and perfectly controlled crescendos," culminating in a second triumphal resolution of tensions already half-released in their appropriate sections. The two strands with which I am presently concerned—thematic strands, as will appear shortly—help prepare in the first and second movements for the final resolution in the third.

The third movement begins with the celebrated catalogue of flowers. One function of this passage is to modulate between St. Peter's angry speech about the corruption of the English Church and the exultant description of Edward King's reception into Paradise. The catalogue interposes a little ease, as Milton himself says, which is to lead ultimately into the fuller and less deceptive comfort accessible through the realization that in its largest implications the drowning has not been tragic. It cannot have been tragic, for earthly life is continuous with eternal, in which temporal misfortunes are recompensed. But the image of flowers banking a drowned man's hearse cannot develop immediately into ecstatic and thrilling joy. The notion is too pretty-pretty, too conventionally poetic to carry a heavy emotional weight. Moreover, in this context the thought of floral offerings is consciously and deliberately delusive. Accordingly the next mood is one of profound spiritual depression; and this, by a natural emotional rhythm, illustrated on the abnormal level by the familiar manic-depressive pattern, passes into the final rapture. The three parts of the final movement are thus organically related, the first being emotionally causal to the second, and the second, and through it the first, emotionally causal to the third. The structure is not logically but emotionally inductive. Much of the value of the first two of the three parts lies in their power to entail the third. The first two parts, however, in their turn have been implied by everything that has gone before. The catalogue of flowers that "sad embroidery" wear picks up and utilizes many preceding references to a blight that has been placed on vegetative nature by King's death, and the description of the sounding seas which hurl his body to and fro is the poetically inevitable culmination of many earlier references to water.

I do not know how many readers have noticed the remarkable consistency with which Milton has made every mention of vegetation in the first 132 lines of the elegy suggest a sympathetic frustration in nature to balance the human frustrations about which the poem is built. The technique goes far beyond the use of simple pathetic fallacies. It extends to descriptions of objects which seem not to be conscious of any involvement in the death of the poet-priest-shepherd.

The theme appears at the very beginning and is resumed several times, usually quite briefly and often glancingly, before the climactic enumeration of mournful flowers. The laurels and myrtles invoked in lines 1–5 have berries which are *harsh* and *crude*. The leaves of both laurels and myrtles are to be *shattered* by Milton's singing before they have an opportunity to reach mature exuberance ("before the mellowing year"). The emphasis now shifts to other matters; but when in the fourth verse-paragraph vegetation again comes momentarily into focus, the connotations are similarly depressing. The woods and caves that lament the accident are overgrown with *wild* thyme and *gadding* vines, the adjectives implying, perhaps not quite rationally, a desperate and uncontrolled abandon to grief. The willows and hazel copses have ceased to react with joyous activity to pastoral songs; their leaves, having left off their "fanning," presumably droop in dejection. The rose is subject to canker; early flowers (Lycidas was a young man) succumb to frost. The tree-covered island of Mona mentioned a few lines later is not verdant but *shaggy*. The sixth paragraph offers a slight touch of relief: the *shade* in which the poet contemplates sporting with Amaryllis is thought of as a cool retreat. But Camus, when he appears, is described as wearing a bonnet of inelegant sedge variegated along the borders by figures which resemble "that sanguine flower inscrib'd with woe," and no further relief is offered. The regularity with which natural growth is made to carry lugubrious associations in the introduction and first two movements is remarkable. So pervasive is the blight that as early as line 78, when Phoebus wishes to praise true fame, he is able to do so effectively by simply dissociating it from plants that grow on mortal soil.

All this would seem easily accountable if it were not for the fact that paragraph three recalls the happier times before King's death. Here one might expect attention to be diverted from gloom sufficiently to permit an avowal that for man's gayer hours (as Bryant said) nature has a voice of gladness and a smile and eloquence of beauty. The avowal is there, but it is phrased in terms of sunlight, the sounds of insects, stars, and other nonbotanical phenomena. The only exception is in the mention of "high Lawns" in the first line of the description. For the rest, there is a studious avoidance of precisely those faces of nature which one would imagine to be most important to a shepherd. The comparative lightness of the paragraph depends not at all on images of energetic or brilliant growth. The opening eyelids of the morn carry the suggestion of an awakening, a stirring in preparation for the day's chores; the winding of the grayfly's sultry horn is associated with a genially warm air; the brightness of the evening star implies fine weather; the dancing of the satyrs and fauns is indicative of high spirits. The green of the pasturage, however, is hinted only by the single word "lawns," and nothing whatever is said at this point about shade trees or flowers. The flocks, which anywhere else would eat grass, in this setting batten themselves on "the fresh dews of night." The association of plants with depression of the spirit is not compromised.

Against this background the catalogue of flowers takes on strong emotional meanings. It resumes and develops an established theme, which, however, is now partly inverted. Although the emotional connotations set up earlier are not exactly denied, they are subdued to provide a poignant contrast to the ease the poet has announced himself to be seeking. The primrose, we are reminded, dies forsaken; the cowslips hang their pensive heads; the daffodils fill their cups with tears. The floral offerings are in fact meant to include "every flower that sad embroidery wears." On the other hand, the coloring is no longer somber. The myrtles addressed in line 2 were *brown,* and throughout the first two of the three movements the visual imagery has been prevailingly dull. The whiteness of the thorn which blows in early spring and the redness of the sanguine flower have only deepened the general murkiness by contrast. Now, suddenly, we are asked to imagine bells and flowerets *of a thousand hues.* Certain colors are specified—the *purple* of enameled eyes, the *green* of the turf, the *paleness* of the jasmine, the *whiteness* of the pink, the *jet* of the pansy, the glowing *violet*—and others are evoked by the names of flowers like the daffodil, which can hardly be visualized in more than one way. The result is that the grief, while remaining grief, is lifted and brightened. For the moment it is made tolerable by association with beautiful objects. At the same time the reader feels relief of another kind. Up to the present he has been under a constraint to imagine nature in only one of its moods; he has been forced, as it were, to consent to a perversion of what he knows to be the full truth. His conscious mind, which is aware of Milton's elegiac purpose, has assented to the fiction that a human death has lessened the objective beauty of woods and fields. But there is a part of his mind which is not controlled by his will, and this part has perhaps been, hardly perceptibly, uncomfortable, like the part of a father's mind which feels guilty about the answers he has given to his child's questions about the wind and the moon. The injustice is now partly rectified. In the catalogue of flowers Milton says not only, "There is brilliance as well as dullness in nature," but also, more indirectly, "The flowers named here are those poetically associated with sadness. I have made a selection to suit my elegiac theme." He is not, then, unhinged by his grief. He does not really distort. The largeness of his mind permits him to acknowledge a partiality in his descriptions; and his reward is the conquest of a tiny but not wholly insignificant scruple.

The second theme is somewhat less peripheral than the first, though it also lies to one side of the poem's exact center. The description of King's body as it is washed far away by the sounding seas, whether northward, toward or beyond the Hebrides, or southward, toward Cornwall, has been even more elaborately prepared for in advance. The first visual image of the dead poet-priest-shepherd is that of a corpse rocked to and fro on ocean swells swept by a dry wind. From the beginning, accordingly, the sea is in the background of the reader's consciousness. Images of water have considerably greater prominence than images of trees and plants and have frequently been noticed by critics. Sometimes the water moves forward into clear focus; again it flashes rapidly across the margin of attention, half-unnoticed and significant chiefly because the glimpses sustain a theme that must not be allowed to lose continuity.

Some of the references to water carry only a very indirect reminder of the sea, and, with it, the manner of King's death. For example, the invocation in the second paragraph calls up the image of a well: "Begin then, Sisters of the sacred well, / That from beneath the seat of *Jove* doth spring." The well is not, however, quiescent; the word "spring" suggests movement, and the movement of water, though now on a small scale, both carries on the visual motif and, by reducing the image's physical and emotional dimensions, modulates into the calmer passage which follows. A somewhat analogous technique is used at five other points: in the mention of Deva's wizard stream, in the apostrophe to the Fountain Arethuse and smooth-sliding Mincius, in the personification of the River Cam, in the description of St. Peter as pilot of the Galilean lake, and in the reassurance addressed to the River Alpheus. Each of these glancing evocations of water helps keep the theme alive by giving the reader's memory of it a little fillip. In a similar way the fountain, the three rivers, and the Sea of Galilee, by faintly echoing the water motif, prevent the reader from ever quite losing sight of the fact that King died by drowning.

I should like to dwell for a moment on a representative passage, that which contains—and surrounds—the laments of the University and the Church. At the beginning of the paragraph the University is represented, appropriately enough, by the personified figure of the leisurely, rush-lined Cam. I should not like to pretend that every reader has a momentary glimpse of a river sliding among reeds when he comes to these lines; nevertheless the complete dissociation of the river from the figure would be difficult. St. Peter next appears as the "Pilot of the *Galilean* lake," the description providing an ironic contrast to the reader's knowledge that King was *not* rescued from the sea. After this introduction comes a thunderous attack on the state of the English Church; but the attack has no sooner ended in the climactic prediction of the two-handed engine than the water theme is again stated: "Return *Alpheus*, the dread voice is past, / That shrunk thy streams." The transition could hardly be more apt. The hint of timidity in the stream lowers the key from indignation at the same time the words "dread voice" carry the last reverberations of anger. Moreover, the ideas of water and fright have been associated before and will be associated again. The relationship in the present passage is curious, however, for now it is the water that is frightened by the man. The effect is somewhat like that of an inverted musical phrase, which remains recognizable despite the fact that it has been turned upside down.

The address to the Fountain Arethuse and smooth-sliding Mincius performs a somewhat analogous function a little earlier. It too uses water imagery to reassert the pastoral medium just when the need for a reassertion is felt. The mention of Deva's wizard stream is incidental to the fixing of a geographical location, but the motor quality of the verb "spread" adds vividness by making the movement seem the result of an act of will. The Dee spreads its waters as a housewife might spread a tablecloth or a bird its wings.

We have seen, then, that there are six muted statements of the water theme besides the more resonant ones to be noted presently. The sacred well, the River Cam, the Galilean lake, the River Alpheus, the Fountain Arethuse and smooth-sliding Mincius (I count them as one because they occur in such close juxtaposition), and the River Dee prevent the Irish Sea from ever quite slipping out of the reader's consciousness. Milton's awareness of the manner in which King died is not wholly suppressed even in parts of the elegy in which he is mainly occupied in talking about something else. Formally, the six passages contribute to a massive harmony without themselves being very distinctly heard. It will be approximately accurate to say that their structural function is similar to that of the middle notes of triads struck on the piano. Only the analytic listener pays careful heed to them, but anyone would feel a slight decrease of tonal richness if they were omitted.

The more resonant statements of the theme begin in the description of Lycidas on his watery bier and continue at lines 50, 62, 89, and 154. At each of these points the drowning is specifically mentioned or water is in some other way made to appear menacing. There are also two later passages, at lines 167 and 183, which perform for the water theme the function performed for the flower theme by the catalogue.

The first statement, already once referred to, has evoked the image of a body rocking helplessly on ocean swells. The second is less grisly but in a way even more distressing, for it recreates briefly the exact instant at which a human life succumbed to an indifferent natural force: "Where were ye Nymphs when the remorseless deep / Clos'd o'er the head of your lov'd *Lycidas?*" The visual image is that of a face sinking for the last time beneath water, the motor image that of a rejoining of fluid edges; and there is perhaps induced also a slight muscular strain, as of an effort to fight one's way upward toward air. To describe small things by large, the effect is now rather that of fright than of nausea. (I hope the reader will understand that the only way in which I can make some of my points at all is by overstating them.)

The third statement picks up the nausea and drops the fright —for I should suppose no one to feel personal danger in the sight of a severed and bleeding head being tumbled down a precipitous river bed by the current. The head is that of Orpheus, who, like Lycidas, was a singer.

> by the rout that made the hideous roar,
> His goary visage down the stream was sent,
> Down the swift *Hebrus* to the *Lesbian* shore.

The cold passivity of the second image has been replaced by the movement of the first; but there are in addition angry sound and the blood that is so frequently an accompaniment of violence. The association of water and death, however, has remained constant.

The same association is present in the fourth statement, which recurs to the passivity of the second image and develops it in considerable detail. The herald of the sea

> ask'd the Waves, and ask'd the Fellon winds,
> What hard mishap hath doom'd this gentle swain? . . .
> And sage *Hippotades* their answer brings,
> That not a blast was from his dungeon stray'd,
> The Ayr was calm, and on the level brine,
> Sleek *Panope* with all her sisters play'd.

The drowning and its circumstances are again set in contrast; death is described as having occurred in a peaceful setting. On the other hand, the feeling appropriate to this statement is neither fright nor nausea but perplexity. Within limits, variations in the emotional demands made on the reader increase the affective pull by activating dormant parts of the psyche. At the same time continuity is provided by the maintenance of the association of water and death.

Up to this point the Irish Sea has been described once as weltering and twice—if I do not misread the connotations of lines 50–51—as tranquil. The tranquillity has been insisted on at greater length than the movement and is probably more vividly present in the reader's imagination. Yet the possibility of movement in the Sea has been strongly asserted by the verb "welter" and implied by the swift motion of the Hebrus. In the longest, and climactic, development of the water theme the vastness of the Sea is brought together with the swiftness of the river to produce an impression of great violence.

> Ay me! Whilst thee the shores, and sounding Seas
> Wash far away, where ere thy bones are hurld,
> Whether beyond the stormy *Hebrides,*
> Where thou perhaps under the whelming tide
> Visit'st the bottom of the monstrous world . . .

The Irish Sea has become a resistless, unsympathetic force which deals with the body of the poet-priest-shepherd exactly as the Hebrus has dealt with the severed head of Orpheus, tossing it about with the indifference with which it would toss a plank broken from the hull of the wrecked ship. The effect is overwhelming (the word is suggested by the passage), and more than one critic has testified that for him this is the most powerful part of the elegy.

Relief, however, is at hand, for the depressing thought of a tossed and ruined body generates immediately, by contrast, that of a redeemed and joyous soul. The flower and water themes, in direct juxtaposition, thus lead directly into the apotheosis, in which all the tensions are finally resolved. Little more needs to be done with the flower theme. It has served its purpose and will appear only once more, disguised almost beyond recognition, in the last line of all: "To morrow to fresh Woods, and Pastures new." The water theme, on the other hand, has carried a much heavier emotional weight and cannot be so easily dropped. Moreover, growing nature has already been adequately purged of blight, whereas the sea continues to hold a menace. It too must be purified. The mourners must be reconciled to the physical world as well as to the turnings of human destiny.

Accordingly the transition from despair to hope is made by images drawn from the very water that we have just been led to believe coldly and impersonally fearful:

> So sinks the day-star in the Ocean bed,
> And yet anon repairs his drooping head,
> And tricks his beams, and with new spangled Ore,
> Flames in the forehead of the morning sky:
> So *Lycidas* sunk low, but mounted high,
> Through the dear might of him that walk'd the waves . . .

The sun is not harmed by the sea. Christ walked on its waves. Indeed, the very man who was killed by water on earth can seek out its Heavenly equivalent as a comfort: "other groves, and other streams along, / With *Nectar* pure his oozy Lock's he laves." Even this is not all. The element *water* has been purified, but the Irish Sea must be especially cleared of threat. Hence we are told that travelers on the Sea will gain composure by recalling the "large recompense" which we now realize to have followed the brief torment of drowning.

> Now *Lycidas* the Shepherds weep no more;
> Hence forth thou art the Genius of the shore,

> In thy large recompense, and shalt be good
> To all that wander in that perilous flood.

For myself—I do not pretend to speak for others—there is a slight dissatisfaction in the reading of these lines. If the source of composure is to be an understanding of the total meaning of King's death, the word *all* provokes resistance. Calmness of mind will be accessible only to voyagers who, having known King, have been led by reflections on his fate to an acceptance of death similar to that expressed in the poem. If, on the other hand, we are to imagine King's spirit as extending physical protection to voyagers on the Sea, the implication that death is to be avoided as significantly bad contradicts the whole drift and meaning of the elegy. The structural function of the passage, however, is clear. A *formal* means of escape from the last tension has been provided. Not only is the poet-priest-shepherd living after all; the mourners can again face nature courageously and take delight in its external beauty. Everything is as it should be, and daily activities can be taken up at the point where they were dropped.

The two minor themes, then, come into prominence at various places in the first and second movements and at other places are hinted in ways that have been described. In the third movement they are developed side by side in preparation for the apotheosis, in which sorrow is finally transcended and the mind restored to peace. There is a difference, however, both in their intrinsic importance and in their usefulness in preparing for the resolution. The flower theme shows a temporary effect of profound grief, the water theme is intimately related to the cause. The distortion of vision must wear off before adjustment to the irremedial cause becomes possible; hence it is altogether proper that the former of the two themes should be resolved a little in advance of the latter. Yet each has its function, and the emotional impact would be weakened if either were omitted from the third movement. The first paragraph of the final movement, unaccounted for by Barker's explanation of the structure, is thus only less necessary than the apotheosis. It fits not only into a design but also into an emotional pattern; not only into a form but also into a response.

Essays in Analysis:
Lycidas

Cleanth Brooks and John Edward Hardy

With *Lycidas*, as so often elsewhere with Milton, Dr. Samuel Johnson's comments form an excellent point of departure. When Dr. Johnson castigates *Lycidas* for the mingling of pagan with Christian references, he puts his finger firmly on the matter of first importance for a reading of the poem, even though it is a finger of the left hand and the gesture is deprecatory. Here again Johnson in failing to appreciate the poem has given us a valuable clue for our own understanding.

The problem of the pagan-Christian conflict has to be faced: the mingling either is turned to account in a rich synthesis, or it is not, and it disfigures the poem as a clumsy confusion. It will not do to write off the discrepancies as due to an improper attention to what Milton meant only as "conventional ornament." We had better side with Johnson in taking the poem seriously, in reading narrowly and precisely, in assuming that the pattern of statement is important, than try to save the poem by ignoring the implications of the pattern. If the poem cannot survive a serious and close reading, we can be sure that Milton least of all would have wished it to survive.

It can, of course, survive the most rigorous reading. It can be closely read, for it has been closely written. We shall certainly need to take certain conventions into account as we read,

From *Poems of Mr. John Milton* (New York, 1951), pp. 169–186.

but it will become clear that the poem does not lean unduly upon
them: rather it reinvigorates and justifies them. The first lines
will illustrate Milton's characteristic treatment of the conventions and the general tightness of the structure he employs.
Milton's praise for Edward King is that "he knew / Himself to
sing, and build the lofty rhyme." Milton's own poem in King's
memory is *built* in every sense of the word, and, if we are to explore the poem, we must be prepared to become acquainted with
its architecture, and an intricate and subtle architecture at that.

The laurel is a symbol of poetic fame. The poet comes to
pluck the berries before they are ripe; that is, the poet apologizes for the fact that his own art is immature. The meaning of
the conventional symbolism is plain. But Milton is not content
to make a conventional *use* of the convention.

> I com to pluck your Berries harsh and crude,
> And with forc'd fingers rude,
> Shatter your leaves before the mellowing year.

Not only are the fingers which pluck the berries "forc'd"; the
unripe berries are themselves "forc'd" from the stem. We have
here a rich and meaningful ambiguity. And so with the whole
passage: the fingers are "rude" not only in their brutal compulsion, but also in their unmannerliness and clumsiness. The
poet is unripe, but Lycidas, "dead ere his prime"; Lycidas for
whom the berries are to be plucked, was also unripe, untimely
dead; and there is therefore a kind of ironic justification in the
poet's being compelled to sing thus prematurely.

We can see in the manner in which this idea is expressed
yet another kind of unconventionality. The passage looks forward to the development of the pastoral mode in the poem—
the plucking of the berries is "appropriate" to the shepherd—
but the poet has taken care that it be sufficiently realistic. We
have not, in the figure of the shepherd here, merely the often
shadowy character of the conventional pastoral. It is, after all,
Milton, the self-conscious young poet, speaking. Evidently this
is not the first time he has come forward with an immature
performance:

> Yet once more, O ye Laurels, and once more
> Ye Myrtles brown, with Ivy never-sear,
> I com . . .

He should know better; but even so,

> Bitter constraint, and sad occasion dear,[1]
> Compels me . . .

The point we are making here is not that the passage is difficult and cannot be understood but that it is rich; that the words are carefully chosen; that the network of connotations is important; that the "poetry" resides in the total structure of meanings. The opening lines, then, give us warning, if we care to heed it, that the various smaller items in the poem are mortised together most cunningly; and they offer the hint that we shall do well to expect, and look forward to, the same kind of careful articulation of the larger elements.

The shepherd imagery, simply as such, hardly calls for any special comment. It is pervasive, and it is important, particularly in helping to provide a basis for the fusion of the Christian-pagan elements: the "pastor" as pagan shepherd and as Christian "pastor." Further consideration of the pastoral machinery may await a discussion of some of the elements that are not ordinarily part of the pastoral convention—elements that we should not be able to predict merely from the assumption that this is a pastoral poem.

One of the most important of these elements—and one of the most startling, once it is seen—is the water imagery. Milton does not forget that King met his death by drowning. He makes much of the sea in this poem, and he makes much of water in general—the tear, the stream, the Galilean lake, etc.

The first instance of the water imagery occurs in the twelfth line:

> He must not flote upon his watry bear
> Unwept, and welter to the parching wind,
> Without the meed of som melodious tear.

The funeral couch is the tossing sea itself. *Welter* means "to roll" or "to toss"—but there was another *welter* in this period, a word which meant "to wither" or "to wilt"; and Milton's phrase, "welter to the parching wind," would seem to indicate that this latter meaning is present too.

[1] The word "dear" here means, of course, *heartfelt, profoundly affecting.* But it can also mean *dire* (see *N.E.D.*). The effect of the ambiguity is to emphasize the inescapable, fatal character of the poet's obligation to Lycidas.

Actually, one can make out a case for the double meaning in terms of the context—and thereby give some point to the otherwise rather pointless statement that Lycidas must not toss upon the waves without one more drop of moisture, the "melodious tear," which must be added to the ocean in which the drowned body is already immersed. The submerged metaphor at which the double meaning of "welter" hints is something like that of a shipwrecked man tossing on his raft, surrounded by water, and yet parching.

The contrast between the salt water of the immensity of the sea and the salt water of the melodious tear may not seem to be of much importance; but as the poem develops it comes to mean a great deal. The "melodious tear" promises to overwhelm the "sounding Seas." Even at this point one can see something of the complexity of the symbol; and a little attention to it here will be very helpful in the important task of defining the theme of the poem.

It has been pointed out that Milton did not necessarily have any close friendship with King and that he therefore took the young man's death as a convenient peg on which to hang his elegy. The expression of grief is thus, we are inclined to say, conventional, and the elegy itself a *conventional* poem. But the term should not imply that Milton's feelings are not seriously engaged: the question is rather, what is the real subject? What theme does engage the poet's feelings? The answer can be found in the poem itself: Milton is at his most conventional in describing his personal association with King ("We drove a field, and both together heard . . .") ; and he can afford to be conventional here, for what counts in the poem is not Edward King as an individual but rather what King stands for, the young poet and pastor. But if Milton is not deeply concerned with King as a person, he is deeply concerned, and as a young poet personally involved, with a theme—which is that of the place and meaning of poetry in a world which seems at many points inimical to it. In the dramatic development of this theme the "conventional" figure of King has, of course, the leading role. It is this theme that dominates the poem, and a variant of it—the relation of the poet to the forces of nature—which shapes the first paragraphs.

Immediately after the reference to the "melodious tear" the

speaker invokes the "Sisters of the sacred well." Is the tear wept
by the sorrowing speaker? Or since it is "melodious," is it drawn
from the well of the Muses? Or is it wept by the Muses themselves? The ambiguity is not a meaningless one: the primary
matter is the relation of the poet to the Muses; or, to put the
question in other terms, whether the personal lament of the
speaker can transcend the *merely* personal. The equivocation is
meaningful and intended, for the speaker carries it further in
the next lines. It is *he* in the first verse paragraph who apologizes for daring to write at this time; but it is the *Muses* to whom
he says in line 18,

> Hence with denial vain, [2] and coy excuse . . .

And in the next line he makes it plain that the "gentle Muse"
who he hopes will sing an elegy at his death is masculine—a
poet like himself.

The relation of the poet to the Muse—even the question
whether the Muse has any existence apart from the poet himself
—is thus crucial for the theme of the poem, though Milton
might be considered merely gracefully conventional in beginning his elegy by invoking the Muses and paying the usual
tribute to the sacredness of the well with which they are associated. On this level the "sisters" are the nine Muses of Greek
mythology, but Milton is careful to relate them to the island of
Britain, and more intimately still to the scene of the disaster, to
the Welsh coast itself. It is true that the beings whom he reproaches (l. 50) for failing to protect Lycidas are the
"Nymphs." But as the phrase "your old *Bards*" suggests, these
nymphs are not merely deities of field and stream; they have
the poets under their care and are thus associated with the
Muses. (If there is any doubt on this point, it is resolved by the
very excuse which the speaker supplies for the nymphs: they
are not to be blamed for failing to protect Lycidas since "the
Muse her self that *Orpheus* bore" could not protect her son.)

There is a sense, of course, in which the nymphs are conventional nymphs. They might have been expected to be playing
"on the steep / Where . . . the famous *Druids* ly" or on the

---

[2] "Vain" means "useless"; "Bitter constraint" forces the tribute. But it also
means "desirous of admiration": the denial is an effect of vanity which asks
for further urging.

"top of *Mona* high" or by the stream of the Deva. They *are* the
deities of hill and stream. However, since in this poem poethood
is first identified with the pastoral, it is only proper that this
should be so. The description of Lycidas's career as a poet has
prepared for just this kind of association, for in his and the
poet's earlier life together

> . . . the Rural Ditties were not mute,
> Temper'd to th'Oaten Flute,
> Rough *Satyrs* danc'd, and *Fauns* with clov'n heel.

The pastoral is a poetry of wild innocence, close to nature, a
part of the music of nature, and the nymphs are its natural
muses and guardians. On the day of Lycidas's death the nymphs
were not playing where one would have expected them to play.
The speaker knows this—because, had they been there, they
would surely have tried to save Lycidas. Calliope is mentioned
simply to emphasize the deeper pessimism into which the elegist
falls at this point—not only were the nymphs absent; even had
they been present they would have been ineffectual, as the Muse
herself (of a higher order, yet of the same kind) was powerless
to save her son.

The point is that *all* the divine guardians of the classical
tradition—from the highest and most remote, the Muse herself, to the lowest and most intimate, the nymphs—appear to
be ineffectual. And one can see an implication of yet deeper
despair. The exclamation, "Ay me, I fondly dream!," placed as
it is *after* the statement that the nymphs were not present and
before the statement that they would have been useless in any
case, could mean either that the existence of the nymphs or their
effectuality is a "fond dream." But the two propositions come
to the same thing; to say nymphs are ineffectual is tantamount to denying their existence. The poet enjoys no special
status. The old intimate relation between the poet and the forces
of nature has lapsed—if it *ever* existed, save as a fable of some
early and lost golden age.

To sum up: by hinting that the Muse cannot save her vota-
ries, the poet has called in question the efficacy of the melodious
tear, for which the poet has turned to the well of the Muses. Is
the tear, after all, other than the waste salt water which it resembles and on the waves of which the body of the dead poet

now welters? Is the sacred well really sacred? Does one not do
better to turn to the flesh-and-blood Amaryllis than to this
"thankles" shadowy being, who seems powerless and who perhaps does not even exist? The poem at this point has moved
dangerously close to a naturalism which divests nature of any
special sanctity and the poet of any supernatural function.

The last statement may seem to read too much into the
passage in question; and yet this is the general meaning up to
which the whole of verse paragraph four leads. In lines 37–49,
nature is represented as mourning. And, with regard solely to
Lycidas himself, one might take the statement that the trees
"Shall now no more be seen, / Fanning their joyous Leaves to
thy soft layes" to mean simply that the sympathetic emotion of
nature has *changed*—from joy to sorrow. But for the elegist it
would seem to be not merely a change, but a *loss* of the sense of
nature's sympathy. Milton has been careful in this stanza *not*
to give us personifications of nature: "Woods . . . desert Caves
. . . And all their echoes mourn." The dancing satyrs and fauns
of the preceding stanza are not represented here as weeping;
neither they nor the nymphs are mentioned at all. When the
nymphs are mentioned in the next stanza, they are referred to
as absent. In this stanza, then, we are presented with an emptied
nature, a nature which allows us to personify it only in the sense
that its sounds seem mournful; and, finally, the interpretation
that they *seem* mournful is justified by the concluding lines of
the stanza:

Such, *Lycidas*, thy loss to Shepherds ear.

It is the *ear* of the shepherd speaker that has been affected.
He is not saying merely that he can no longer hear the song of
Lycidas. The music of nature which accompanied that song, and
(it is implied) which prompted the song, has also been stilled.
But the voice of nature is not silenced by her own grief. The
change which the death of Lycidas has brought is not actually a
change in nature itself; the death is not a loss to nature, but a
numbing of the poet's sensitivity to nature. What has happened
to the ear is particularized quite explicitly: it is the same sort
of thing that happens to the sheep when the taint-worm attacks
them or that happens to early flowers cut off by a late frost. It
is as though the shepherd in his grief, though he still calls him-

self "Shepherd," sees himself reduced to the level of his charges, the sheep themselves, in his relation to the forces of nature. In the elegist's compliment, Lycidas is made a kind of shepherd to him, without whom now he is abandoned and helpless. Nature is no more sympathetic with him in his sorrow than it would be with the sheep if their keeper should die and leave them to fend for themselves. Nature has no apparent respect for the memory of Lycidas. And it is questionable whether she had any for him alive. For Lycidas too, beyond the terms of the present compliment, is just such a shepherd as the speaker himself—as much as he, one of the helpless sheep.

The entire passage *can* be read simply as a compliment to the music of Lycidas; and the next stanza, with its implied comparison of Lycidas to Orpheus, whom "Universal nature" also lamented, carries the compliment further. But the passage, including again its reference to the fate of Orpheus, also reads as a dark commentary on any hopeful view of the relation of the poet to nature. The poet enjoys no special status. To judge by the fate of either Lycidas or Orpheus, the poet's name is literally written in water.

The poet is shrewd enough not to appeal to the justification of fame. That, too, is an effect of pride, "That last infirmity of Noble mind." Men live laboriously and stringently in the hope of fame; they endure a life of hardship, only to have that life extinguished by the "Blind *Fury*"—"blind" in the sense that she cannot see they are about to burst into a blaze of light, and could not see the blaze even if it had already flared forth. Better to eschew the light altogether, therefore, and "sport with *Amaryllis* in the shade."

It is here that the pastoral tone is first broken by a "strain . . . of a higher mood," by the voice of Apollo himself, who, touching the poet's deadened ears, points out that true fame transcends this world. (True fame here is distinguished from "broad rumour" or "report," the sense in which the term is first used in the passage. The fame of which Phœbus speaks has taken on something of the meaning of "praise"—"But not the praise, / Phœbus repli'd"— a word retaining from its Latin root a much stronger sense of evaluation and judgment than *fame* usually carries. The effect of *pronounce* may also be noted— "*Jove* . . . pronounces lastly on each deed"—with its sense of an authoritative judgment behind the "speaking" which, again, *fame* does not ordinarily have.) True fame is immortal, and does not grow on mortal soil.

This passage makes a distinction between the pagan deities of wood and field and stream—the genii of the place—and the higher deities—the gods of "heaven"—and therefore seems an anticipation of the specifically Christian doctrine with which the poem is to end. But we should be careful to remember that Apollo and Jove, even so, are *pagan* deities. The shock of transition from pagan to Christian is being cushioned by the poet's having one of the classic gods proclaim in effect that his "Kingdom is not of this world." But "cushioned" really overstates the case. Milton obviously wants us to feel some kind of clash in all three places: between the high utterance of Apollo here and the pastoral world of the poem; between St. Peter's words and that same pastoral mood; and between, in the largest terms, Christian and pagan, at the moment of St. Peter's entrance.

By addressing the "fountain *Arethuse*" and the river Mincius (ll. 85–86) he calls attention to the interruption of the pastoral, before proceeding again in that mode:

> But now my Oate proceeds
> And listens to the Herald of the Sea . . .

The transition is not one to a more hopeful mood. Nature cannot protect the poet, as the section reproaching the nymphs has indicated. But the sea is a part of nature too, and as the next section shows, if nature does not protect man, it is at least neutral: there is no culprit to be found among the sea deities. The disaster must be attributed to something outside nature, something supernatural, as is hinted by the dark reference to—

> . . . that fatall and perfidious Bark
> Built in th' eclipse, and rigg'd with curses dark.

But, again, if the sea deities are not actively hostile to man, the sea over which they preside is consistently presented in the poem as unfriendly and alien. It covers the "monstrous world." Its waters are presented several times as something which is sterile and meaningless: the first picture of the drowned man "welter[ing] to the parching wind"; the second, of the "sound-

ing Seas" which "hurl" the drowned man's bones; the third,
of "that perilous flood."

In this poem, for obvious reasons, the sea is associated with
death—the death of King, and also with the death of Orpheus.
But, in relation to the theme of fate as announced in the earlier
sections of the poem, it is associated with a kind of aimless confusion, type of nameless oblivion in which the known and familiar human world is swallowed up. The streams and fountains
which run throughout the poem flow with life-giving water:
they are "crown'd with vocall reeds," or flowers. They flow
to some purpose—they go somewhere—whereas the seas flow
chaotically without pattern—mere tumbling water. (It is ironical, of course, that the streams all have for their destination
the sea, and seem to lose themselves in its purposeless waste:
but this is the very point of the analogy: the lives of men, too,
with their purposes and meanings, spill themselves finally into
the sea of oblivion.)

But whatever the precise meaning of the sea symbol, it can
hardly be an accident that all the "resurrection images" have to
do with a circumvention of the sea, or a rising out of the sea:
Alpheus, in his love for Arethusa, flowing under the sea to come
up again in Sicily and mingle his waters, still fresh and life-
giving, with hers; the day-star rising from the sea; "the dear
might of him that walk'd the waves." On the purely naturalistic
level, all life eventually ends in the sea, and thus far in the poem
we have had a naturalistic account of the state of affairs. Devotion to nature—devotion to the muses, in Milton's deliberate
confusion of these figures with the nymphs—cannot save the
poet. Nature is neutral: it is not positively malignant, but
neither is it beneficent. The only answer that can suffice to
justify "the homely slighted Shepherds trade" is an answer that
does not fall properly to the rural deities at all. It has had to
come from the lips of Apollo, and it has had to consist of an
affirmation of value that transcends this world.[3]

---

[3] Even Phœbus's words, to speak very strictly, do not really "suffice." This
is perfectly apparent from the mere fact that the elegy continues from this
point. And one insufficiency of the pronouncement is immediately clear, that
which is remedied by St. Peter. But something still more complex is involved in the allusion to the traditional conflict of Apollo and Pan implied
in the words, "and touched my trembling ears." (Pan with his flute and Apollo

The pastoral mode, restored so briefly, is, of course, soon broken again—this time, more decisively, by a voice that transcends not only those of the deities of stream and field, but those of the whole classic order. But Milton attempts to bring St. Peter on the scene in accordance with the forms of the occasion. The "Oate proceeds," as it must, since the conventions required by the pastoral form of the poem cannot yet be abandoned. Neptune has called up Æolus to make his report. Next comes Camus, attired as a river god, "His Mantle hairy, and his Bonnet sedge." (Whether he comes also in answer to "Neptune's plea" is left ambiguous. Presumably he does not, but he is presented as a river god just as St. Peter is introduced as the "Pilot of the *Galilean* lake.")

Yet, though Milton has thus accommodated the Christian figure to the classical procession, he does not attempt to conceal his Christian character. St. Peter's locks are "mitred"; he carries his keys. Moreover, if the University under the guise of Camus utters a plaint which can easily be called a conventional pastoral lament, St. Peter emphatically does not. He is talking about "pastors," it is true, but not the *pastores* of Virgil.

By Dr. Johnson's time, the two meanings of *pastor* had, for a serious mind, become so far divorced that Johnson must have thought Milton was taking advantage of a connection as frivolous as that which joins the discrepant meanings in a pun. But we must try to avoid prejudging what Milton is doing. Milton's age felt, and Milton himself felt, that the classic ages and Chris-

with his lyre were fabled to have engaged in a musical contest in which Apollo was the victor. But Midas dissented from the decision, preferring the music of Pan, and Apollo turned his ears into ass's ears as a sign of his inferior taste.) In the passage of *The Shepheardes Calender* (June, ll. 65 ff.) in which Spenser makes a similar allusion the influence of the Muses is dissociated entirely from the pastoral. The Muses are allied with Apollo in *disdaining* the inferior mode of the pastoral. It is important to note that Milton does *not* so dissociate them. In *Lycidas* the pastoral is true poetry, and its guardians, effectual or ineffectual, are ultimately the same as those of the higher modes of the classical tradition. It is precisely the failure of Apollo here that he speaks from his conventional attitude of *disdain* for the "earth" of the pastoral, its earthly values and earthly concerns. Something different, therefore, is required to satisfy the elegist, an affirmation which transcends but does not disdain the natural world—such consolation in short as that presented in the figure of Christ Himself, heroic and yet pastoral, the divine shepherd. We may see Milton, in his resolution of this problem, exploring again that favorite theme—the relation of heroic and pastoral ideals, and the paradox of the pastoral-heroic—and finding, as usual, the solution of the difficulties of the pagan tradition in the truth of Christian revelation.

tianity could be united—that classic thought foreshadowed
what Christianity had revealed, and that the men of the Renaissance were the heirs of both traditions, as indeed they were.

Actually, we beg the question if we assume that St. Peter
can a priori have nothing to do with the pastoral tradition. He
qualifies it, to be sure, by his very presence. And Milton, as
lines 132–33 indicate, expects us to feel a shock. (Milton is
simply more keenly aware of the implications—for both the
conflict and the larger synthesis—of what he is doing than
were his pastoral predecessors who introduced references to the
corrupted clergy. The evidence, again of lines 132–33 especially,
is that he is one step ahead of Johnson in awareness of the
"pun.") But what St. Peter does is to bring in a note not so
much completely alien as realistic. The shepherd's life, he reminds us, is not merely one of singing and meditating the muse,
though he mentions singing. After all, there are the sheep to
be fed and protected. It is a life of some difficulties and dangers:
it requires knowledge and diligence. There are worthless shepherds who have their pipes too, oaten pipes like those on which
Lycidas played and on which the protagonist now plays, but
in St. Peter's angry description they are called "scrannel Pipes
of wretched straw."

The worthless shepherds are "blind mouthes"; and the bold-
ness of Milton's metaphor has caused some comment. How can
a mouth be blind! Everything that is not specifically an eye
is blind, and this is so obvious that some critics have won-
dered why Milton felt it necessary to imply the eye at all. Yet,
even on the literal level, the yawning mouth resembles an eye,
a monstrous sightless eye. And when we remember the shepherd's function (much more when we remember the Christian
shepherd's function), the shepherds whose watchfulness has become simply a gluttonous and selfish desire are rightly "blind
mouthes." Incidentally, the figure is balanced by an equally bold
one which occurs a few lines below, but which has not excited
critical comment. The poet asks the valleys to throw hither "all
your quaint enameld eyes, / That on the green terf suck the
honied showres." The "blind mouthes" are thus balanced by
"sucking eyes." We shall not claim that Milton has consciously
worked out the contrast: such a claim would be difficult to prove.
But the patterning, whether it has been arrived at consciously

or unconsciously, by design or by chance, confronts us in the poem. And the reader does not have to dismiss either passage as a mere strained conceit. The poet seems to be saying that even the flowers, nature's nurslings, which one expects to do nothing more than "suck the honied showres," by contrast with the worthless shepherds who have failed in the responsibilities of their high office, have the kind of spiritual life and awareness we attribute to a seeing eye.

But to argue this is to anticipate, and we must say a final word on St. Peter's speech before taking up the function of the flower passage. St. Peter, as we have said, brings in a grim and realistic note. Lycidas was a good shepherd in a world in which there are too many bad shepherds. But though the speech as a whole praises Lycidas, in terms of the larger theme it makes his death even more meaningless. The good shepherd has been taken; the wicked remain. And even the warning to the wicked shepherds hardly helps Lycidas's case or that of those who mourn for him. Thus, if St. Peter's speech, like Apollo's, transcends the pastoral mode, it carries us away from the hope that Apollo's words had suggested. For the speech, taken literally, indicates that Lycidas was needed and should have lived: many others could better have been taken. The theme has moved simply from Apollo's hint of individual reward to that of general retribution.

The poet recognizes the disruption the speech has brought. He tries once more to establish the pastoral mode. Just as he invokes the "Fountain *Arethuse*" after the Apollo speech, in line 132, he here invokes the river Alpheus.

> Return *Alpheus,* the dread voice is past,
> That shrunk thy streams . . .

The dread voice has been endowed with something of the effect of blazing light—a hot sun inimical to the cool shadows of mythology and the flowers of pastoral poetry. The voice has shrunk the pastoral stream. In trying to re-establish the conventional mode, the poet attempts to conjure up a cool scene of secluded beauty—

> Of shades and wanton winds, and gushing brooks,
> On whose fresh lap the swart Star sparely looks.

He lavishes upon it all the resources of floral decoration. It is almost as if the poet had said: Very well. I admit that with the intrusion of St. Peter, I have deserted the pastoral. But I'll try to make it up. I'll pick up all your scattered flowers—even the pathetic fallacies.

The flower passage is beautiful, granted. But we mistake its function in the poem if we think that it is merely to add a touch of decorative beauty. Actually, its function in the full context of the poem is ironic. The poet improvises beautifully as he attempts to recapture the pastoral spirit, but the *"Sicilian Muse"* will not return—does not return. Indeed, the poet himself gives over the attempt with lines 152–153:

> For so to interpose a little ease,
> Let our frail thoughts dally with false surmise.

With these words he cuts the ground from under the whole elaborate and beautiful structure. The flowers are not really wearing "sad embroidery" for Lycidas; the cups of the daffadillies are not filled with tears for him. Nature is neutral: it does not participate in grief for the dead man. And since it is a "false surmise" to assume that it does, the surmise can give no real comfort. There is, perhaps, some source of comfort yet remaining—St. Peter's speech has no more finally resolved the problem than has Apollo's—but it is not to be found in this wishful return to the conventional pastoral.

It is entirely proper, therefore, that the flower passage should be followed immediately by a realistic picture of the dead body:

> Ay me! Whilst thee the shores, and sounding Seas
> Wash far away . . .

On the literal level, of course, the very physically real absence of Lycidas, of his body, makes the "surmise" of comfort in the funeral ceremony, the strewing of flowers [4] on the bier, a "false" surmise—the "hearse" is empty. And though the absence and the falseness of comfort are, as we have seen, of a significance far larger than the merely physical and accidental, yet this literal "realism" of the passage gives it much of its strength. This is a realistic passage even in its geography—always a point to which Milton gave careful attention. Since King was

---

[4] And poems—the "posies" of the convention.

drowned in the Irish Sea, his bones may have been washed out
through the northern passage into the Atlantic beyond "the
stormy *Hebrides*," or perhaps through the southern channel out
beyond Land's End. The poet appeals to the dolphins to "waft
the haples youth" as one of them once in Greek fable carried
the body of the drowned Palæmon to the shore.[5] The poet does
not ask the angel Michael to lift the drowned body from the
sea: his petition goes no further than to ask him to feel pity
for Lycidas and his sorrowing friends:

> Look homeward Angel now, and melt with ruth.

We would seem to be at this point at the nadir of despair.
Even if we can, by looking ahead in the poem, read "homeward"
as "heavenward" and see the gaze of the angel as guiding
Lycidas thither, an unyielding irony remains in the very char-
acter of the spirit to whom the appeal for "ruth" is addressed—
Michael, the warrior prince.

The recovery begins with the next lines. With the command,

> Weep no more, woful Shepherds weep no more

the poet makes the first direct appeal to the Christian supernatural. With all false comforts rejected, the true hope may at
last be entertained. Lycidas is not dead. The sun too sinks into
the sea, only to rise again, and

> Flames in the forehead of the morning sky,

and this flaming is not the "sudden blaze" to be ended igno-
miniously by the "blind *Fury* with th' abhorred shears." Other
symbols of the poem find a restatement here too. The day-star
that flames in the forehead of the morning sky is after all the
same sun which in the season of the "swart *star*" shrinks the
pastoral stream. It is the full blaze of truth in which the poetic
fancies seem to shrivel. In this final passage however it is not a
sultry and parching light, but cool and brilliant as the morning.
And even the sea participates in the resurrection image—is

---

[5] The reference, as T. O. Mabbott has shown [see *infra*, p. 244], is to Palæmon, not to Arion as most editors have interpreted it. When the poet Arion
was cast overboard by the sailors, the dolphins, who loved his music, brought
him safe to shore. But Lycidas, like Palæmon, is dead: there is no question
of his being saved from the sea.

the "bed" in which the sun repairs its strength for the new day's
journey.

Indeed, Lycidas moves through a pastoral scene as the elegy
closes, a scene where there are

> . . . other groves, and other streams along

which Lycidas walks, surrounded by the flock of his fellows,

> In solemn troops, and sweet Societies.

The shepherds, under the Good Shepherd, have become the
sheep. And since much has been made in the poem of the shepherd as poet and of the shepherd's song, the final passage is
pastoral too in that the "sweet Societies"

> . . . sing, and singing in their glory move.

To sum up: the scene is pastoral in that the world of competition and distraction is done away with. It is "simple" in that
it is quiet, peaceful, undisturbed, harmonious. But there is the
suggestion—if we have attended the earlier sections of the poem
—that only here can the true pastoral life exist; only here do
the sheep feed perpetually by the still waters in an ideal and
beautiful shepherd's world. This is the world which the ancient,
pagan pastorals faintly adumbrate. The synthesis which is
finally accomplished in *Lycidas* is a typically baroque mingling of Christian and pagan materials: the latter are not made
completely false—they remain true insofar as they suggest the
final truth of Christian revelation.

But Milton is unwilling to end the poem on just this note.
And there follows, consequently, the curious last paragraph of
eight lines. There is no third-person section at the beginning
of the poem in which the "uncouth Swain" is introduced, and to
which this last section recurs. The poem begins with the uncouth swain speaking. It is something of a surprise, therefore,
to have this asymmetrical bit at the end.

The anomalous ending has been pointed out before, but we
do not believe that its function has ever been adequately com-
mented upon. Actually, it has a most important function: its
effect is to throw the whole poem back into perspective. After
all, the poem is the utterance of an "uncouth Swain," an un-

known poet, and perhaps an awkward and unpolished one. His thought is "eager"—ambitious, ardent, even enthusiastic, it is suggested—but the instrument is rustic, and the mode is the countrified and old-fashioned Doric, the limitations of which the poet has been defining throughout the performance. If the "uncouth Swain" who speaks up to this point is carried away by his own utterance, Milton is not. He has not submerged his total personality as a poet in the character of the "Swain."

The last bit of natural description participates in the general qualification. Only a few lines earlier, the day-star, rising out of the sea, tricking "his beams . . . with new spangled Ore," had become the sign of Lycidas's own resurrection. But now, as the swain prepares to leave, it has

> . . . dropt into the Western bay

and is, along with the bones of the drowned poet,

> Sunk . . . beneath the watry floar.

The effect is not to deny the radiant vision of promise with which the elegy concludes, but only to place it definitely in that perspective which must be an essential part of its truth. Actually it is a perspective of realism, as we have already seen if we have read carefully, but here it is defined precisely and finally. We are simply *reminded* that the vision is one of hope, not yet fulfilled, that the elegy has been composed and delivered in a real world in which suns rise and set, day follows day, the flood remains perilous to all those whom Lycidas has left behind, and the young shepherd has to bethink himself of the duties of the new day. It is realism, but not a narrowing realism—"To morrow to fresh Woods, and Pastures new."

The Italian Element
in *Lycidas*

F. T. Prince

Lycidas is the most impressive of Milton's minor poems and one of the chief glories of English lyrical verse. **Dr.** Johnson's severity towards the pastoral convention of the poem has had little effect upon its reputation and its appeal, and has been sufficiently answered by criticism from the early nineteenth century to our own time. His denial of beauty to the verse may be felt to be equally a revelation of the sharp limits of his sensibility; but it is somewhat more difficult to rebut, since the structure of the verse is indeed peculiar. We are not likely to find that "the diction is harsh, the rhymes uncertain, and the numbers unpleasing." Yet the fact that the principles of structure of *Lycidas* have never been applied by later poets suggests that they have never been completely understood, however much the poem has been admired.

This, the last poem of Milton's youth, and the most perfect, in fact shows him as more conscious than ever before of the possibilities of moulding English verse by Italian methods. *Lycidas* cannot be dissected without a knowledge of the Italian poetry of the sixteenth century. But it must be said that there is no exact parallel in Italian literature to the pattern of Milton's poem; there is no single model to which we can point. The poem results from Milton's appreciation of several different

From *The Italian Element in Milton's Verse* (Oxford, 1954), pp. 71–88.

kinds of Italian verse, and his application of certain first principles to form a new combination of familiar elements. And, indeed, how could it be otherwise, if the poem was to be what it is, a unique utterance wrung from the poet by the event and the circumstances? Much of the power of *Lycidas* flows from the impression it gives of being thus shaped by a particular occasion: Milton's personal participation in the poem gives it its greatest strength. This impression is one with the form of the poem—a development of the disciplined improvisation of the lines *On Time* and *At a Solemn Musick*. Such a method of writing verse must necessarily produce poems which have a unique shape and movement.

It is possible nevertheless to detect the discipline which guides such poems, and in *Lycidas* it is the discipline of the *canzone*, as it was modified and adapted in lyrics and eclogues of the *Cinquecento*.

Some aspects of this relationship are obvious enough. W. P. Ker pointed out that "you cannot fully understand . . . *Lycidas* without going back to Italy and the theory and practice of the *canzone*," and insisted that the whole tradition of solemn odes in English, from Spenser's *Epithalamion* to the nineteenth century, rested upon Dante's description of the *canzone* in the *De Vulgari Eloquentia*, and in particular on his consecration of the harmony between hendecasyllables and heptasyllables. The combination of ten-syllable and six-syllable lines in *Lycidas* of course represents that Italian harmony, but the connexion with the tradition of the *canzona* goes farther than that.

The wide deviations from the strict form of the *canzone* are, however, the first thing to be noticed. A *canzone* consisted of a complex, fully rhymed stanza of some length, repeated several times and followed by a shorter concluding stanza, the *commiato*. *Lycidas* consists of eleven "verse-paragraphs" of lengths varying from ten to thirty-three lines, closely but irregularly rhymed, and including ten lines, scattered throughout, which do not rhyme at all; the last verse-paragraph is of eight lines, rhymed like an *ottava rima*, and undoubtedly corresponds in its own way to a *commiato*. The six-syllable lines are disposed as irregularly as the rhymes, but are governed nevertheless by certain limitations: they are used somewhat sparingly, and they always rhyme, and always with a ten-syllable line which has gone before.

II

Milton must have been well acquainted with the liberation of some Italian lyric verse from stanzaic form which took place in the latter half of the sixteenth century and which had produced a great flow of facile writing by his own time. There is no need to undertake the difficult task of tracing how this liberation came about, for there can be little doubt that Milton's first and clearest impression of it would have come from two works, Tasso's *Aminta* and Guarini's *Il Pastor Fido*. Tasso's famous pastoral drama must have established the use, for certain purposes, of such irregularly rhymed passages, though it seems that his father Bernardo had experimented with such forms in eclogues and some other elaborate poems. Guarini developed this feature of *Aminta* with great success; among his choruses are to be found, together with the normal use of regular *canzone* form, several examples of a sustained improvised pattern of rhymes. From this type of irregular lyric, and from the partially rhymed semi-lyrical passages of dialogue found both in *Aminta* and *Il Pastor Fido*, Milton would have seen the possibilities of this liberation of the *canzone* for dramatic and lyrical verse. These pastoral dramas were among the most brilliant and most admired works of Italian poetry in the late sixteenth and early seventeenth centuries. Their artistic authority would certainly have been acknowledged even by a poet of so different a temper as Milton.

Nevertheless, the technical innovations of *Aminta* and *Il Pastor Fido* do not in themselves account for the structure of *Lycidas*, though they may help to explain how Milton arrived at his own methods. For with *Aminta* the Italian pastoral began to move away from its dependence on Virgil's example, and entered a new world of its own, preoccupied with the affairs of the Amaryllis and the Neaera who are allotted two lines in Milton's poem. As Italian pastoral poetry became less learned and more facile, it became less evocative of any associations other than erotic. *Lycidas*, with its repeated invocations of the "Sicilian Muse," intends to remain within reach and touch of Theocritus and Virgil; and this intention it shares with the

Italian eclogues of the earlier sixteenth century rather than
with those of the later. The seriousness of the poem, however
personal its intensity may be, is a quality it shares with the
even earlier Latin pastoral tradition; in Italy, as the sixteenth
century ran its course, such allusions as those of Milton to the
Church became impossible.

Lycidas therefore takes advantage of the technical freedom
of the later *Cinquecento;* but it uses that freedom in ways which
recall also the Italian eclogues of the High Renaissance, when
vernacular poetry was absorbed in its imitation of Greek and
Latin.

III

The Italian eclogues of Sannazaro (1458–1530) and Berardino Rota (1509–1575) illustrate some of the technical developments by which it was sought to recreate Greek and Roman
pastoral verse in traditional Tuscan forms. The chief distinction between the methods of these two poets is that by Rota's
time the diction of Italian verse had learned how to reproduce
the movement of Latin syntax, and this made possible a freer
handling of verse-forms.

Sannazaro's eclogues in Italian are interspersed throughout
his pastoral romance, the *Arcadia;* the more lyrical of them
preserve the fixed forms of the *canzone* (including the *sestina*),
but for the purposes of dialogue Sannazaro uses *terza rima*, the
form which was always favoured for colloquial or familiar verse.
The mixture of metres in individual eclogues, and the use of
various elaborate lyric forms, show the problems facing Italian
poets when they set out consciously to rival classical pastorals.
There was no single vernacular metre which could be made
the equivalent of the Virgilian hexameter, moving from dialogue
to song without any change of structure.

Sannazaro does not attempt any profound modification of
the movement of the *canzone* in the elegy which forms his Fifth
Eclogue; he is content to infuse into the diction as much as he
can of the elegiac fluidity and fullness already introduced by
Petrarch in echo of Latin verse:

> *Altri monti, altri piani,*
> *Altri boschetti, e rivi*

> *Vedi nel cielo, e più novelli fiori;*
> *Altri Fauni, e Silvani*
> *Per luoghi dolci estivi*
> *Seguir le Ninfe in più felici amori,*[1]

sings Ergasto to the shade of Androgeo. And a passage which points forward to *Lycidas* describes the grief of Nature:

> *Pianser le sante Dive*
> *La tua spietata morte;*
> *I fiumi il sanno, e le spelunche, e i faggi:*
> *Pianser le verdi rive,*
> *L'erbe pallide e smorte;*
> *E 'l Sol più giorni non mostrò suoi raggi:*
> *Nè gli animai selvaggi*
> *Usciro in alcun prato;*
> *Nè greggi andar' per monti,*
> *Nè gustaro erbe, o fonti:*
> *Tanto dolse a ciascun l'acerbo fato;*
> *"Androgèo, Androgèo" sonava il bosco.*[2]

The diction and the placing of the words here are no more complex than in Petrarch; but they are more consciously used, as they are used also by Milton, to reproduce specific Latin effects.

The same modulation of the flow of the sentences is to be seen in some of Sannazaro's *terzetti*:

> *Talor mentre fra me piango, e ragionomi*
> *Sento la lira dir con voci querule:*
> *"Di lauro, o Meliseo, più non coronomi."*
> *Talor veggio venir frisoni, e merule*
> *Ad un mio roscigniuol, che stride, e vocita:*
> *"Voi meco, o mirti, e voi piangete, o ferule."*
> *Talor d'un alta rupe il corbo crocita:*
> *"Absorbere a tal duol il mar devrebbesi,*
> *Ischia, Capri, Ateneo, Miseno, e Procita."* . . .[3]

[1] "Other mountains, other plains, other thickets and banks, thou view'st in Heaven, and yet fresher flowers: other Fauns and other Silvans throughout sweet summer places follow the Nymphs in happier loves."

[2] "The holy Goddesses wept for thy despiteful death; the rivers know it, and the caves and beeches: the green banks wept, their grasses pale and withered; and the sun for many days concealed his rays: nor did the wild beasts come forth in the meadows, nor the flocks go to the mountains, nor tasted they grass nor fountain: so greatly each was grieved by thy bitter fate; 'Androgeo, Androgeo' the wood resounded."

[3] "Sometimes while to myself I weep and talk, I hear the lyre that says

The double rhymes of these lines are characteristic of Sannazaro's *terza rima:* their effect is to give the dialogue a sustained
cleverness and a monotony of rhythm, which are both somewhat irritating. Such verse has a certain charm, and a flavour of
common speech; but it is more suited to humorous writing than
to serious, and Sannazaro on the whole uses it for such lighter
passages as this exchange of abuse between rival shepherds:

OFELIA.   *Dimmi, caprar novello, e non t'irascere,*
           Questa tua greggia, ch'è cotanto strania,
           Chi te la diè sì follemente a pascere?
ELENCO.   *Dimmi, bifolco antico, e quale insania*
           Ti risospinse a spezzar l'arco a Clonico,
           Ponendo fra' pastor tanta zizzania?
OFELIA.   *Forse fu allor, ch'io vidi malinconico*
           Selvaggio andar per la sampogna, e i naccari,
           Che gl'involasti tu, perverso erronico.[4]

This jocular intricacy of surface betrays an inner emptiness.
But Milton had a leaning toward this verbal type of humour.
His sardonic sonnets on the reception of his divorce tracts and
on the Long Parliament have roots in this kind of satire in
Italian. There is surely an echo of this manner of rustic raillery
in the description of the singing of the bad shepherds in *Lycidas:*

> And when they list, their lean and flashy songs
> Grate on their scrannel Pipes of wretched straw.

The eclogues of the *Arcadia* display a balance between traditional Tuscan forms and the sustained imitation of Virgil's
diction and manner. This balance is upset in the Italian eclogues
of Berardino Rota, written some forty years later. The form
and diction of these *Egloghe Pescatorie* show what progress
Bembo and his disciples had made towards a close imitation of

---

with querulous tones: 'O Meliseo, I crown me no more with laurel.' Sometimes I see finches and blackbirds come to a nightingale of mine, that cried
and calls out: 'O myrtles, weep with me, and weep, ye fennels.' Sometimes
from a high rock the raven croaks: 'At such a sorrow the sea should swallow
Ischia, Capri, Ateneo, Miseno, and Procita.'"

[4] OFELIA. "Tell me, new goatherd, and be not angry: this flock of thine,
    that is so odd, who gave it thee so foolishly to graze?"
ELENCO. "Tell me, old ox-driver, and what madness impelled thee to break
    the bow with Clonico, so setting such discord among shepherds?"
OFELIA. "Perhaps it was then when I saw Selvaggio go sadly lacking his
    pipe and castanets, which thou robbedst him of, thou wicked stray."

Latin verse in the vernacular. Rota was a younger contemporary of Della Casa, and the latinization of the style in his eclogues recalls Della Casa's infusion of Horatian and Virgilian gravity into the sonnet, and probably owes something to Della Casa's methods.

Neither in Rota's sonnets nor in his eclogues do we find any vivid or concentrated poetic power; but the very conventionality of his matter deflects attention to the small innovations of manner and method which give his eclogues their distinction. Himself a Neapolitan, he imitates and develops in the vernacular the Latin Piscatory Eclogues of Sannazaro. As Virgil invokes the Sicilian Muses, Rota invokes the Nymphs of Mergellina; he derives as much from Sannazaro as from Theocritus and Virgil.

His chief effort is directed towards making a new adjustment between Italian verse-forms and Latinate diction; the result is that the still surviving predominance of the rhymed patterns found in Sannazaro is here replaced by the predominance of diction as an element of structure. Intricate word-order, carefully sustained repetitions, and lengthy periods tend to relegate rhyme to a secondary position. Such writing is relevant, in however minor a degree, not only to *Lycidas*, but to Milton's blank verse.

In most of the lyrical parts of his eclogues Rota continues to use stanzaic forms; but for dramatic and descriptive dialogue, and for some lyrics, he devises a new formula. His hendecasyllables are built on a submerged pattern of six-line stanzas: a b c a b c e f g e f g, and so on. The use of *terza rima* in pastoral verse is perhaps reflected in the ternary structure of this pattern; but Rota succeeds in eliminating the strongly stanzaic movement of *terza rima* by spacing his rhymes as widely as he does. Moreover, the sense and the diction so habitually disregard the limits of the lines and the "stanza," they profess to observe but really transgress the rhyme-scheme with such consistency, that there is little difference in the effect when, as in the Second Eclogue, submerged rhyme is abandoned for blank verse.

The only satisfactory way to read Rota's rhymed hendecasyllables is indeed as if they were *versi sciolti;* the diction is elaborated in such a way as to impose its own movement on the metre. The following passage from the Eleventh Eclogue will illustrate this effect; Triton sings of various fables of the sea, *a guisa del Sileno di Virgilio:*

A questo aggiunge poi perchè nell' acque	a
Ino col suo figliuol già si sommerse;	b
Come le fu cangiato, il viso, il nome	c
Dal Re del mar: che così a Vener piacque,	a
E in questo e quel Dio poi li converse;	b
E quanto pianta fu la Nimpha, e come	c
Giunone irata le compagne sue	d
Augelli e sassi fece. E di te disse	e
O Scilla ancor, qual fur dannose e vane	f
Le prighiere di Glauco; e quanto fue	d
Circe crudele, e'n quanto duol poi visse	e
L'amante, quando in mar rabbioso cane	f
Latrar t'intese a torto, e poichè scoglio	h
Ti vide, quanto pianse e quanto ancora	i
Ogni nocchier ti fugga, e perchè festi,	j
Rimembrando di Circe il fiero orgoglio,	h
Senza compagni Ulisse. E come fora	i
O Vener bella tu dal mar sorgesti	j
Nata di spume: onde 'l bel nome hai preso.[5]	k

Yet, for all its careful modulations, there is something mechanical about such verse. Rota has fluency, but little energy, and this is perhaps why he clings to a regular scheme of rhyme, when blank verse would seem to be the logical development of his style. His formula is a compromise, and the opposition between the repeated pattern of rhymes and the irregular current of the diction is too constant to be satisfying: it leaves a faint impression of artistic dishonesty or cowardice. Rota's methods point the way to Tasso's *Aminta*, in so far as his eclogues suggest that blank verse on the one hand, or a greater freedom of rhyme on the other, would open up new possibilities; Tasso's "eclogue" combines these more logical methods.

[5] "To this he adds then why Ino with her son was dipped in the waters; how she had her face and name changed by the King of the sea, for so it pleased Venus, and into this and that God then he changed them; and how much bewept was the Nymph, and how angry Juno made her companions stones and birds. And of thee he said, O Scilla, again, how harmful and vain were the prayers of Glaucus; and how cruel Circe was, and in what pain then lived thy lover, when he heard thee bark in the sea as a raging dog, and when he saw thee as a rock, how much he wept and how yet every sailor flees thee; and why thou deprivedst Ulysses of his comrades, remembering the fierce pride of Circe. And how it was that thou, O lovely Venus, rose from the sea, born of foam, whence thy fair name is taken."

A knowledge of Sannazaro's and of Rota's eclogues enables one to distinguish the main factors in the development of Italian pastoral poetry in the sixteenth century. Taken together with *Aminta* and *Il Pastor Fido*, they point to the underlying compulsions of Milton's "monody," why it seeks, and how it achieves, a reconciliation between rhyme and fluent elegiac diction. *Lycidas* is more powerful than any of these elegant literary amusements; but without the technical discoveries they represent Milton would have been unable to give his pastoral its combination of freedom and discipline.

IV

Two technical experiments—the attempt to evolve a poetic diction equivalent to that of Virgil, and the attempt to combine the tradition of the *canzone* with that of the classical eclogue—marked Italian pastoral verse in the sixteenth century. In England both these experiments bore fruit in *Lycidas*. But before considering Milton's poem more closely, it is worth looking at the degree to which these Italian experiments are traceable in earlier English pastoral poetry. The only previous English poet worth considering in this connexion is Spenser, the only poet to show, in *The Shepheardes Calender*, that he believed the pastoral to be capable of "high seriousness." The general Elizabethan and Jacobean notions of pastoral, however delightfully they might enrich plays and lyrics, or narrative and topographical verse, were too popular and superficial to affect Milton's poem.

Spenser's methods in *The Shepheardes Calender* are akin to those of the earlier type of Italian eclogue written by Sannazaro rather than to those tried out by Rota. Roughly speaking, we may say that he is not interested in the problem of metrical unity of effect that began to interest Rota and was solved by Tasso. Writing in stanzas (except in the three "Chaucerian" eclogues), Spenser either preserves the same stanza throughout or introduces songs or "layes" in different measures. The only reflection of *canzone* form in *The Shepheardes Calender* is in the dirge in November, and this, though of some interest in relation to Milton, has no prosodic affinity with *Lycidas*.

It seems clear that Spenser's technique in pastoral verse was formed without reference to the particular Italian technical advances summarized above. This is confirmed by the form of his later pastorals, *Colin Clout's Come Home Againe, Daphnaïda,* and *Astrophel. Colin Clout* indeed uses a metre not found in *The Shepheardes Calender,* continuous "heroic" quatrains; and the way in which Spenser handles these, so that the limits of the quatrains have little correspondence with the flow of the verse, is faintly suggestive of Rota's device of submerged rhyme. But the analogy is slight because, for one thing, Spenser's quatrains are a shorter and more emphatic pattern than Rota's pattern of six lines and are more difficult to submerge; and for another, Spenser seems to make no effort to submerge them. He does not attempt, by means of a complex word-order or of strong pauses within the lines, to disguise the rhyme-scheme, but rather proceeds with his usual mellifluous facility and produces an effect of his own. There is, moreover, an English parallel to the verse of *Colin Clout,* and that is the verse of Raleigh's surviving fragment of *The Book of the Ocean to Cynthia.* Since the two poets were closely associated at about this time, and Spenser alludes to Raleigh's poetry in *Colin Clout,* it is possible that the quatrains of this poem were suggested by Raleigh's lost poem *Cynthia,* which may have been in the same metre as the later fragment.

Daphnaïda and *Astrophel* were the finest pastoral elegies written in English before *Lycidas,* and must be reckoned important features of Milton's poetic background. Yet in these later and more lengthy poems Spenser does but apply the verse technique he had devised more than a decade before: here, as in the bulk of his poetry, the characteristic rhetoric and music are due to his genius for writing in stanzas. Milton had not attempted to write in stanzas of Spenserian type since he relinquished his poem on *The Passion;* what else *Daphnaïda* had to give him—an example of flowing melody—he must have appropriated long before composing *Lycidas.* The chief interest of a comparison between Spenser's pastoral elegies and Milton's would consist in their divergences: Spenser's regularly woven patterns and leisurely embroidery make an instructive contrast to Milton's more compressed and more passionate variety of movement.

V

It remains to show what specific means Milton employed "to build the lofty rhyme." The final clue to the structure of *Lycidas* is to be found in principles derived from the architecture of the *canzone*.

The structure of the *canzone* was fully explained by Dante in the *De Vulgari Eloquentia;* Tasso also discusses it in his dialogue *La Cavalletta*, and claims to discover some discrepancy between Dante's theory and his practice. But the principle of structure which is relevant to *Lycidas* is never in dispute: it is that the stanza of a *canzone* is most commonly built of two sections, which are linked by a key line or *chiave*. Such a stanza was also called a *stanza divisa*. One or the other of the two parts of such a stanza might also be divided, but not usually both. If the first part was undivided it was called the *fronte* or brow; if it was divided the sub-divisions were called *piedi* or feet. If the second part of the stanza were undivided it was called the *sirima* or *coda;* if divided, the subdivisions were called *versi*. The first part of a *stanza divisa* must be linked to the second by a line rhyming with the last line of the first; this line was the *chiave* or key. The two *versi*, where these existed, might also be linked by a *chiave*.

It is the sense of movement, and the habits of rhetoric, deriving from these divisions, which determine the methods of Milton's poem. Just as in the original use of the sonnet the divisions and subdivisions between quatrains and tercets were observed by the diction and only transgressed for some special purpose, these divisions in the *canzone* were present to the writer and the reader and gave a distinctive emphasis and movement to the different parts of the stanza. And just as with the divisions of the sonnet, the divisions of the *canzone* were often deliberately overridden by sixteenth-century poets, but only because, even when the diction did not follow them, they remained in mind, and the effect was one of counterpoint between the rhyme-pattern and the diction, such as Milton reproduces in his sonnets. The divisions in both sonnet and *canzone* made possible a kind of rhetoric of rhyme: lines which rhymed had differing weight and emphasis according to their position and function. It is impossible to follow Milton's methods in *Lycidas* without perceiving that he makes use of such a rhetoric of rhyme, combining it and contrasting it with the more usual rhetoric of sentence-structure.

The most obvious feature which this method gives the poem is the failure of Milton's sentences to correspond to the pattern of rhymes; the ebb and flow of statement, the pauses and new departures, appear to be independent of any necessity but their own. To give two examples:

Next *Camus,* reverend Sire, went footing slow,	a
His Mantle hairy, and his Bonnet sedge,	b
Inwrought with figures dim, and on the edge	b
Like to that sanguine flower inscrib'd with woe.	a
Ah; who hath reft (quoth he) my dearest pledge?	b
Last came, and last did go,	a
The Pilot of the *Galilean* lake,	c

Weep no more, woful Shepherds weep no more,	a
For *Lycidas* your sorrow is not dead,	b
Sunk though he be beneath the watry floar,	a
So sinks the day-star in the Ocean bed,	b
And yet anon repairs his drooping head,	b
And tricks his beams, and with new spangled Ore,	a
Flames in the forehead of the morning sky:	c

In the first of these passages there is a strong pause at the end of the fifth line, yet the next line, introducing a new series of rhymes, takes its own rhyme from those of the completed statement; in the second passage the first strong pause comes at the end of the seventh line, yet this line introduces a new rhyme. Everywhere in the poem we find such effects, and they are due to the working of a positive principle, not to a mere negative overriding of a casual rhyme-scheme. Milton has in mind the chief principle resulting from the *stanza divisa* of the *canzone:* that each new group or series of rhymes must be linked to its predecessor by a key line. In the first example given, either the fifth or sixth line (but preferably the latter) may be regarded as such a key, taking up a rhyme from the first four lines. In the second example the fifth line is such a key, though again it is followed by a line which also takes up a rhyme from the first four lines. A clearer example is the fifth line of the following paragraph:

Return *Alpheus,* the dread voice is past,	a
That shrunk thy streams; Return *Sicilian* Muse,	b
And call the Vales, and bid them hither cast	a
Their Bels, and Flourets of a thousand hues.	b
Ye valleys low where the milde whispers use,	b
Of shades and wanton winds, and gushing brooks,	c

Milton is using the principle of articulation of the *canzone;* and he has liberated it from its association with repeated *piedi* or *versi* within his paragraphs. This principle of articulation is therefore free to affect any part of his paragraphs, not only certain transitions, like the *volta* or, as Dante calls it, the "diesis."

The rhetoric of rhyme derived from the *canzone* has thus provided Milton with an invaluable instrument—a type of rhyme which looks both back and forward. His ear had been so trained by the *canzone* as to appreciate this effect not only in the key, or *chiave*, where it is most obvious, but in subtler details. One of these is the use of the six-syllable lines, which are also placed so as to give a sense of expectation: they not only always rhyme with a previous longer line (thus looking back), but they give the impression of a contracted movement which must be compensated by a full movement in the next line (which is always of full length), and they thus look forward. This effect is most marked when, as in most cases, these short lines rhyme with the line immediately preceding them.

Milton has constructed *Lycidas* by means of these very precise principles, though they are principles which not only allow him a certain freedom of improvisation but even facilitate it, in a way that would be impossible if the verse were not closely controlled. He has made his own rules for this poem, but made them out of his knowledge and enjoyment of the strictest Italian practice. Thus he appears to have decided that his rhymes must not generally be separated by more than two lines. For the scattered unrhymed lines he had sufficient Renaissance authority. He has also accepted from Dante the preference for a couplet to end his paragraphs; according to the *De Vulgari Eloquentia,* "the endings of the last lines are most beautifully disposed if they fall with a rhyme into silence."

Indeed, the only true couplets in *Lycidas* are those which conclude verse-paragraphs; and one of the best ways to appreciate the articulation of the poem is to analyse the effect of those rhymes coming together elsewhere, which might appear to be couplets, but which are not, because the second rhyming line always looks forward to what comes next. The following examples illustrate this effect in varying degrees:

Begin then, Sisters of the sacred well,	a
That from beneath the seat of *Jove* doth spring,	b
Begin, and somwhat loudly sweep the string.	b
Hence with denial vain, and coy excuse,	c
It was that fatall and perfidious Bark	a
Built in th' eclipse, and rigg'd with curses dark,	a
That sunk so low that sacred head of thine.	b
Fame is no plant that grows on mortal soil,	a
Nor in the glistering foil	a
Set off to th' world, nor in broad rumour lies,	b
But lives and spreds aloft by those pure eyes,	b
And perfect witnes of all judging *Jove;*	c

To analyse *Lycidas* in the light of the *canzone* and the Italian eclogues is to realize with vividness that only a poet of Milton's intellectual energy could have devised and successfully applied such a formula. The poem is built upon movements of thought and emotion; Milton is able to use the methods of repeated transitions, of a continuous unfolding and developing, because his mind and emotions naturally moved with power and confidence, with a sustained strength. Even when other poets who have attempted solemn odes in English have had some of this capacity for embodying mental and emotional energy in verse, they have lacked a technical formula so appropriate to such a task. The discipline of *Lycidas* has left little mark on the tradition of the English ode; it has proved to be inimitable. And this is scarcely surprising, if the peculiarly combined forces described in this chapter are among those which went to its making.

Theme, Pattern, and Imagery in *Lycidas*

Rosemond Tuve

Lycidas is the most poignant and controlled statement in English poetry of the acceptance of that in the human condition which seems to man unacceptable. I do not of course refer simply to the calm ending of the elegy, but to its whole poem-long attempt to relate understandably to human life the immutable fact of death—the pain of loss, the tragedy of early death, the arraignment of the entire natural world that did not avert this unnatural concluding of what was unfulfilled, the passionate indictment of an order that sets a fatal stop upon even man's Orphean task and the good report that would crown it, the depositions one after another of those who carry out the higher commands in orderly fashion, the accusers who still press for an answer, and finally the center and heart of the matter: the questioning of a justice that would take the young and leave the ripe, take the devoted and leave the self-indulgent, so too would take the shepherd and leave the destroyer. What answer? What order? to what end a human life, struck down and ended by an immutable will even as it consecrates itself to God's own uses on an earth sick and famished under the hand of His enemy? Disorder, no answer, death is our answer; the slit life, the ravaged commonwealth.

From *Images and Themes in Five Poems by Milton* (Cambridge, Mass., 1957), pp. 73–111.

Indictments of the unfathomable total moral order, and answers to them, are matter of tragedy, not of pastoral, and Milton twice recognizes this and twice returns from that higher mode back into the different music of the pastoral. Each question has its answer before he makes this return. The questions are cognate. One is in terms of the folly of the poet's devotion (since Death ends it, irrelative of fulfillment), and one in terms of the flat impossibility of the priest's task, when an inscrutable power extinguishes those who alone would do its work here. The answers are not so much cognate as the same, that judgement is the Lord's. In each case the meaning of the answer transcends man's unaided wisdom, and it is properly spoken by an unearthly voice. This last is simply one aspect of the imagery which keeps each answer exactly suited to the nature and philosophical weight of the question.

In the first climax of question and answer Milton moves unobtrusively through related types of images: from the pastoral images which can signify to us all that is careless, not responsible for ends, in a life that sports with Amaryllis in the shade, all that is symbolized by "Delight" in a *Roman de la rose*, on through images with a sure romance connotation, spur and guerdon. The *guerdon* which as tangible token marks a course run with honor at the tournament or at the end of an entire knightly life[1] is not, I think, equated with the *spur* of honorable report (honor, not its by-product prestige) which impels to action. For a poet it impels to self-discipline and laborious days. Thence to the simpler figure used for what the care and labor bring forth, the *sudden blaze* of a poetic achievement worthy those years of fire tended and fostered; but instead of this comes the other suddenness, irretrievable, of Atropos' action. The terror that attends our powerlessness lies in the image, *"thin spun* life"; the ease of this end is an ironic comment on our attention to ends.

The secrets of the otherworld, of those who create and who judge, have been thought of as epic matters by Milton ever

---

[1] For example, Malory's last book was called by him "The Piteous Tale of the Morte Arthure *saunz Gwerdon,*" and the reader will recall its import. *Blaze* in the next sentence is apparently an image from fire, not originating at any rate in the verb or noun *blazon, blaze.* The usual reading takes the *blaze* as *the becoming famous.* In support of my different one: the fire which smoulders or is tended in a poet bursts out at last in great poetry, only a smouldering *reputation* breaks forth into a blaze of *fame.*

since *Vacation Exercise,* 30–54. Yet it is fitting and necessary that the answer which enlightens his servant, and negates "the *thankless* Muse," should be fully spoken out here by shining *Phoebus,*[2] to whom the allegiance of all poet-shepherds is due, both him whose life is slit and the living ones who are left to write of it. In this answer, through the extended metaphor of the heavenly plant, which *lives and spreads* as the great final pronouncements echo through heaven, Phoebus extracts and throws away the irony and the powerlessness, reduces to instrument the inimical shears, redefines the spur, promises due guerdon when all real guerdons are given, "lastly." Not ignoble, the other conception had yet not been truly a conception of *Fame.* Artifice and vulnerability are the character of all garlands where soil is *mortal,* witness *im*perfect, eyes *im*pure; and "Fame" is neither rightly understood by men, nor conferable by them, nor measurable by their imperfect faculties, nor at all touchable by death; ineffable, unwithered, and immortal.

It is a perfect instance of subtle literary judgement that Milton did not phrase this, as he might have done, in the imagery of "And when the chief Shepherd shall appear, ye shall receive a crown of glory that fadeth not away" (1 Peter v. 4). He saved for his second great answer the overtly Christian terms of St. Peter's speech, by which time the sudden blaze and clear light of unequivocal terms is wanted. This is not a matter of "Christian" and "pagan" but of direction and indirection, of a less or a more figurative functioning in the language. Both are Christian. The question of Milton's pagan imagery in *Lycidas* here comes up in its first form, and we make the first answer to it, that such *terms* do not make images non-Christian. The additional element of indirection in the first question and answer was of a kind endeared to the Renaissance reader by long habit. Nor have Milton's Phoebus and Jove and amaranthine plant lost their classical suggestions to become exactly and solely what Peter and Paul talk about in God's conferred "crown of righteousness." The two terms of any metaphor both add meaning to that which is being given significance through its use. We must turn later to the full

[2] Milton's other uses of *Phoebus,* from *Elegy i* on, illuminate this one; the sense of a responsibility to poetry apparent here comes out especially in *Manso,* 35: "not profitless to Phoebus"; and the reminiscence of Virgil's Sixth Eclogue is pertinent. Modern over-personal readings are to be questioned.

importance of this, but the point that should be made before we leave Phoebus's *first* of the *three* overt "consolations" in *Lycidas* is this one concerning the metaphorical weight of classical allusion and figure. This does not deny the judgement that the unambiguously full statement of Christian consolation in Christian terms may shine out with a more splendid and luminous clarity, in Milton's own imagination and to us toward the end of the poem.

St. Peter both makes evident and answers the second great question which draws Milton into the epic and tragic realm, where doubts raised by resentful human bewilderment ask for ultimate answers, secrets known only to a wisdom above nature. Camus, though he is a river god like the rest, wears the clothing of grief and stands like the song itself among the mourners who question rather than among the accused who state their innocence, and it is he that asks the forthright *"Who* hath reft him?"* which closes the inquiry; we hear no more of second causes, and nature is acquitted. The last personage is neither accuser nor accused, but the emblem of a just and final judgement, vicar of Christ. Peter speaks first as type, bishop, and head of all priests, of the living ones he could better have spared no less than of the faithful one cut off.[3]

From here onward the bitter, despairing and violent description, of "our corrupted Clergie then in their height," of its own weight poses the further accusation which the situation in fact in November 1637 had certainly brought Milton to make. It is Job's outcry against incomprehensibility in the moral order and in the "justice" of its Author; added, to turn the knife in the wound, is the irony of the death he here bewails, typifying all hopes cut off in the bud and all faithful devotion silenced. The indictment is expressed, not spoken; the very stones of these harsh facts cry out for reason and justice. After the rage and despair of the fierce "and nothing sed," Peter's answer is the terrible one of God's final doom, when all that is to be said will be said. He speaks little more

[3] Milton does not use precisely Dante's symbolism of Peter's gold and his white key, but there are interesting connections with the way Dante uses them (*Par.* v) in condemning private inconstancy to vows made to the Church; *cf.* also *Purgatorio,* ix. 127. *Paradiso,* xxvii, has Peter's own more famous diatribe, which also employs the common image of rapacious pastors as wolves, and also keeps to the tone of castigation that accompanies a still-anticipated judgement by the source of power that gave the keys.

of the divine justice than this, that judgement of evil is the Lord's and that it will come; that is the answer, for man's question in the face of the riddle of allowed evil is: WILL it? It seems difficult to press the image, as many critics do, to answer also the question *"when* will it?"; this is a vision of judgement, not a picture of it, and if it "foretells the ruine" of evil men for whom an earthly fall is even now preparing, it also (or therefore) contains indubitable reference to the last and perfect judgement. As the first climactic resolution in the poem touched primarily the living greenness of an eternal justice accorded to faithful shepherds, heirs of Orpheus, by the perfect witness of all-judging Jove, the second embodies that other side of justice, when those upon the left hand shall know the power of the sword that issues from the mouth of God.

These two apocalyptic lines [4] carry images, inseparable from the Biblical imagery whence they spring, which make them more than lines of triumph felt at the spectacle of just judgement, to be done at long last upon evil. Several considerations make this trumpet note of prophetic vindication necessary. But still—especially as we remember that we listen to Peter not Milton—that fear which shakes also the "just" man when he confronts the perfect judge, is felt too, if only in the power of the image in the awful "at the door, *Stands ready"* and in the dreaded finality:

> Stands ready to smite once, and smite no more.

This inner tremor of even the less guilty, of every natural creature, before the vision of doom, we know to be in the poem, for the lines following are "Return, Alpheus, the dread voice is past, That shrunk thy streams. . . ." The end of all judging, when the sword shall smite *no more,* is the end of our world, when by the dread voice announcing a final justice even Alpheus' innocent streams shall indeed be forever shrunk, and all the living rivers of the earth be dried up, when "the elements shall melt with fervent heat, the earth also and the works that are therein shall be burned up" (2 Peter iii. 10). The turn to the reviving sweetness of the passage in which all fresh and growing things give their loveliness to strew the hearse where Lycid lies, is of an extreme beauty.

[4] [See the essays by LeComte, Howard, Robins, *et al.,* cited *infra,* p. 241.]

It is a turn from one kind of "consolation" to another, for all that. Milton never does turn in this poem from a non-Christian sense that death may be the only answer given for the riddle of life to a Christian belief in eternal life. He turns, more than once, from what seems senseless in death to death made tolerable. Where he must go outside the human world to find what makes endurable an "order" that commands the death of the unripe and the death of the consecrated, he leaves his chosen mode, but not his subject. Neither excursion is in the remotest degree digressive except in the first sense. There is no single "Christian consolation" in the poem; the whole texture of it is replete with these, and the imagery is the major voice carrying that constant burden. If it seem a fantastic misuse of words to call Peter's "dread voice" a consolation, the rest of the poem adds its witness to our own experience that the stab at the heart of loss is that it denies conceivable order. All that reaffirms order consoles. The image of life may seem to be more than balanced by the vision of death, the symbol of the mystical plant that lives and spreads to make a crown so different from the laurels and the myrtles brown may seem less adequate to its function than is the great engine of doom which metes out another due measure of "meed." However, not only is the poem a structure of cumulative, not contrasted, insights into the meaning of life and death, but also there is yet to come the vision of the nuptial union of the soul with the source of love, a third vision of judgement. Moreover, though it is notable that symbols are chosen at these three crucial points to convey great fundamental oppositions like growth and destruction, life and nothingness, union and sundering, fruition and annihilation, there is also the whole continuing web of the poem with its living and tender sense of imperishable sweetness in all moving and growing things. The affirmations of *Lycidas* begin with its first line.

The imagery within the great speech of St. Peter is different from any other in the poem. It has a different purpose: denigration, an almost magniloquent diminishing ("depraving") of its subjects—the exact formal parallel and the exact evaluative opposite of the "praise" or magnification which is the natural function of most images in Milton's as in any funeral elegy. This, combined with their satirical purpose and resultant "roughness," lowers the style violently (*within* the great symbolic parent image), paradoxically enough considering the elevation of subject. But for the one factor of their dependence, this would be intolerable, and is indeed some excuse for those who have called it digression. The crowd of lesser images, being all of one kind rhetorically (*meiosis*) set going so strong a current of defamation that the one line where this movement halts ("The hungry Sheep look up, and are not fed") derives thence an accent of most piteous blamelessness and vulnerability, and compassion converts to generosity what might have been arrogance. Comment can be spared on this group of images; their vitality, a series of direct shocks from a charged wire, is felt by any reader; the directness results from their pronounced logical simplicity (based on comparable quality: *lean, flashy, scrannel;* or compared manner of acting: *creep, devours, scramble*). The unifying pastoral figure which governs the passage gives their metaphorical depth and thence their universality to the terms within it. And this, not merely the type of particulars used, is the character of allegory.

The passage would be allegorical even if there were no topical reference to the events of the late 1630s in England; that simply doubles its allegorical reference. Since other treatments of *Lycidas'* "allegory" assume that it resides in these historical relationships, some general remarks are in order. They are best made with this passage under our eyes.

The gradual figurative amplification of the Good Shepherd in scores of pastoral figures throughout the Old and New Testament, the constant liturgical emphasis in all centuries and all churches, the accretions and interpretations through centuries of use, Petrarch, Mantuan, Spenser's powerful satirical use in May of *The Shepheardes Calender* (Milton quotes twenty-nine lines of it) [5]—these are what have given its allegorical power to Milton's figure, that is to say, made a metaphor of it. This is why rereading them makes us see more than history in it. Like all metaphor, the figure is "dark"; this re-

[5] In *Animadversions upon the Remonstrants Defence against Smectymnuus* (see Columbia *Milton* III, 165–166) Milton quotes lines 103–131 of *S. C.: May;* he is speaking of one's learning "to renounce the world and so give himselfe to God," and says that "our admired Spenser" "personates our Prelates, whose whole life is a recantation of their pastorall vow, and whose profession to forsake the World . . . boggs them deeper into the world. . . ."

sults from one term being left open, its meaningfulness left to the experience and wit of the reader. Like all allegory, it is *continued* metaphor. That is, in Spenser's phrase, "a dark conceit" in which profound conceptual meanings are gradually figured forth (to be read only in the figures), providing thus the deep-diving plunge into significance which the language of discursive reason cannot provide. Such figures carry conceptions not propositions, essences not phenomena, and shadows of that which we know the-substance-of only through its shadows. The allegorical (contrast the illustrative, the exemplary) aspect of the figure of shepherd as type of Christ we penetrate only through the figure's history, developing as it did in intimate connection with all else that happened to pastoral poetry; Milton does not provide its metaphorical senses but depends upon and uses them. A modicum of knowledge about the life of a sheep, with its needs, perils, and protectors, will tell us what sort of things the bad clergy did in 1637; but only knowledge of what that allegorical figure was accustomed to carry will make to shine out before our eyes the enormity (to Milton) represented by what they did, and relate it to all the other issues and griefs and joys of the poem. The enormity because of the relation is Milton's point.

Such possible changes in sensibility (that is, of the receiving mind in reading) can be pointed to but not really accomplished by explanations, and I shall dwell upon this figure only long enough to clarify these general principles about the working of allegorical imagery through the poem's simplest example. Powerful as it is, St. Peter's arraignment of those who by vow were Christ's shepherds pledged to lead his flock out of death into life, for their treacherous betrayal of the idea of Christlike love, is not the most complex or moving use of the methods of allegory in the poem. One point which touches this passage primarily and two which will be important later may be made fairly swiftly.

The first concerns the relation of historical allegory to the other figurative senses. Through its long Jewish and Christian history, this Biblical figure of the shepherd had come to command ways of reading which are variously fruitful. Rather simply parabolic sometimes, it was used in ways that ask a tropological reading (that is, the metaphor leads to moral in-

sight and different conduct: *quid agas*); and an allegorical
reading in the strictest mediaeval sense (typological, with
Christ as the head of his hierarchical Church); and an anagogical reading (speaking, like the Shepherd's unfading crown in
1 Peter, quoted earlier, of last things and eternal life). Milton's *Lycidas* asks for all three kinds of reading. In addition a
less precise way of reading, which I believe may be included in
what was loosely referred to as taking the letter *spiritualiter*,
could open the way to ideas less homiletically moral or specifically Christian than metaphysical, Platonic or timeless. Milton early became a great master of the last (that is of writing
that asks it of us), but save for his very largest figures in
the long works, he is no match for his master Spenser in the
first, the creation of vast and extremely complex figures which
when read tropologically provide moral insight of unparal-
leled delicacy, and a universality unarrested by time.

Historical allegory is a special offshoot, which habit he borrowed not only specifically from Spenser's May and its like
but generally from the whole tradition of pastoral, to which
it now seemed indigenous because of mediaeval practice. Not
Dante's and Boccaccio's and Petrarch's eclogues alone (stem-
ming ultimately from Virgil) but dozens of Carolingian and
later pastorals enter the world of affairs thus, and give the lie
to any notions we in later ages may have of Arcadian "escape."
But historical allegory doubles the figure back upon itself to
provide a second *literal* reading, a way of making the metaphor give birth to an intended series of historically true significances, factual and interpretative. Spenser of course used
this, but only with the secondary importance of assisting clarity and inescapable convincingness in his universal meanings.
This Milton too has done in the passage in question. As readers interested in all the workings of his images, we have two
helpful courses to follow: when read not as sources *but as
pieces in their own right*, other literary works using any allegorical figure widen and deepen for us its metaphorical possibilities, for these possibilities are a common heritage, and
are often recognized through the merest color of specialized
diction or familiar allusion. This will be exemplified presently.
And secondly, because historical allegory is both literal history
(put figuratively) and active metaphor timelessly applicable,

we read history, in order that clear understanding of two sets of literal terms may make this activity large and free. The reading of ecclesiastical history during Laud's time reveals without our taking thought for it the universality, more than the historicity, of Milton's massive indictment.[6]

Two points touching the imaginative power of topical suggestions in allegorical figures are as relative to other parts of the poem as to that here discussed. Only experience as direct as possible of the second term of any metaphor provides both the peculiar pleasure derived from the "translation" of terms and the capacity to follow out the suggestions other than sensuous which are thus drawn in. Even "What time the Grayfly winds her sultry horn" remains a poorer thing if one has never heard a horn, and the carefree languor and peace that come with the music (metrical skill suiting) have changed the thermal quality of *sultry*. In figures where many suggestions enter, the avenues to such "direct experience" may sometimes seem odd enough. An example is in the passage which begins "Ay me! Whilst thee the shores, and sounding Seas / Wash far away." It culminates in the headland where "the great vision of the guarded Mount" looks (from the Celtic tip of Britain that Druids and giants had guarded before Michael) straight across the unbroken water to Spain; and it comes to an end with the unexpected figurative turn in "Look homeward Angel now, and melt with ruth." "Direct experience" here involves not only the imagined wash and murmur of the cold seas down the whole western coast of Britain from the Hebrides to Land's End. It asks that we should have thoughts like those awakened in Milton by Drayton's *Polyolbion*, by legends of Cornish might and of Orphean druidic seers prefiguring Christianity, by Spanish strongholds seen on Ojea's map and recalling ecclesiastical tyrannies once escaped, by the

---

[6] Plentiful knowledge of contemporary events is not always so useful to image-study as in this case, but the eclogue is a compressed form in Milton's hands, requiring much inner particularization from a reader, and moreover no antidote to a too-personalized way of taking Milton's vigorous style is easier to take than the old-fashioned specific: Book iii in Masson's first volume. (Strict correctness, in either writer, or our agreement, is not in question here.) Another seemingly but not truly paradoxical result accrues: a vivid sense of the parallels between *Lycidas*, 108–131, and our contemporary history, in this case secular. This is a normal result when reading historical allegory, unless of course it is not read as allegory but simply as history.

events of the centuries during which the venerable unmoved
Mount opposite had stood, guarded, with its angelic defender
who looked only outward across the sea toward Namancos and
Bayona's hold. It is with such reflections that we stand "where"
Milton stood, conscious of the ancient integrities and remembering the ancient threats, to see the fragile body which he
has made to typify England's frail integrity against present
threat, and see it *"sleep,"* inactive, unmarked, and pitiable, "by
the fable of Bellerus old." In highly allusive poetry books
must become our five senses, to make our experience direct.[7]

The second point is this. The reader must have noticed that
it has proved almost impossible to avoid considering the whole
theme of the poem whenever discussion of the functioning of
any topically suggestive image was attempted. Each, no matter how small, was enmeshed in a web—which I have cut by
simply not finishing the treatment of the full metaphorical
meaning of any. Even the gray-fly's horn we left as if it were
a line describing noonday, which nowhere nearly covers the
matter; we allowed the Phoebus image to seem primarily a
discussion of the poet's reward, whereas Lycidas' death *sans
guerdon* has meanings that flow out of the image of Orpheus's
unpreventable death, just before; we all but ignored St. Peter's
speech as lament while noting it as diatribe. It is the metaphorical force of each image which was slighted. And the omis-
sion in the Hebrides-St. Michael's Mount passage was gross.
For Lycidas is not only Lycidas, nor not only our own Edward
Kings who die young; the passage speaks of the whole crush-
ing human isolation and fragility, of the unreachable dumb
body that goes out alone as it came, and of the slender thread
of belief—in the loving and pitying superhuman "guard," in
ideas of some meaningful harmony and order—which is all

[7] Therefore the debt of the student of *metaphor* to the annotator is not
measurable, being an aesthetic debt. This is a linguistic point, and has little
to do with a "historical" attitude or a "scholarly" reading. Full understanding
of a poet's language is crucial for metaphor; diction affected by ancient conventions, and allusions no longer recognized as such, are words which are not
quite in our vocabulary. To be sure, historical and scholarly criticism is
oftenest responsible for our fully understanding the second terms of metaphors, when they are not primarily sensuous, and hence catching the relations
which are the secret of their power. *Polyolbion,* Song i, and Selden's "Illustrations" discuss Christian use of a "Genius," the Druids, a speech by St.
Michael's Mount; compare, with *Lycidas,* 53 ff., Songs ix, x, and Illustrations,
and note 15 of this essay.

man has spun to secure him from the deep on which he wanders undefended and as much in peril while he lives as when he dies, unless the cry does indeed not echo back to mock his ideas of meaning and of powerful allies, "Look *homeward* Angel *now*, and melt with ruth. / *And, O ye Dolphins.* . . ." A rephrased metaphor never keeps decorum, and Milton's statement does not like mine seem to talk merely about whether angels and dolphins exist and listen; I have allowed the indecorum in order to point out the major fact about the imagery of *Lycidas*: that the entire poem is grounded in metaphor. It is figurative speech from first to last.

This is the gift to Milton of the pastoral tradition. It means that every group of images functions as a large figure, these all within the largest; that each of the so-called pastoral conventions is, like any metaphor, open at one end to allow interpretations that go as deep as a man's knowledge of life will take him. It is time to see in a more deliberate way how this operates. It cannot be seen very clearly (in our century) by reading *Lycidas* alone, since we have lost a once truly widespread sophistication able to catch allusions far more numerous and subtle than the references normally so designated, and we have lost the Renaissance and mediaeval and baroque habit of following the multiple senses of long-continued metaphors— for of course I am now speaking of the important kind of allegory in pastoral. The history of the criticism of *Lycidas* shows what happened as obscurity overtook first the habit (eighteenth- and nineteenth-century criticism) and later the knowledge (twentieth-century criticism). We are just beginning to get them back together again. Several kinds of recently emphasized knowledge are involved, but all work primarily to change a reader's expectations and presuppositions, and thence his way of taking images rather than his capacity to construe them.

The most important loss suffered by the general reader of *Lycidas* since Milton's time is the loss of pleasure taken in a familiar long procession of great pastoral elegies which preceded it. Study of sources and "classical background" have always received attention, but scholars have had to restore (and chiefly to scholars) sympathetic knowledge of the great Italians and the prolific French and English writers of similar

elegies, and the reader is rare who brings to *Lycidas* that natural enjoyment of the form and immediate grasp of its modes
of feeling which come with wide and sympathetic reading—
of Castiglione and Sannazaro as well as Virgil, of Ronsard and
Spenser and Marot, of Petrarch and Boccaccio and nonelegiac
pastoral. Yet Milton wrote *Lycidas* in a continuing tradition,
for those to whom finding pleasure and emotional immediacy
in the similar works of just such famous predecessors was a
genuine and usual experience. It is more possible now than
it was fifty years ago to be such a reader.[8] I refer to something
considerably on the farther side of a mastery of parallels and
borrowings.

This essay cannot discuss the images of *Lycidas*, seriatim,
and that is not necessary or advisable. I should like instead
merely to suggest slowly by example the kind of reading of
pastoral imagery which comes naturally if we make use of its
inheritance. This inherited wealth was not created by Theocritus or Virgil but very slowly built. Milton's poem is the
supreme example of the fullest use of it; he misses nothing, he
wastes nothing. He fell heir to a way of reading as well as ways
of writing, and though the chief point about both is the seemingly simple one that his poem moves entirely on a metaphorical plane, this will prove to be (I think) the secret of that
mysterious attraction which has stirred readers of *Lycidas*
throughout the vicissitudes of three centuries. It is through
this power in the imagery that Milton can present, with the
greatest reticence, tact, power and depth, certain great and
moving conceptions, universally felt states of mind and meanings, not usually conveyable except in symbols; I point to this
power at work in a few instances. His method is not primarily
symbolic (differing here from that of the *Nativity Hymn*),
and no archetypal symbol such as those of purgation, rebirth,
love (water, fire, cave, garden, or the like) pervades or organ-
izes his poem. It is necessary to get into the poem by some
consideration of its first fourteen lines.

This is Milton's third English elegy, and all had put upon
him the irony of "*well* finished" to be said in the teeth of the
fact of early death, the interruption seemingly rather than

[8] See the fundamental study by J. H. Hanford [*supra,* pp. 27 ff.] and
the essays by Sandys, Norlin, *et al.* [cited *infra,* pp. 239–240].

the conclusion of life. It is through the imagery of the pre-ceding lines, not line 8 ("dead, dead ere his prime . . .") that we look at what bitter comment this death makes on human aims. With a lasting garland men show honor to immortal Poetry, crowning her mortal exemplar. But in this one shat-tered leaves displace those symbols long thought of as fit for Poetry because it, too, matures *not* to die but live on. It is *Lycidas'* garland which, like his poetic promise, is cut while it is still harsh and unready; everything in the image is dis-rupted, plucked before it can ripen, finished before it can be-gin—but finished, ended, this crown or none. I do not read in Milton's first lines the note of apology for his own unripe verses familiarly referred to in commentary and criticism. This poem brings honors, does not constitute them; the garland is a symbol, and Milton does not pluck his *own* unripe honors. He says overtly why he is compelled to disturb the due season of leaves and berries destined thus never to ripen—*"For"* the one whose poetic gift they exalt is dead ere his prime, and he does not leave his like, to ripen the crown for. "Bring the rathe Primrose that forsaken dies" (corrected from "unwedded dies," 142) touches the same note; and throughout the poem there are shadows of such ironic connections. These symbols of "immortal" honor are at once too incongruous and too suit-able to the fulfillment they signalize, torn from the plant and made as mortal as what they crown. *Unripeness*—the flaw is in our entire condition, and to read it as "my art as yet un-ready" seems too literal and too confined.[9] All is unperfected

[9] Even for line 18. The *Muses* are entreated to lament "loudly" even though it be for a stripling youth rather than for one ripe in their service, not "deny" their aid when *any* of their shepherd servants lie dead. When Milton hopes that so too some gentle Muse will remember him, it is no longer, in this second paragraph, of garlands and praises that he speaks, but of the "good speed" of a companion, said where he in his turn will lie ready to be put from men's sight. The usual very different interpretation of all these images depends from an emphasis usual in Milton criticism since (roughly) the period of Coleridge's "John Milton himself is in every line. . . ." Perhaps it is we who intrude Milton's personality, not he; more than once this happens in criticism when we underrate the largeness of reference that is an inherited virtue of pastoral language (*human* ears must tremble, not just Milton's, when Phoebus hears and answers our bitter accusation of the futility of serving him; with "To morrow to fresh Woods, and Pastures new" we with Milton take up again not The Epic but our human hopes—he too had others). Possibly Tillyard's "the abnegation of self by the great egoist" [*supra,* p. 63] has been more influential during the last twenty-five years of criticism, and his careful reservations less so, than he intended.

still, one thing like another—but plucked, nevertheless. What can the unripe do but fade? "Who would not sing for Lycidas?" who indeed? when he is all that sorry load of human hopes, every early death, every quietus said too soon upon promise?

The title alone establishes certain delicate understandings with any reader even of English poetry, by Milton's time, and the chief of these is that Lycidas is both Edward King and all that he signifies. A death is one form of the whole danger; it is the principle of death in human life that is lamented. This is felt when, later, decay and disease, the worm that dooms the rose, all that destroys in the bud the promise of fruit, are "such" as was the news of this loss, *to Shepherds ear*. To the ear, that is, of the one who is guardian over "the weanling Herds," who sings the beauty of the white-thorn when first it blows, whoever in that group of Cambridge men thought that Orpheus' lyre could tame, and move, and make immortal, but who in a sudden event saw youth and beauty and dedication powerless against the hidden worm.

The pastoral figures for which so many critics apologize make it possible for Milton to engender in us the exact quality of feeling and the exact reference to universal realities with which men receive the first death that breaks rudely in upon any group, however loosely associated, who have lived together in youth. As Milton begins that pastoral day, "Together both, ere the high Lawns appear'd . . . ," we are not to make a one-to-one equation, detail by detail. That is not the way allegory works (lines 25–49 are a pure though simple example of the rhetorical figure *allegoria*). The most which is made of this passage usually is that it describes, "conventionally," a Cambridge association with King—unintimate to be sure but justifiably somewhat heightened for the occasion—in the borrowed cold pastoral terms of Greek, Latin, and Renaissance poetry, borrowed but decorous. But the image was not read this way (certainly of course not written this way); its "conventions" wake too many echoes to leave it so empty of passion. We may if we like read it so that something resembling the full feelings that are in it can appear. If we choose we may read it as did those who, weeping with Iolas, had mourned for Alcon that had borne the cold and heat of the day with him, worked, sung, talked, only to be taken by the fates in

the first flower of his youth. We may read as one who with
Simichidas has walked under the trees talking poetry with
Lycidas; one who has seen how Astrophel piped and danced at
the shearing feast, and has seen him untimely cropt, clean de-
faced; one who has remembered how the crowd of shepherds
had sat carefree a long day in the shade by the great cypress,
their craft of poetry protected by Argus, and how the cypress fell and they fled. Pastoral imagery did not remain a
game of allusions in minds familiarly accustomed to read thus
of Castiglione's friendship for a brother writer dead, of Theocritus comparing poems under an elm, of what English poets
looked forward to when Sidney, chief hope in certain high endeavors, would never write again, of how storms, intrigue and
murder, broke out for poets at the death of Petrarch's patron
Robert, of a score of other "shepherds" who had to leave the
flocks they battened. The pre-eminent result was then as now
that these figures for intellectual companionship fertile in life
or interrupted by death became inescapably, habitually, mov-
ingly metaphorical in their operation. "Battened their flocks"
is not a synonymn; it is a figure. Likewise all the rest.

Not the direct experience of a metaphor's terms is in question here but the habit of reading figuratively, of reading not
about history but about reality. (This is the habit the great
Doctor did not have, when he read pastorals.[10]) Since all our
experience of reality flows together, this has the further result
that these pastoral figures are not only pregnant with the feel-

[10] Dr. Johnson, in the passage on *Lycidas* which made "no flocks to batten"
so famous, clearly thinks of allegory as a set of synonymous correspondences,
and when he says "the true meaning is so uncertain and remote that . . . it
cannot be known when it is found," he marks as a vice what provides the
strength of allegory as it does a metaphor; that which speaks of things in
their universal consideration must of necessity present meanings not certainly
limited. It is *not* the associations, connoted second terms, of a metaphor which
are left free for a reader to assign as he fancies—hence the importance of
scholarly criticism, for here we should follow the author's slightest indication
—but the reality to which these point is necessarily undefined and limitless.
Dr. Johnson said some of the wisest and truest things of Milton which have
ever been said, but these are not they. It is idle to inflate into careful criticism
(as has become customary) his remarks on the pastoral mingling of pagan
"trifling fictions" with Christian "awful and sacred truths"; he indicates no
pagan-Christian conflict (rather deplores the absence of one), no tensions,
ambiguities—but quite simply does not realize that pastoral "fictions" are
metaphors in nature and function. They *became* thus through their history,
and he has not sympathetically lived through that history. The sympathy
again possible, if we add the history we may see again one of the faces of
truth which was turned aside from the eighteenth century.

ing and thought their own authors had and we experience
with them; metaphor plunges the arrow of its very precise
meaning into our own present selves and situations. I have
called what Milton wrote in this typical passage an *allegoria*
—not continued equations, but continued metaphor. Whether
there were high lawns near Cambridge, an inn at Grantchester
for cakes and ale after some village revel, is not of moment
except as our knowing some real or fancied detail makes it
all happen again, wearing its meanings in its face; and metaphor, by which we think about all real things together in the
one thought, brings back to life as well our own picnics at our
own Grantchesters. This is not the aim of the image, but only
the way it works; metaphor no more imprisons one in one's
own history than another's, but makes us look at the meanings
which give experience its quality. All the adventure and freshness of Milton's morning, all the endless noons when the gray-
fly's languorous horn stops only to start over—these all say
with one voice *life without time*, man without his mortality, the
rose without the thorn and the garden before what happened in
it. Nothing so sentimental as that youth *is* this; only that in
those moments, when with others "upon the self-same hill"
young poets saw in Orpheus' tasks and delights the highest
use of a life, nothing in the universal framework of things
spoke of the thorn, not on their rose. "But O the heavy change."
It was spoken of.

The monstrousness of death is stressed at first in the un-
naturalness of this death, and stressed at first in the imagery
alone. It appears in certain longer subtler images besides those
mentioned of the unripe honors and the denial of nature's
rhythm (frosts out of season, the young of the herd not the
old poisoned where they fed). It is stressed also in all the multi-
tudinous intimations of man's questioning in the face of every
form destruction takes. Earlier in the poem this questioning
has the shape of "why must man go unready," and a man's fear
that he may die too soon is surely no stronger than the fear
and the pity for that which he loves and loses too soon. But
the question is absent from few lines of the poem. It dwells in
the cadences and inhabits the frail and lovely figures. We are
shaken because we know the fear—by the shadow of the un-
suspected death to come which darkens one figure among those

who drove out under the opening eyelids of the morn, by the vine that overgrows the unkempt woods the shepherd meant to keep, by the blind hands which hold the abhorred shears. The monstrousness of the fact that death the unmanageable (*"What could the Muse her self?"*) should be our single certainty is in the early part of the poem heightened by the wild incalculable-ness of this death at once early and by "accident."

The subject of all this first portion of *Lycidas* is what King's death meant (still means); not "King's death" nor "Milton's fears of death" nor "his poetic aspirations," but the pathos, un-naturalness, disorderliness, and impotence, hidden and revealed, in the fact of all early death. As Milton pursues the sub-ject, it comes closer to the tragedy than the pathos of the destruction of promise, for the poem almost defines this as the nature of human life. The pursuit will not only integrate this theme with all the tragic human questionings discussed in my first pages, but will arrive at them through poignant considerations of the nature of loss, considerations of the ob-scure reasons why tribute paid to the dead eases grief, of the scheme of nature which includes man—whether inimical to him, indifferent, or loving, and of the relation of humane and nat-ural; and finally will transform the questions into affirma-tions through a stronger opposing principle than that of death —and when this is stated we perceive it to be at one with that sweetness which has run underneath all the poem like a strong current, flooding these lines and those, now at the end running open and clear. It is a travesty thus to restate crassly what the poem says so delicately and fully, almost entirely through the metaphorical force of its figures. They could not do this were they not pastoral figures.

What is the nature of the loss? Reserve, dignity, and full expression with neither risk of bathos nor slighting of per-sonal intensity of feeling are but the first gifts of metaphor: greater still is its universalizing power. It is the pastoral tra-dition that allows *Lycidas* to be a lament for the death of Poetry. So stated, this frightens no man. But metaphor does not state it so. Again we see this for what it means when a par-ticular stance of the mind is habitual. I do not refer only to the fact that we expect the theme when we recall Spenser's October and Theocritus 16, though our doing so restores to

Lycidas a breadth it possesses but lost for a time in some eyes.
I mean rather that (for example) we cannot miss the tragedy
of what Milton says by looking at the point upside down,
when we are told that King was but a poor poet; and that we
cannot think the matter is esoteric, or see Milton as a self-
conscious poetaster, managing his clashes and planning his
ironies yet dismayed lest his own garland also wither. We cannot in fine read images without seeing the full depth and time-
lessness of the ancient themes they carry, if we have sorrowed
for the death of song when music itself dies in the death of
Bion its exemplar, known why Apollo left the fields and thorns
grew in them when Virgil's Daphnis died, wept that with
Adonis all things die (the beauty of Love herself becoming un-
fruitful), believed that order goes to wrack when the eddying
flood washed over the man beloved of the Muses, the first
Daphnis. This image has never meant that song stops, poets
never sing more, creatures never couple again, meadows never
become green—only that they do so in vain. It means that
deathless poetry is not deathless, that nothing is. The death
of any the humblest exemplar of that "civilization" man has
wrested from disorder tells us that Orpheus will die, and order
with him; nothing is exempt, not man's dearest hope or highest
achievement; the principle of death in the universe has worsted
what he thought confirmed his immortality, and nothing can
outwit, nothing negate, that dark power. "What could the
Muse her self that Orpheus bore?"—not even the mother and
source of that which allied him to the creating gods. All alike;
down the swift Hebrus. "Persephone," says Love out of whom
all things spring, "thou art stronger than I, and every lovely
thing must descend to thee."

How, starting from all this, should Milton not go on to
consider the mortality of Poetry, and the withering that awaits
all its laurels? And when the Protectors themselves are powerless, and the Poets put to a check, and dozens of poems down
the centuries point as does life itself to good that dies, and to
evil, decay, all death's lieutenants that take over the flock and
the fields, how should Milton not go on to the Bad Shepherds
and the sheep that rot inwardly? Men could not have seen
these as digressions except by not taking seriously the poets
Milton read with an intensity that burns through his language.

The pastoral images in Lycidas point to men's deepest trusts and despairs; time had got them ready to mean all Milton was able to say.

No claims of a critic can thus get them ready. But when, reaccustomed to the old habits, we no longer think of all pastoral in terms of Arcadian "fancy," a related late-born misunderstanding will likewise disappear. We remove from the images of *Lycidas* the obscuring distortions they have worn because a late Romantic separation of man from "Nature" supplanted that living continuity in the fabric of all created things whence, in *Lycidas* as in its predecessors, spring the deepest pain of the lament and the noblest sublunar echoes of a final and divine consolation.

Almost all pastoral elegies ask man's permanent question, "Was this death Natural?" Sometimes with angry amazement, as of Petrarch's Argus, "Did earth dare this?"; or with sad contrasts as in Castiglione's *Alcon* ("the rude husbandman does not pluck the unripe fruit"); sometimes obliquely as in Marot's accusation: "*Hà Mort facheuse! onques ne te meslas Que de ravir les excellentes choses.*" It takes no poem to make a man ask these questions; he asks them of every death that touches him. But the answers are another matter. Milton has learned, and uses, them all, and it is all but impossible to tell some of the "pagan" ones from the other Christian ones, as it had been for many hundreds of years. The answers are complicated, ranging from the merest color on an image to great figures occupying fifty lines. We have noticed the simplest appearance of the question, the un-Naturalness of decay that is untimely. And in all those images the human death and the others were seen as like flaws, in the one fabric.

One later image might seem to place man in a "Nature" hostile or indifferent to him, until we remember that the sea beyond the stormy Hebrides is no more "Nature" than the daffodils, the willows, or the singer himself. It is the human pain over the remembered body wandering untended and unstrewn that gives the sense of wild displacement to that image which most mixes grief with pity: "Whilst thee the shores, and sounding Seas / Wash far away . . . ." The cold indifferent blows of "where ere thy bones are hurl'd" are only less powerful to give this sense than are the two lines:

> Where thou perhaps under the whelming tide
> Visit'st the bottom of *the monstrous world.*

That underseas world is peopled by creatures which carry their primitive alienation in their names (monsters: outside nature) and the irony of the intimate communication in *visit'st* is less grim than piteous. The body comes, goes again, not even a prey, not "at the mercy of," but a thing with no place, unheeded, meaningless, and alone. This rightly appears just before the tenderness of "And, O ye Dolphins, waft . . . ," so that a flood of sweetness accompanies the double assurance of a nonhuman concern for man. The love and rescuing pity which had long been thought of as the beauty of Arion's story [11] are like in character to the saving heavenly Love that walk'd the waves; but with the allusion to Arion's enchanting song Milton puts a close to the lament for the death *of poetry* more specifically, and the consolation (paralleled in "Look homeward Angel") is that assurance of natural and supernatural powers on the side of those the Muses loved which is in every pastoral elegy, pagan or Christian.

The ancient figures through which man's death is lamented as a great flaw in the fabric of nature are structurally used by Milton, by his attaching them to the other ancient motif fixing responsibility for a particular death. Because it is so familiar an echo, his "Where were ye Nymphs?" [12] can and does carry all its old weight of a sympathy that extends throughout the great frame, and that connects natural powers specifically with poets. We accepted the sympathy when we recognized the genre, for it is perhaps the greatest and most moving conception pastoral has borne down the ages. That this is true in *Lycidas* will appear gradually; here we but notice how Milton can count upon this meaning and make double structural use

[11] I see little reason for excluding Palaemon from this reference but none for substituting him. Parallels in fact (Palaemon died and Arion did not) make less difference to poetry than parallels in significance; both the echo of Orpheus, and Arion's winning harmonies that won the dolphins' love, are too valuable for Milton to forego them; Arion's dolphin was familiar in graphic arts.

[12] Echoing Theocritus 1, Virgil 10, Baïf 2, Alamanni 1, and others less exactly. I do not usually cite title or numbers of earlier elegies, since I confine my references to the great stream of well-known pastorals to which scholars have pointed as Milton's sources in articles I have cited; I have made them easily identifiable, in, for example, Harrison and Leon's anthology [cited *infra,* p. 239], whence I usually take translated phrases.

of the lamenting natural creatures and powers. His procession is not quite, or not only, a procession of mourners, but of innocent underlings who make depositions that exonerate great Neptune, and exonerate Natura herself. Yet it is partly the long history of these and all aspects of the natural world *as mourners* (the rivers and woods and winds that weep and sigh, the spirits of all places that join shepherds in laments, the myriad fruitful creatures that will no longer bear nor blossom) that rules out here in *Lycidas* any sense of a framework of "Nature" inimical or indifferent to "Man" or from which he is separable; a pure gentleness like cool balm breathes through all these passages. That is, as usual, the acceptances to which pastoral has accustomed its readers allow Milton to speak all by indirection. He prefers not to say outright as does Spenser and many another, "Ay me that dreerie Death should strike so mortall stroke, / That can undoe Dame natures kindly course" (kindly: deriving from her own essential nature; Nov., 123). But twice his images state this: in the poet's death which "Universal nature did lament"; in the perfidious Bark that sank where Panope in quiet played. The despairing sense of a whole powerful creation powerless before one ultimate threat is the ground of the final vision of love's conquest of death. Not truly sudden, or new, not opposed by but joined underneath to the image of the strewn flowers, this consolation—the only one Milton finds—has been shadowed throughout the poem. The ebb and flow of love and hostility in the universe is the secret of *Lycidas'* obscure and almost primitive power.

Such conceptions and such poetic powers remind us that we do not deal with an author whose sole remaining testament regarding the meaning of human life lies in the single text before us. The complication and the restraint of the images we have now to speak of more fully suggest that it is well to speak first of certain other kinds of assistance, besides a deepened understanding of pastoral poetry, to a fuller comprehension of *Lycidas*. It is one result of the subtlety of Milton's organization and the restraint of his style that the imagery resists a consideration in separation from more general matters; we have repeatedly come to a halt before points which are so related to the rest of our knowledge about Milton, or so recurrent in general criticism of this poem and others, that they ought to be made with recognition of that background rather than with the seeming innocence of plain exegesis.

Another kind of knowledge which like studies of the pastoral mode has received recent emphasis, is important to imagery for the steady balance it provides, hence for depth without waywardness in interpretations: the study of chronologically related poems of Milton's and of relations to some single other one, notably in this instance the *Epitaphium Damonis*.[13] As in the case of the poet Yeats, Milton himself wrote—in his earlier and later poems—some of the most important commentary on the images of *Lycidas*. There is a marked present tendency to criticize by the analysis of imagery within the single poem, but when studies with this approach (including the present one) are allowed to supplant more general studies of the kinds I have mentioned, profound understanding of the figurative language of the poem is not a result.[14] Some exception must be made for studies of the history of single great images, such as that of Orpheus.[15] But only the large substructure of recent extensions of knowledge in general scholarship on Milton and his period can protect the analysis of imagery from irresponsibility (both in its reader and its writer), or from turning into a mere "reading the poem *for* one" in a sort of question-begging paraphrase embodying explication of image. Even the explication necessary in order to relate themes to the formal nature of figures can be the bane of a discussion emphasizing imagery, and this I also am not able to escape entirely. But the following points, like some earlier ones, deal constantly with

[13] See especially A. S. P. Woodhouse, "Milton's Pastoral Monodies" [cited *infra*, p. 246].

[14] J. E. Hardy on *Lycidas* in Brooks and Hardy, *Poems of Mr. John Milton* [*supra*, pp. 136 ff.] contributes an occasional careful detail rather than a fully trustworthy reading, and at least three studies of the poem's imagery since 1949 base interpretations on overreading "lines concerned with water." An exception to these strictures is Barker's analysis [cited *infra*, p. 242]. D. C. Allen's chapter in *The Harmonious Vision*, which I read after this essay was written, avoids various abuses through critical use of many kinds of learning.

[15] See particularly D. P. Walker, "Orpheus the Theologian and Renaissance Platonists," *Journal of the Warburg and Courtauld Institutes*, XVI (1953), 100–120 (the druids also belong to *prisca theologia*). C. W. Mayerson [cited *infra*, p. 244] brings together references from Sandys, Fletcher, Drayton, etc., and shows Orpheus as poet-prophet, symbol of civilizing order. But Milton draws upon yet other connotations of Orpheus as a symbolic figure, such as the denial of death through soul or form (of civilizing forces or of individuals), and cf. the ascetic self-discipline of the "aged Orpheus" in *Elegy vi*.

images whose *bases* in Milton's thought and poetic habits have received comment in very many discussions; their wider general concerns, and knowledge, underlie any reading of the imagery proper which wishes to avoid starved or capricious interpretations. I touch upon all the cruxes which have caused much debate, but generally incorporate answers to the questions thus raised without describing the arguments. Breadth of knowledge pre-eminently affects our sense of a poet's tone of voice, and with the point made in the last paragraph but one this factor began to show as crucial.

The sensitivity to Milton's own suggested themes and patterns, with which we can come prepared through the help of recent comparative and chronological studies, aids especially our sense of direction, as we find ourselves carried unobtrusively along by certain hidden tides of comfort and of desolation which meet violently several times within *Lycidas*. One sort of imagery which persistently carries the consolatory stream of generosity, alliance, and love is rather obscurely figurative. All the images *that present tributes* flow in one stream with the final vision of the blest kingdom of joy and love (this last a favored kind of figure in Milton's other elegies). Something more "natural" than Death, in the universe of which man is one member, has been stressed since the first *he must not float unwept*.

The poem is a tribute, is like some but not like all elegies in that it is not an object but an act, offered, and speaking allegiance; and a tribute to the dead is part of a rite that assuages and reaffirms. Milton calls his poem, by the time-honored *metaphor*, a "tear," a public tear that goes down into the grave with the body, and signifies sorrow for a loss of something that body once signified which still deserves undying honor and receives unquenchable love; nothing more damaging than to read this image *literaliter* as "water imagery," nor are tears water symbols, nor chiefly wet. They are chiefly salt and bitter; but this one is whatever the metaphor asks, and is what Milton calls it elsewhere, a "vow." Symbols do not work through mentionings, but through believed meanings.[16] Symbols that

---

[16] On the other hand, line 175 ("With Nectar pure . . .") does seem to me a use of those symbolic meanings of water with reference to purification, rebirth, giving of life, of which we have heard so much in *Lycidas* criticism of

work naturalistically in this poem are few and simple, and archetypal significances working otherwise are generally so deep-caught in a web of historically understood meanings (classical and Christian) that these are the best way into them. This is early apparent, and the web itself is very moving.

It is as poet, first, that Lycidas must not go unwept (unsung); the Muses must know their own, and all poets have drunk with those heavenly companions of the well whose source is Deity. But also, all images wherein Milton sees Lycidas' physical self (as here on his watery bier) are touched with a deep human pity, and that sense of human community by which our tributes deny the aloneness of the dead makes each such tribute by him an affirmation of love, of strong and responsible ties. The tribute is due (*meed*, 14) not as praise but as memorial is due; and the obscure consolation that is handed down from human creature to human creature by this ritual remembrance of the human tie is deliberately strengthened in "So may some gentle Muse. . . . And as he passes turn, / And bid fair peace be to my sable shrowd."

"Obscure" consolation—even primitive; and certainly both pagan and Christian. To be sure, the classical clothing reminds us of particular songs born of special ties between poets, and certain echoes—"fair peace to Daphnis," "peace to Gallus," fair peace to Alcon, to Astrophel—sound with sweetness in our minds to bulwark them against "What boots it with uncessant care" when the hostile tide sweeps in. A simpler sweetness lies in the universal human act so directly phrased: *and, as he passes—turn*. The pause which the living make for the dead is made in tribute to what has not died. But they make it in sorrow; Milton's next image following without paragraph break—the reason why, like that other fellow-servant of the Muses later, *he* must turn as he passes—is pierced through with that poignancy which loss has when it breaks open earliest unities: "*For* we were nurst upon the self-same hill, / Fed the same flock; by fountain, shade and rill." These lines are com-

---

the last ten years. Whether or not language is being symbolically used can often be detected by applying the principle: that such use always "presents" something the poem, as written, can use, and in that precise place. Symbols do not get in the way, in great poets; the relation to stated meanings may be obscure, ironic or unexpected, but it is real. On the possibly connected sun-sunk-beneath-water, see n. 21 of this essay.

pletely and perfectly metaphorical; they touch all earliest human allegiances, and shared endeavors which bind even scarce-known men in unity, and they are at once so particular that a single speaking voice seems to dwell upon the alliterative and rhetorically intensified phrases, and yet so universal that the pastoral landscape comprises our human world. The affirmative force of these declarations of loyal relationship and responsibility (for there are others) flows on to the image of heavenly love seen not in shadow but in essence, where all the saints in paradise sing tributes of joy to the new soul, "And wipe the tears for ever from his eyes." The fountains, shades, and rills of this incomplete and transient place have their transcendent counterpart in those "other groves, and other streams"; the loving guardianship of heavenly beings which has appeared at intervals throughout the poem continues now secure and sure, and Lycidas' "large recompense" is felt to be with no sense of dissonance or incongruity both the angel's propitious watch and the grateful love returned to earthly petitioner by Genius or Muse or any of Jove's sacred company.[17]

I have dealt especially with human tributes. There is a more subtly tender feeling in certain other images with this same avowed function—of which we may take the so-called flower passage as typical—and the reasons for their consoling power lie more deeply hidden. This passage is less accurately termed "metaphorical" than simply a portion of the poem where the great metaphors that underlie the whole pastoral conception, as it developed more than as it originated, must govern our reading or we read with a most unhappy superficiality. Its place is deliberately just after the great vision of judgement upon human evil, the self-aggrandizing betrayal of the flock by those who were to have been the earthly types of the Good Shepherd himself, that is of love which throws itself away for the sheep. The reasons why our grief *even for this* is assuaged

---

[17] As with Sannazaro's Androgeo or Ronsard's Henriot. The latter is *"un Ange parfait"* in heaven—*un ange* to whom green turf altars are to be built, on which *"comme . . . Aux Faunes, aux Satyrs, te ferons sacrifice."* If such "fusion" is to be called "baroque," the term loses its meaning—for a Boccaccio, too, merely expects to be *read* as cultivated men of the Middle Ages had grown accustomed to reading, when he sings in Eclogue 14 of Christ sent from Olympus into the Virgin's womb to bring back the Golden Age, and of the fields of Elysium where Mary, *alma Iovis genitrix,* is honored by virgins and martyrs, nymphs and fauns and Apollo himself (this is dependent on Dante's Earthly Paradise, of course).

by the twenty-five lines which follow, "Return Sicilian Muse, / And call the Vales, and bid them hither cast / Their Bells . . . ," are not so much complicated as deep. Pastoral has its ways of reasserting a fundamental and harmonious sympathy, and of proclaiming that not decay and death but life and creativity and love is the universal principle, one which is seen (especially, but not solely, as pastoral was Christianized) as having the strength of a divine intention.

No person brings in tribute these heaped and countless flowers, but the fresh and shady vales bring them to make the same acknowledgement as the other tributes. They are the preciest possible counterpart of the offered-up verses which men strew upon a laureate hearse; all alike mourn for the death of a part (as poet, an Orphean part) of that fabric to which all belong, and all alike, reaffirming life, make an answer to death's power. The valleys are bid by the Muse (the Muses have always spoken through men of these harmonies and these mysteries) to bring all their flowers, to cast here every flower that can weep; this passage is for good reason elaborate with tiny particulars, as are all images where significance is not to be said outright, and the actual effect of assuagement depends much upon tone. For the sense that there is such a thing as loving pity in the natural universe (of which evil men and good are a part), seeping in after the inimical violence which preceded, becomes a calm strong tide carried by the generous abandon of these lines. This sense, "consolation" almost by definition, is at its height when Milton writes a line which gives so quietly the sudden shock often produced by extreme beauty in music that one is tempted to use the word "occult":

Bid *Amaranthus* all his beauty shed . . .

The sudden depth of the image is unexpected; amaranth is the deathless flower, later to be used by Milton as a symbol of the flawless world before the Fall, but long known as the immortal plant, that one blossoming thing whose "beauty" is never quenched or withered [18]; and he is bid to give over his

[18] The verb whence the flower's Greek name was formed appears to make it carry the sense not-quenched-light-or-flame, and the red spires revive in water long after plucking and last many years (as Pliny describes, xxi. 23, or Gerard's *Herball,* ii. 42: Floure-gentle or Floramor). The attendants of Persephone in *Fasti,* iv. 39, picked amaranth.

exemption from the mortality which all natural things share with Lycidas, and lay his red spires in symbolic tribute on the bier to go down with it.[19] This is not hyperbole of praise, but a glint of light upon the subterranean river that runs under the long image making a connection between sacrifice and immortality born of death—in a way which my explanation travesties almost unpardonably, except that it may shed light on why and how these whole multitudes of plucked and offered flowers do indeed interpose the "ease" Milton says they give.

They are to strew the bier "where Lycid lies"—"Ay me!," where does he lie? This passage is very closely articulated with the next one, and that Lycidas is "to our moist vows deny'd" is not a simple grief, as the pain of the following passage shows. How can we not come with tributes, though there is no place to lay them? The much-discussed "For so . . . Let our frail thoughts dally with false surmise" seems to me to have this clear reference, and not to be an indication that Milton repudiates the truth of preceding reflections—because he finds that his "pagan" and his Christian comforts conflict and therefore asks us to throw away, as "false surmise," solace we have all felt to be real as we read. There is not much evidence that Milton was a man to let even innocent counterfeit stand because he had once thought it provided "a little ease." The two contrasted passages of imagery work upon a very deep level of feeling.

In the flower passage, it is indubitable that we respond, and that he did, to symbolisms immemorially ancient, not only feeling life in essence symbolized peculiarly by the moment of

[19] It should be stressed that consciousness of the kind of thing I speak of in these paragraphs is at a minimum (in *writer* and *reader:* these relations are nothing like so "known" within the thinking mind as description of them must be) and there is much pleasure in these images for those who love at lower rate. I do not think Milton consciously related this line to the spreading heavenly plant which symbolizes immortal honor in lines 78 ff., nor perhaps that he had yet the idea (image) in *Paradise Lost,* iii. 353 ff., where the angels cast down their crowns inwove with amaranth.
Cf. also xi. 78: the blissful bowers "Of *Amarantin* Shade, . . . By the waters of Life" where sit the angelic Sons of Light. He was probably *having* the idea; symbolic images grow slowly, like all ideas involving complicated relationships of much experience. The relations hold so solidly, as with a kind of inner truth, that we can as it were see them coming—this characteristic I believe Milton would have referred not to his originating mind but to the structure of "reality"; perhaps such revealing (Invention, uncovering) is what one asks for from a "Heavenly" Muse.

blossoming (promise of fruit, not fruit), but equally feeling the necessity of giving over to death these symbols of life-to-be-born-of-death. This is far from being unrelated to the dear might of him that walk'd the waves. It is also indubitable that part of the valid sense of assuagement which human beings feel in symbolic actions that asssert the continuity of life despite the fact of death does disappear when the action is not possible. This did not make nonsense of the symbol. It made another form of the assertion more consoling, and to that Milton proceeded. He proceeded by way of another of those passages—here, the body under the whelming tide—of imagery like direct experience of the reality of death (decay, evil, impermanence). Throughout the poem these bitter tides meet, and are drowned in, the full-flowing stream of symbolized life, faithfulness, creativity, eternal flowering, earthly and heavenly pity, aid, sacrifice, and love. The vision in heaven, his last such answer to the inimical principle in all its forms—for that is the theme of *Lycidas* —touches the "tender stops" of all these various Quills, and when the singer's "eager thought" is closed in the tranquil light of an ordinary dying day human life is once again "fresh Woods, and Pastures new," a harmony accepted, hopeful, and dear.

It is now possible to see with more exactness and force that we disturb and nullify this entire design of images that discuss meaning and destiny in the universe when we import into pastoral even subconsciously that special and quite recent way of thinking which takes "Man" out of "Nature." The very ground of the imagery in pastoral writing is the integrity of the great fabric of created nature, and a chief contribution of reading to saturation in Milton's predecessors and fellows is a posture of the mind, an immediate and unreflecting readiness to feel this assumption true. If Ruskin's term, "pathetic fallacy," accurately represents our subconscious presuppositions, it is folly to expect understanding of this poetry except in ways which stand coldly outside it. The very simplest form of imagery which assumes a living tie between all creatures including man is used sparingly by Milton, but he uses complicated forms of it at every point in his poem. Such complications of structure and feeling as I have touched on are erected upon the same assumption that gives us the simple "Thee

Shepherd, thee the Woods, and desert Caves, / With wild Thyme
and the gadding Vine o'regrown, / And all their echoes mourn."

Why do the woods mourn for human deaths in pastoral
poems? the vines lament in their untended wildness? Several
accustomed meanings of such images provide for Milton the
very conceptions of the universal order without which others
of his great metaphorical figures could not move and work.
I speak from examples. Other natural things mourn with men
in pastorals for the death of the Orphean singer, of the order-
bringer, the one who teaches men and quiets animals and prunes
vines and moves rocks (all four the same thing), of the theo-
logue who knows the nature of the creator and preserver of
life—all those he delights and all those he instructed mourn;
they mourn for the protector and helper, the Wise Shepherd;
they mourn for the death of their peace, because thorns choke
growth, and sterility and drought possess the land where death
has intruded.

"The Shepherd" is poet and priest, certainly, but *these* figure
forth, *being shepherds*, something more still. Especially this is
true as Christian ideas transmuted the ancient ideas and extended them; man brought in death, as "shepherd" he helps
to mend it. We have not finished reading when we read how
Marot's Loyse, *la bergère de paix*, had wisdom to protect
"Contre le temps obscur et pluvieux"—and see its reference to
troublous persecutions. Or when we read Alamanni's *"Ahi
quanto con ragion piangon . . . e greggi"* for that if the
shepherd had remained alive their young might be safe from
rapaci pastor e feri lupi—and see therein a reference to why
he mourned Cosimo Rucellai. The universal use of figurative
terms from the pastoral life for these literal historical meanings makes our *history itself present* to us much profounder
significances of storm and wild ravager, and we read constantly
in pastoral of two worlds, both that of our particular human
disasters and that which we can organize only through our
symbols of a Waste Land, of Garden given over to thorns, Harmony become chaos—and, of the Garden of Adonis, the Earthly
Paradise, and the perfect music of the spheres. When Boccaccio's Olympia says, "All of us who are created in the wood-
lands are born to death," she speaks in the language of pastoral as well as in Dante's metaphor, and of the whole vast

universe of created things. When Milton writes (*PL*, ix. 782) how at the instant of Eve's deed "Earth felt the wound, and Nature from her seat / Sighing through all her Works gave signs of woe, / That all was lost," and how the roses of Adam's garland faded as they dropped, he says what the pastoral woods mourn for. For the flaw, and mourn again for all who die mending it.

The harmony among the creatures is by no means necessarily pagan even when its terms are so; the point around which the matter turns is rather whether the metaphors which express it are believed or not. Figures which adumbrate it use the so-called pathetic fallacy as their natural language, but they mean what they say. Such language neither denies a hierarchy among creatures nor a special tie between man and divinity; its giving man's form of sentience or will or *pathos* to other creatures is a metaphorical way of putting unity not identity.[20] The phrase that makes pastoral trivial is "*a mere* metaphor." For, as pastoral developed, all its greater figures clearly call for the kind of reading termed "allegorical," and such reading is only possible to men who believe that metaphor does present the real.

Milton of course did not "write an allegory" in *Lycidas*. The phrase is fruitful of misconceptions; "allegorically" refers primarily to a way of understanding, reading, a thing. Proof that this way had become habitual and secular lies in what men wrote, over several hundred years and extending well into Milton's time and to his own work. An *allegoria* is a figure asking such reading for its comprehension, and a whole poem can be one, but *Lycidas* is not. And we find in it few of the most usual sort—moral allegories; we have not been reading tropologically, and the chief wisdom in *Lycidas* has little directly to do with "how men should act."

Much of the classical imagery of Christian pastorals ask to

---

[20] Nor is the unity in a sympathetic harmony contradicted by the famous figure of the "riddle" of man's short earthly life (his never coming again contrasted with the cyclical renewal of other creatures); Man is no more seen as outside "Nature" because he does not sprout again like the tree than the tree is fallaciously made "Man" when the metaphor of human responses (it sighs, mourns) is used. The conceptions really antipathetic to these ways of thinking and using language are nominalistic conceptions of metaphor, or naturalistic or positivistic conceptions of what meanings can be real. Milton did not share them.

be read allegorically in the stricter mediaeval sense, for classical figures retain their truth in being read as types of a later revelation. There would be some truth in saying that the Middle Ages made of classical literature one great old testament, for the New Dispensation is with little sense of displacement read in the figures of an older shadowed truth; so read, man sees from it "what to believe," as readily and truly as one could from reading the great book of the universe itself. And, one might add, as uncalculatingly, unself-consciously, and delightfully, for the forms in which we are meeting these habits of mind are only solemn because they are elegiac; no Planned Movement was needed to "save the classics" in the eras we speak of, and a good deal of exuberant gaiety accompanies the mediaeval and Renaissance pleasure in plurality of meanings. Reading allegorically for moral meanings merged with the stricter kind, and as Dante pointed out in the Letter to Can Grande, all these functions fall together in the supreme distinction between literal and figurative ("allegorical"). Pastoral early isolated itself as a genre which by reason of a basic figure for presenting universal harmonies and discords was fundamentally and formally "continued figure"; the largely mediaeval development toward historical allegory and satire in disguise was an expectable result, and Milton builds images on all these accepted forms of indirection.

The use of anagogy—which is writing that when read figuratively yields ideas of ultimate destiny, of the eschatological, of the other world—is equally natural to the form. Milton uses it for just the function it serves in his predecessors: to express in symbols the ultimate triumph of life over death. Such imagery is archetypal wherever we find it; the soul's home is that place where the conditions of our exile do not obtain. The place where Harmony, Love, Peace (all the same) are not threatened by Discord or Mutability or Death (all one enemy) is an otherworld where the details of music and growing things and endless spring and living waters simply tell over and over the same tale of the conquest of that one unconquerable flaw whence spring all the others. In Milton's anagogical figure for the complete victory of that principle which he has shadowed forth in all the consolations throughout his poem, the terms are largely Christian, and one Christian symbol, a usual one, is basic—the marriage between the human soul and Heavenly Love. He does not choose to use the symbol of Light save in the reference to the saints "in their glory," and his simile of the Sun (which like Lycidas rises from the waters to flame in the forehead of the morning sky) is probably not to be symbolically extended.[21] At any rate he does not choose to use the great numbers of Earthly Paradise details familiar from Dante, Boccaccio, Ronsard, Marot; in these as in Spenser or Sannazaro the homogeneity of classical and Christian details is assumed, and Milton had himself assumed it in those Latin elegies whose visions of paradise are among the best commentaries upon this in *Lycidas*. Where symbols are archetypal these differentiating terms lose their meaning. Spenser is not baroque but simply nursed on old habits when he says his Dido "raignes a goddesse now emong the saintes," but when he calls his paradise the Elysian fields he is, more simply still, just in the right. There is no incongruity and certainly no surprise in the classical close of Milton's image.

The close of the poem is properly kept strictly within pastoral bounds in language and imagery, even to the degree of a quite usual final realism in the Coventry-blue of the shepherd's mantle. Restraint and tranquillity are native possessions of writing which by definition shadows further meanings but does not say them. In one last quiet and delicate image of the shepherd, intentionally as well as deceptively pictorial, Milton makes the vast human world which pastoral writing can denote with so economical a pen seem to us that tranquil place which his vision of man's end makes of it.

What we call "pastoral imagery" was a great achievement of

[21] Of course it speaks metaphorically of resurrection, life born of death; but it is difficult in fact to tell whether it includes what we might well expect: that it rose again because it sank into the water. There are many difficulties with it as a naturalistically based rebirth symbol (familiar as this must have been to Milton, since natural-philosophy meanings offer one of the commonest forms of allegorical interpretation throughout Middle Ages and Renaissance). Among these difficulties are the emphasized literal meaning in line 167 ("Sunk though he be beneath the watry floar"; there is no special rebirth for the drowned); and the immediate other symbolic use of water in "walk'd the waves." The unextended simile (as ostensibly written) avoids what I should call a *true* incongruity otherwise present: i.e. that the only Sun-figure large enough for this context would have been God-as-Light. On these old and common images and on the language of other poets in the King volume see R. Wallerstein, *Studies in 17th Century Poetic* (Madison, 1950), for example pp. 104–105.

the human imagination. In eighteen centuries no man used it
with more power and grace than Milton in *Lycidas.*

Literature as Context:
Milton's *Lycidas*

Northrop Frye

I should like to begin with a brief discussion of a familiar
poem, Milton's *Lycidas*, in the hope that some of the inferences
drawn from the analysis will be relevant to the theme of this
conference. *Lycidas*, then, is an elegy in the pastoral convention,
written to commemorate a young man named Edward King who
was drowned at sea. The origins of the pastoral are partly
classical, the tradition that runs through Theocritus and Virgil,
and partly Biblical, the imagery of the twenty-third Psalm, of
Christ as the Good Shepherd, of the metaphors of "pastor" and
"flock" in the Church. The chief connecting link between the traditions in Milton's day was the Fourth or Messianic Eclogue of
Virgil. Hence it is common enough to have pastoral images echoing both traditions at once, and not surprising to find that *Lycidas* is a Christian poem as well as a humanistic one.

In the classical pastoral elegy the subject of the elegy is
not treated as an individual but as a representative of a dying
spirit of nature. The pastoral elegy seems to have some relation
to the ritual of the Adonis lament, and the dead poet Bion, in

From *The Proceedings of the Second Congress of the International Comparative Literature Association,* edited by W. P. Friederick, University of
North Carolina Studies in Comparative Literature, XXIII (1959), 44–55.

Moschus's poem, is celebrated with much the same kind of imagery as Bion himself uses in his lament for Adonis. The phrase "dying god," for such a figure in later pastoral, is not an anachronism: Virgil says of Daphnis, for example, in the Fifth Eclogue: *"deus, deus ille, Menalca."* Besides, Milton and his learned contemporaries, Selden, for example, or Henry Reynolds, knew at least as much about the symbolism of the "dying god" as any modern student could get out of *The Golden Bough*, which depends mainly on the same classical sources that were available to them. The notion that twentieth-century poets differ from their predecessors in their understanding or use of myth will not bear much scrutiny. So King is given the pastoral name of Lycidas, which is equivalent to Adonis, and is associated with the cyclical rhythms of nature. Of these three are of particular importance: the daily cycle of the sun across the sky, the yearly cycle of the seasons, and the cycle of water, flowing from wells and fountains through rivers to the sea. Sunset, winter, and the sea are emblems of Lycidas' death; sunrise and spring, of his resurrection. The poem begins in the morning, "Under the opening eyelids of the morn," and ends with the sun, like Lycidas himself, dropping into the western ocean, yet due to rise again as Lycidas is to do. The imagery of the opening lines, "Shatter your leaves before the mellowing year," suggests the frosts of autumn killing the flowers, and in the great roll-call of flowers towards the end, most of them early blooming flowers like the "rathe primrose," the spring returns. Again, the opening invocation is to the "Sisters of the sacred well," and the water imagery carries through a great variety of Greek, Italian, and English rivers to the sea in which the dead body of Lycidas lies.

Lycidas, then, is the "archetype" of Edward King. By an archetype I mean a literary symbol, or cluster of symbols, which are used recurrently throughout literature, and thereby become conventional. A poetic use of a flower, by itself, is not necessarily an archetype. But in a poem about the death of a young man it is conventional to associate him with a red or purple flower, usually a spring flower like the hyacinth. The historical origin of the convention may be lost in ritual, but it is a constantly latent one, not only in literature but in life, as the symbolism of the scarlet poppies in World War I shows. Hence in *Lycidas* the "sanguine flower inscrib'd with woe" is an archetype, a symbol that recurs regularly in many poems of its kind. Similarly Lycidas himself is not only the literary form of Edward King, but a conventional or recurring form, of the same family as Shelley's Adonais, the Daphnis of Theocritus and Virgil, and Milton's own Damon. King was also a clergyman and, for Milton's purposes, a poet, so, having selected the conventional archetype of King as drowned young man, Milton has them to select the conventional archetypes of King as poet and of King as priest. These are, respectively, Orpheus and Peter.

Both Orpheus and Peter have attributes that link them in imagery with Lycidas. Orpheus was also an "enchanting son" or spirit of nature; he died young, in much the same role as Adonis, and was flung into the water. Peter would have drowned too without the help of Christ; hence Peter is not named directly, but only as "The Pilot of the Galilean Lake," just as Christ is not named directly, but only as "Him that walked the waves." When Orpheus was torn to pieces by the Maenads, his head went floating "Down the swift Hebrus to the Lesbian shore." The theme of salvation out of water is connected with the image of the dolphin, a conventional type of Christ, and dolphins are called upon to "waft the hapless youth" just before the peroration begins.

The body of the poem is arranged in the form ABACA, a main theme repeated twice with two intervening episodes, as in the musical rondo. The main theme is the drowning of Lycidas in the prime of his life; the two episodes, presided over by the figures of Orpheus and Peter, deal with the theme of premature death as it relates to poetry and to the priesthood respectively. In both the same type of image appears: the mechanical instrument of execution that brings about a sudden death, represented by the "abhorred shears" in the meditation on fame and the "grim two-handed engine" in the meditation on the corruption of the Church. The most difficult part of the construction is the managing of the transitions from these episodes back to the main theme. The poet does this by alluding to his great forerunners in the pastoral convention, Theocritus of Sicily, Virgil of Mantua, and the legendary Arcadians who preceded both:

O fountain Arethuse, and thou honour'd flood,
Smooth-sliding Mincius, crown'd with vocal reeds . . .

and later:

> Return, Alpheus, the dread voice is past
> That shrunk thy streams: return, Sicilian Muse.

The allusion has the effect of reminding the reader that this is, after all, a pastoral. But Milton also alludes to the myth of Arethusa and Alpheus, the Arcadian water-spirits who plunged underground and reappeared in Sicily, and this myth not only outlines the history of the pastoral convention, but unites the water imagery with the theme of disappearance and revival.

In pastoral elegy the poet who laments the death is often so closely associated with the dead man as to make him a kind of double or shadow of himself. Similarly Milton represents himself as intimately involved with the death of Lycidas. The theme of premature death is skilfully associated in the opening lines with the conventional apology for a "harsh and crude" poem; the poet hopes for a similar elegy when he dies, and at the end he accepts the responsibilities of survival and turns "To morrow to fresh woods, and pastures new," bringing the elegy to a full rich *tierce de Picardie* or major chord. By appearing himself at the beginning and end of the poem, Milton presents the poem as, in a sense, contained within the mind of the poet.

Apart from the historical convention of the pastoral, however, there is also the conventional framework of ideas or assumptions which forms the background of the poem. I call it a framework of ideas, and it may also be that, but in poetry it is rather a framework of images. It consists of four levels of existence. First is the order revealed by Christianity, the order of grace and salvation and of eternal life. Second is the order of human nature, the order represented by the Garden of Eden in the Bible and the Golden Age in classical myth, and which man in his fallen state can, up to a point, regain through education, obedience to law, and the habit of virtue. Third is the order of physical nature, the world of animals and plants which is morally neutral but theologically "fallen." Fourth is the disorder of the unnatural, the sin and death and corruption that entered the world with the Fall.

Lycidas has his connections with all of these orders. In the first place, all the images of death and resurrection are included in and identified with the body of Christ. Christ is the sun of righteousness, the tree of life, the water of life, the dying god who rose again, the saviour from the sea. On this level Lycidas enters the Christian heaven and is greeted by the "Saints above" "In solemn troops, and sweet societies," where the language echoes the Book of Revelation. But simultaneously Lycidas achieves another apotheosis as the Genius of the shore, corresponding to the Attendant Spirit in *Comus*, whose habitation is said to be a world above our own, identified, not with the Christian heaven, but with Spenser's Gardens of Adonis. The third level of physical nature is the world of ordinary experience, where death is simply a loss, and those who mourn the death have to turn to pick up their tasks again. On this level Lycidas is merely absent, "to our moist vows denied," represented only by the empty bier with its flowers. It is on this level too that the poem is contained within the mind of the surviving poet, as on the Christian level it is contained within the body of Christ. Finally, the world of death and corruption holds the drowned corpse of Lycidas, which will soon come to the surface and "welter to the parching wind." This last is an unpleasant and distressing image, and Milton touches it very lightly, picking it up again in an appropriate context:

> But swoln with wind and the rank mist they draw,
> Rot inwardly . . .

In the writing of *Lycidas* there are four creative principles of particular importance. To say that there are four does not mean, of course, that they are separable. One is convention, the reshaping of the poetic material which is appropriate to this subject. Another is genre, the choosing of the appropriate form. A third is archetype, the use of appropriate, and therefore recurrently employed, images and symbols. The fourth, for which there is no name, is the fact that the forms of literature are autonomous: that is, they do not exist outside literature. Milton is not writing an obituary: he does not start with Edward King and his life and times, but with the conventions and archetypes that poetry requires for such a theme.

Of the critical principles illustrated by this analysis, one will be no surprise to the present audience. *Lycidas* owes quite as much to Hebrew, Greek, Latin, and Italian traditions as it does to English. Even the diction, of which I have no space to speak, shows strong Italian influence. Milton was of course a learned poet, but there is no poet whose literary influences are entirely confined to his own language. Thus every problem in literary criticism is a problem in comparative literature, or simply of literature itself.

The next principle is that the provisional hypothesis which we must adopt for the study of every poem is that that poem is a unity. If, after careful and repeated testing, we are forced to conclude that it is not a unity, then we must abandon the hypothesis and look for the reasons why it is not. A good deal of bad criticism of *Lycidas* has resulted from not making enough initial effort to understand the unity of the poem. To talk of "digressions" in *Lycidas* is a typical consequence of a mistaken critical method, of backing into the poem the wrong way round. If, instead of starting with the poem, we start with a handful of peripheral facts about the poem, Milton's casual knowledge of King, his ambitions as a poet, his bitterness against the episcopacy, then of course the poem will break down into pieces corresponding precisely to those fragments of knowledge. *Lycidas* illustrates, on a small scale, what has happened on a much bigger scale in, for example, the criticism of Homer. Critics knowing something about the fragmentary nature of heroic lays and ballads approached the *Iliad* and the *Odyssey* with this knowledge in mind, and the poems obediently split up into the pieces that they wished to isolate. Other critics came along and treated the poems as imaginative unities, and today everyone knows that the second group were more convincing.

The same thing happens when our approach to "sources" becomes fragmentary or piecemeal. *Lycidas* is a dense mass of echoes from previous literature, chiefly pastoral literature. Reading through Virgil's Eclogues with *Lycidas* in mind, we can see that Milton had not simply read or studied these poems: he possessed them; they were part of the material he was shaping. The passage about the hungry sheep reminds us of at least three other passages: one in Dante's *Paradiso*, one in the Book of Ezekiel, and one near the beginning of Hesiod's *Theogony*. There are also echoes of Mantuan and Spenser, of the Gospel of John, and it is quite possible that there are even more striking parallels with poems that Milton had not read. In such cases there is not *a* source at all, no one place that the passage "comes from," or, as we say with such stupefying presumption, that the poet "had in mind." There are only archetypes, or recurring themes of literary expression, which *Lycidas* has recreated, and therefore re-echoed, yet once more.

The next principle is that the important problems of literary criticism lie within the study of literature. We notice that a law of diminishing returns sets in as soon as we move away from the poem itself. If we ask, who is Lycidas? the answer is that he is a member of the same family as Theocritus' Daphnis, Bion's Adonis, the Old Testament's Abel, and so on. The answer goes on building up a wider comprehension of literature and a deeper knowledge of its structural principles and recurring themes. But if we ask, who was Edward King? What was his relation to Milton? How good a poet was he? we find ourselves moving dimly in the intense inane. The same is true of minor points. If we ask, why is the image of the two-handed engine in *Lycidas?* we can give an answer, along the lines suggested above, that illustrates how carefully the poem has been constructed. If we ask, what is the two-handed engine? there are forty-odd answers, none of them completely satisfactory; yet the fact that they are not wholly satisfactory hardly seems to be important.

Another form of the same kind of fallacy is the confusion between personal sincerity and literary sincerity. If we start with the facts that *Lycidas* is highly conventional and that Milton knew King only slightly, we may see in *Lycidas* an "artificial" poem without "real feeling" in it. This red herring, though more common among third-rate romantics, was dragged across the study of *Lycidas* by Samuel Johnson. Johnson knew better, but he happened to feel perverse about this particular poem, and so deliberately raised false issues. It would not have occurred to him, for example, to question the conventional use of Horace in the satires of Pope, or of Juvenal in his own. Personal sincerity has no place in literature, because personal sincerity as such is inarticulate. One may burst into tears at the news of a friend's death, but one can never spontaneously burst into song, however doleful a lay. *Lycidas* is a passionately sincere poem, because Milton was deeply interested in the structure and symbolism of funeral elegies, and had been practising since adolescence on every fresh corpse in sight, from the university beadle to the fair infant dying of a cough.

If we ask what inspires a poet, there are always two answers. An occasion, an experience, an event, may inspire the impulse to write. But the impulse to write can only come from previous contact with literature, and the formal inspiration, the poetic structure that crystallizes around the new event, can only be derived from other poems. Hence while every new poem is a new and unique creation, it is also a reshaping of familiar conventions of literature, otherwise it would not be recognizable as literature at all. Literature often gives us the illusion of turning from books to life, from second-hand to direct experience, and thereby discovering new literary principles in the world outside. But this is never quite what happens. No matter how tightly Wordsworth may close the barren leaves of art and let nature be his teacher, his literary forms will be as conventional as ever, although they may echo an unaccustomed set of conventions, such as the ballad or the broadside. The pretence of personal sincerity is itself a literary convention, and Wordsworth makes many of the flat simple statements which represent, in literature, the inarticulateness of personal sincerity:

> No motion has she now, no force:
> She neither hears nor sees.

But as soon as a death becomes a poetic image, that image is assimilated to other poetic images of death in nature, and hence Lucy inevitably becomes a Proserpine figure, just as King becomes an Adonis:

> Rolled round in earth's diurnal course
> With rocks, and stones, and trees.

In Whitman we have an even more extreme example than Wordsworth of a cult of personal statement and an avoidance of learned conventions. It is therefore instructive to see what happens in *When Lilacs Last in Dooryard Bloomed*. The dead man is not called by a pastoral name, but neither is he called by his historical name. He is in a coffin which is carried the length and breadth of the land; he is identified with a "powerful western fallen star"; he is the beloved comrade of the poet, who throws the purple flower of the lilac on his coffin; a singing bird laments the death, just as the woods and caves do in *Lycidas*.

Convention, genre, archetype, and the autonomy of forms are all illustrated as clearly in Whitman as they are in Milton.

Lycidas is an occasional poem, called forth by a specific event. It seems, therefore, to be a poem with a strong external reference. Critics who cannot approach a poem except as a personal statement of the poet's thus feel that if it says little about King, it must say a good deal about Milton. So, they reason, *Lycidas* is really autobiographical, concerned with Milton's own preoccupations, including his fear of death. There can be no objection to this unless Milton's conventional involving of himself with the poem is misinterpreted as a personal intrusion into it.

For Milton was even by seventeenth-century standards an unusually professional and impersonal poet. Of all Milton's poems, the one obvious failure is the poem called *The Passion*, and if we look at the imagery of that poem we can see why. It is the only poem of Milton's in which he is preoccupied with himself in the process of writing it. "My muse," "my song," "my Harp," "my roving verse," "my Phoebus," and so on for eight stanzas until Milton abandons the poem in disgust. It is not a coincidence that Milton's one self-conscious poem should be the one that never gets off the ground. There is nothing like this in *Lycidas:* the "I" of that poem is a professional poet in his conventional shepherd disguise, and to think of him as a personal "I" is to bring *Lycidas* down to the level of *The Passion*, to make it a poem that has to be studied primarily as a biographical document rather than for its own sake. Such an approach to *Lycidas* is apt to look most plausible to those who dislike Milton, and want to see him cut down to size.

One more critical principle, and the one that I have written this paper to enunciate, seems to me to follow inevitably from the previous ones. Every poem must be examined as a unity, but no poem is an isolatable unity. Every poem is inherently connected with other poems of its kind, whether explicitly, as *Lycidas* is with Theocritus and Virgil, or implicitly, as Whitman is with the same tradition, or by anticipation, as *Lycidas* is with later pastoral elegies. And, of course, the kinds or genres of literature are not separable either, like the orders of pre-Darwinian biology. Everyone who has seriously studied literature knows that he is not simply moving from poem to poem, or from one æsthetic experience to another: he is also entering into a coherent and progressive discipline. For literature is not simply an aggregate of books and poems and plays: it is an order of words. And our total literary experience, at any given time, is not a discrete series of memories or impressions of what we have read, but an imaginatively coherent body of experience.

It is literature as an order of words, therefore, which forms the primary context of any given work of literary art. All other contexts—the place of *Lycidas* in Milton's development; its place in the history of English poetry; its place in seventeenth-century thought or history—are secondary and derivative contexts. Within the total literary order certain structural and generic principles, certain configurations of narrative and imagery, certain conventions and devices and *topoi,* occur over and over again. In every new work of literature some of these principles are reshaped.

Lycidas, we found, is informed by such a recurring structural principle. The short, simple, and accurate name for this principle is myth. The Adonis myth is what makes *Lycidas* both distinctive and traditional. Of course if we think of the Adonis myth as some kind of Platonic idea existing by itself, we shall not get far with it as a critical conception. But it is only incompetence that tries to reduce or assimilate a poem to a myth. The Adonis myth in *Lycidas* is the structure of *Lycidas.* It is in *Lycidas* in much the same way that the sonata form is in the first movement of a Mozart symphony. It is the connecting link between what makes *Lycidas* the poem it is and what unites it to other forms of poetic experience. If we attend only to the uniqueness of *Lycidas,* and analyze the ambiguities and subtleties of its diction, our method, however useful in itself, soon reaches a point of no return to the poem. If we attend only to the conventional element, our method will turn it into a scissors-and-paste collection of allusive tags. One method reduces the poem to a jangle of echoes of itself, the other to a jangle of echoes from other poets. If we have a unifying principle that holds these two tendencies together from the start, neither will get out of hand.

Myths, it is true, turn up in other disciplines, in anthropology, in psychology, in comparative religion. But the primary business of the critic is with myth as the shaping principle of a work of literature. Thus for him myth becomes much the same thing as Aristotle's *mythos*, narrative or plot, the moving formal cause which is what Aristotle called the "soul" of the work and assimilates all details in the realizing of its unity.

In its simplest English meaning a myth is a story about a god, and Lycidas is, poetically speaking, a god or spirit of nature, who eventually becomes a saint in heaven, which is as near as one can get to godhead in ordinary Christianity. The reason for treating Lycidas mythically, in this sense, is conventional, but the convention is not arbitrary or accidental. It arises from the metaphorical nature of poetic speech. We are not told simply that Lycidas has left the woods and caves, but that the woods and caves and all their echoes mourn his loss. This is the language of that curious identification of subject and object, of personality and thing, which the poet has in common with the lunatic and the lover. It is the language of metaphor, recognized by Aristotle as the distinctive language of poetry. And, as we can see in such phrases as sun-god and tree-god, the language of metaphor is interdependent with the language of myth.

I have said that all problems of criticism are problems of comparative literature. But where there is comparison there must be some standard by which we can distinguish what is actually comparable from what is merely analogous. The scientists discovered long ago that to make valid comparisons you have to know what your real categories are. If you're studying natural history, for instance, no matter how fascinated you may be by anything that has eight legs, you can't just lump together an octopus and a spider and a string quartet. In science the difference between a scientific and a pseudo-scientific procedure can usually be spotted fairly soon. I wonder if literary criticism has any standards of this kind. It seems to me that a critic practically has to maintain that the Earl of Oxford wrote the plays of Shakespeare before he can be clearly recognized as making pseudo-critical statements. I have read some critics on Milton who appeared to be confusing Milton with their phallic fathers, if that is the right phrase. I should call them pseudo-critics; others call them neo-classicists. How is one to know? There is such a variety of even legitimate critics. There are critics who can find things in the Public Records Office, and there are critics who, like myself, could not find the Public Records Office. Not all critical statements or procedures can be equally valid.

The first step, I think, is to recognize the dependence of value-judgments on scholarship. Scholarship, or the knowledge of literature, constantly expands and increases; value-judgments are produced by a skill based on the knowledge we already have. Thus scholarship has both priority to value-judgments and the power of veto over them. When Thomas Rymer called *Othello* a bloody farce, he was not making a bad value-judgment; he was making a correct value-judgment based on impossibly narrow scholarship. Most of the famous howlers of criticism are of this kind. The second step is to recognize the dependence of scholarship on a coordinated view of literature. A good deal of critical taxonomy lies ahead of us. We need to know much more than we do about the structural principles of literature, about myth and metaphor, conventions and genres, before we can distinguish with any authority a real from an imaginary line of influence, an illuminating from a misleading analogy, a poet's original source from his last resource. The basis of this central critical activity that gives direction to scholarship is the simple fact that every poem is a member of the class of things called poems. Some poems, including *Lycidas,* proclaim that they are conventional, in other words that their primary context is in literature. Other poems leave this inference to the critic, with an appealing if often misplaced confidence.

Five Types of *Lycidas*

M. H. Abrams

Most modern critics base their theories on the proposition that a poem is an object in itself. And all critics endorse enthusiastically at least one statement by Matthew Arnold, that the function of criticism is "to see the object as in itself it really is." The undertaking is surely valid, and laudable; the results, however, are disconcerting. For in this age of unexampled critical activity, as one poetic object after another is analyzed under rigidly controlled conditions, the object proves to be highly unstable, and disintegrates. In the pages of the critics we increasingly find, under a single title, not one poem but a variety of poems.

Milton's *Lycidas* is a convenient case in point, because it is short enough to be easily manageable, has been explicated many times, and is almost universally esteemed. If not every reader goes all the way with Mark Pattison's judgment that it is "the high-water mark of English Poesy," still critics agree about its excellence as closely as they ever do in evaluating a lyric poem. My point is that, on the evidence of their own commentaries, critics agree about the excellence of quite different poems. They present us not with one *Lycidas* but with discriminable types of *Lycidas*—five types, I have announced in my title. I feel confident that with a little more perseverance I could have distinguished at least seven, to equal William Empson's types of ambiguity. But in these matters distinctions, as Mr. Empson's pro-

---

This essay is based on a lecture given at the Columbia Graduate Union in 1957 and elsewhere.

cedure demonstrates, can be rather arbitrary. And even five types of *Lycidas* are enough to confront the literary theorist with an embarrassing problem: Is a poem one or many? And if it is one, how are we to decide which one?

I

For the first type, take *Lycidas* as it was commonly described in the period between the first volume of Masson's monumental *Life of Milton* (1859) and the critical age ushered in by T. S. Eliot and I. A. Richards a generation ago. This traditional reading (in which I was educated) was conveniently epitomized by J. H. Hanford in his *Milton Handbook*. Individual discussions varied in emphasis and detail; but when in that lost paradise of critical innocence readers looked at *Lycidas*, they agreed that they saw an elegiac poem about Edward King, a contemporary of Milton's at Christ's College, who had been drowned when his ship suddenly foundered in the Irish Sea. To depersonalize his grief and elevate its occasion, Milton chose to follow the elaborate conventions of the pastoral elegy, as these had evolved over the 1800 years between the Sicilian Theocritus and the English Spenser; he ended the poem with a traditional consolation at the thought of Lycidas resurrected in heaven, and found in this thought the strength to carry on his own concerns. In two passages, many commentators agreed—they often called them digressions—Milton uttered his personal concerns in a thin fictional disguise. In one of these Milton expressed his own fear that "th' abhorred shears" might cut him off before he could achieve the poetic fame to which he had dedicated his life. In the other Milton, through St. Peter, voiced a grim warning to the corrupt English clergy of his time.

Writing in 1926, on the extreme verge of the New Criticism, Professor Hanford was so imprudent as to close his discussion with the statement that "*Lycidas* bears its meaning plainly enough on its face." It contains, to be sure, a minor verbal crux or two, such as the nature of the "two-handed engine at the door"; but, he roundly asserted, "there has been little room for disagreement regarding its larger features."

Only four years later E. M. W. Tillyard published in his *Milton* an analysis of *Lycidas* which in its opening tucket sounded the new note in criticism:

Most criticism of *Lycidas* is off the mark, because it fails to distinguish between the nominal and the real subject, what the poem professes to be about and what it is about. It assumes that Edward King is the real, whereas he is but the nominal subject. Fundamentally *Lycidas* concerns— [1]

But before we hear what *Lycidas* is really about, we ought to attend to Tillyard's distinction between "nominal" and "real" poetic meaning. For this modern polysemism, which splits all poems—or at least the most noteworthy poems—into two or more levels of meaning, one overt and nominal (which other readers have detected) and the other covert but essential (whose discovery has usually been reserved for the critic making the distinction) is extraordinarily widespread, and we shall find it repeatedly applied to *Lycidas*. The lamination of poetic significance is variously named. Tillyard elsewhere distinguishes between conscious and unconscious, and direct and oblique meanings. Other critics make a parallel distinction between manifest and latent, ostensible and actual, literal and symbolic, or particular and archetypal significance. And at the risk of giving away a trade secret, it must be confessed that most of the time, when we critics come out with a startling new interpretation of a well-known work, it is through the application of this very useful interpretative stratagem.

The procedure is indispensable in analyzing works for which there is convincing evidence that they were written in the mode of allegory or symbolism. But it is worth noting that the distinction was developed by Greek commentators, interested in establishing Homer's reputation as a doctor of universal wisdom, who dismissed Homer's scandalous stories about the gods as only the veil for an esoteric and edifying undermeaning. The same strategy was adapted by Philo to bring the Old Testament into harmony with Greek philosophy, and by the Church Fathers to prove that the Old Testament prefigured the New Testament, and by medieval and Renaissance moralists in order to disclose, behind Ovid's pagan and ostensibly licentious fables, austere ethical precepts and anticipations of the Christian mysteries. From the vantage of our altered cultural prepossessions, it appears that the distinction between nominal and real meaning has

[1] Quotations without page references are from essays reprinted in this volume.

not frequently been used as a handy gadget to replace what an author has said with what a commentator would prefer him to have said.

We are braced now for Tillyard's disclosure of the real subject of *Lycidas*. "Fundamentally *Lycidas* concerns Milton himself; King is but the excuse for one of Milton's most personal poems." The main argument for this interpretation is that *Lycidas* is generally admitted to be a great poem, but "if it is great, it must contain deep feeling of some sort"; since this feeling is obviously not about King, it must be about Milton himself. Milton, Tillyard maintains, expresses his own situation and feelings and attitudes, not only in the obviously allegorical passages about driving afield and piping with Lycidas, or in the passages on fame and the corrupt clergy which had been called personal by earlier critics, but from beginning to end of the poem. How radical Tillyard's formula is for translating objective references to subjective equivalents is indicated by his analysis of the poem's climactic passage:

> The fourth section purports to describe the resurrection of Lycidas and his entry into heaven. More truly it solves the whole poem by describing the resurrection into a new kind of life of Milton's hopes, should they be ruined by premature death or by the moral collapse of his country. . . . Above all the fourth section describes the renunciation of earthly fame, the abnegation of self by the great egotist, and the spiritual purgation of gaining one's life after losing it.[2]

Only such an interpretation, Tillyard claims, will reveal the integrity of the poem, by making it possible "to see in *Lycidas* a unity of purpose which cannot be seen in it if the death of King is taken as the real subject." Furthermore, the value of the poem really resides in the ordered and harmonized mental impulses for which the objective references are merely a projected correlative: "What makes *Lycidas* one of the greatest poems in English is that it expresses with success a state of mind whose high value can hardly be limited to a particular religious creed."

From this interpretation and these grounds of value John Crowe Ransom (to speak in understatement) disagrees. His premise is that "anonymity . . . is a condition of poetry." Mil-

[2] See also Tillyard's analysis of *Lycidas* in *Poetry Direct and Oblique,* revised edition (London, 1948), pp. 81–84.

ton very properly undertook to keep himself and his private concerns out of his memorial verses, and to do so assumed the identity of a Greek shepherd, the "uncouth swain" of the last stanza, who serves as a dramatis persona, a "qualified spokesman" for the public performance of a ritual elegy. As for the problem with which Tillyard confronted us—if the passion is not for King, for whom can it be except Milton himself?—Ransom solves it by dissolving it. There is no passion in the poem, and so no problem. "For Lycidas [Milton] mourns with a very technical piety." The pastoral conventions are part of the poetic "make-believe," and the whole poem, whatever more it may be, is "an exercise in pure linguistic technique, or metrics; it was also an exercise in the technique of what our critics of fiction refer to as 'point of view.' "

This is the poem, at any rate, that Milton set out to write and almost succeeded in writing. But his youth and character interfered and forced into the writing three defiant gestures of "rebellion against the formalism of his art." One of these is the liberty he took with his stanzas, which are almost anarchically irregular and include ten lines which do not rhyme at all. Another is St. Peter's speech; in Ransom's comment on this passage, we hear a voice out of the past—the Cavalier critic gracefully but firmly putting the stiff-necked and surly Puritan in his place: it expresses, he says, "a Milton who is angry, violent, and perhaps a little bit vulgar . . . Peter sounds like another Puritan zealot, and less than apostolic." The third instance of Milton's self-assertion is his "breach in the logic of composition"; that is, he shifts from the first-person monologue with which the poem opens to dialogues with Phoebus and others, then abruptly to the third person in the last stanza, where the uncouth swain is presented in "a pure narrative conclusion in the past [tense]." It follows that Ransom's concluding evaluation turns Tillyard's precisely inside-out. The sustained self-expression, on which Tillyard had grounded both the unity and excellence of the elegy, according to Ransom breaks out only sporadically, and then so as to violate the integrity and flaw the perfection of the poem. "So *Lycidas*, for the most part a work of great art, is sometimes artful and tricky. We are disturbingly conscious of a man behind the artist."

One might, of course, demur that given Ransom's own criteria,

two of the items he decries as arrogant gestures of Milton's
originality are exactly those in which he closely follows established conventions. The scholarly annotators—at whom, as he
passes, Ransom turns to smile—tell us that the models for Milton's stanzas, the elaborate *canzone* employed by several Italian
lyrists of the sixteenth century, were not only variable in structure, but also included unrhymed lines for the sake of that seeming ease and freedom which is the aim of an art that hides art.
As for St. Peter's diatribe, Milton inherited the right to introduce rough satire against the clergy into a pastoral from a widespread convention established by Petrarch, who was hardly vulgar, nor a Puritan, nor even a Protestant. In Ransom's third
exhibit, one element—Milton's putting the elegy into a narrative
context in the conclusion, without a matching narrative introduction—is not, apparently, traditional. But it is at any rate
odd to make Milton out to assert his own egoism in the passage
which specifically assigns the elegy to another person than himself; a person, moreover, who is the entirely conventional rural
singer of a pastoral elegy.

But this begins to seem capricious, and does not represent
the measure of my admiration for the charm and deftness of Mr.
Ransom's essay, which thrusts home some important and timely
truths about the dramatic construction of *Lycidas* by the artful
device of overstatement. It is, one might hazard, a virtuoso exercise in critical point of view.

Let the commentary by Cleanth Brooks and John Hardy, in
their edition of Milton's *Poems* of 1645, represent *Lycidas*, type
four. At first glance it might seem that to these explicators the
poem is not really about King, nor about Milton, but mainly
about water. They turn to the first mention of water in lines
12–14 and discover at once the paradox that the "tear" which
is the "meed" paid to Lycidas by the elegiac singer is of the
same substance, salt water, as the "wat'ry bier," the sea on which
the body welters. As the poem develops, they say, "the 'melodious
tear' promises to overwhelm the 'sounding Seas.'" For the tear
is the elegy itself, which derives its inspiration from the "sacred
well" of the muses, and flows on through a profusion of fountains, rivers, and streams, in richly ambiguous interrelations of
harmonies, contrasts, and ironies, until, by the agency of "resurrection images," all of which "have to do with a circumvention

of the sea," we are transferred to a transcendent pastoral realm where Lycidas walks "other streams along" and the saints wipe the tears forever from his eyes.

The base of the critical operation here is the assumption that "the 'poetry' resides in the total structure of meanings." The primary component in this structure is "imagery," of which the component parts are so organically related, through mutual reflection and implication, that it does not matter where you start: any part will lead you to the center and the whole. The key to both the form and value of *Lycidas,* then, which Tillyard had found in the ordering of mental impulses, and Ransom in the all-but-successful maintenance of impersonal elegiac conventions, Brooks and Hardy locate in the evolution and integration of the imagery: "*Lycidas* is a good poem not because it is appropriately and simply pastoral and elegiac—with . . . all the standard equipment—but because of its unique formal wholeness, because of the rich 'integrity' of even such a single figure as that in the lines 'He must not flote upon his wat'ry bear / Unwept. . . .'" [3]

It turns out, however, that these images are only provisionally the elements of the poem, since in Milton they are used as vehicles for a more basic component, "certain dominant, recurrent symbolic motives." The fact, hitherto mainly overlooked, is that "Milton is a symbolist poet to a considerable extent." [4] Accordingly we must again, as in Tillyard's essay, penetrate the ostensible meaning to discover the real meaning of *Lycidas,* though a real meaning which in this case is an abstract concept. "What," they ask, "is the real subject" of *Lycidas?*

> If Milton is not deeply concerned with King as a person, he is deeply concerned, and as a young poet personally involved, with a theme—which is that of the place and meaning of poetry in a world which seems at many points inimical to it.

Specifically, the early part of the poem presents the despairing theme that nature is neutral, emptied of the old pastoral deities ("to say nymphs are ineffectual is tantamount to denying their existence"); and this concept is transcended only by the movement from philosophic naturalism to Christian supernaturalism, in the pastoral imagery of the conclusion in heaven.

---

[3] *Poems of Mr. John Milton* (New York, 1951), p. 259.
[4] *Ibid.,* pp. 256, 250.

Perhaps other readers share my disquiet at this discovery. Leaving aside the validity of assuming that *Lycidas* is essentially a symbolist poem of which the real subject is a theme, there remains the difficulty that the theme seems to be startlingly anachronistic. Milton, we are told, writing in 1637, and echoing a complaint about the nymphs which is as old as Theocritus' first Idyll, presents us with the world-view involving "an emptied nature, a nature which allows us to personify it only in the sense that its sounds seem mournful. . . . The music of nature . . . has also been stilled." But wasn't it Tennyson who said this, in an elegy published in 1850?

> And all the phantom, Nature, stands—
> With all the music in her tone,
> A hollow echo of my own,—
> A hollow form with empty hands.

As for the concept imputed to Milton, with respect to the place of poetry in an inimical world, that "Nature is neutral: it is not positively malignant, but neither is it beneficent"—isn't this exactly the thesis laid down in 1926 by I. A. Richards in a very influential little book, *Science and Poetry?* In our own age, Mr. Richards said,

> the central dominant change may be described as the *Neutralization of Nature,* the tranference from the Magical View of the world to the scientific. . . . There is some evidence that Poetry . . . arose with this Magical View. It is a possibility to be seriously considered that Poetry may pass away with it.[5]

At any rate, it is by a notable sleight of explication that Brooks and Hardy convert to the real meaning that Nature does not sympathize with the poet's sorrow and "has no apparent respect for the memory of Lycidas" the very passage in which Milton explicitly states the contrary: that nature, which had responded joyously to Lycidas' soft lays when he was alive, now mourns his death:

> Thee Shepherd, thee the Woods, and desert Caves,
> With wilde Thyme and the gadding Vine o'regrown,
> And all their echoes mourn.

We go on to the fifth type of *Lycidas,* the archetypal version, which entered the critical ken after the vogue of the writings

[5] *Science and Poetry* (London, 1926), pp. 47–48.

in comparative anthropology of James G. Frazer and in analytical psychology of C. G. Jung. This mode of criticism, like the last, begins by isolating images or patterns of imagery; now, however, the focus is on images which reflect the agents and events of myth or folklore. The favorite legends are those which (according to some folklorists) concern beings who were once nature deities—the dead and risen gods of Syria, Egypt, and Greece associated with the dying or reaping of the crops in the fall and their revival in the spring.

Richard P. Adams, investigating "The Archetypal Pattern of Death and Rebirth in *Lycidas*," discovers that the poem is throughout "a remarkably tight amalgam of death-and-rebirth imagery." These images begin with the initial reference to the evergreen plants, the laurel, myrtle, and ivy, and continue through the allusions to the hyacinth, the rose, and the violet, which had their mythical genesis in the blood of a mortal or deity. The many water-images are here interpreted as fertility symbols; the allusion to the death of Orpheus is said to bring in a myth whose similarities to "the deaths of Adonis, Attis, Osiris, and other fertility demigods have been pointed out by modern scholars"; while the poet's speculation that the body of Lycidas perhaps visits "the bottom of the monstrous world" parallels the descent into water and the dragon flight "which is often a feature of death-and-rebirth cycles." [6]

Adams is content with a fairly traditional interpretation of the subject of *Lycidas:* Milton's concern was not with Edward King, but "with the life, death, and resurrection of the dedicated poet, and specifically with his own situation at the time." Northrop Frye, however, in his essay on "Literature as Context: Milton's *Lycidas*," contends that the "structural principle" of the poem, the formal cause which "assimilates all details in the realizing of its unity," is "the Adonis myth," and that "Lycidas is, poetically speaking, a god or spirit of nature, who eventually becomes a saint in heaven." The archetypal reading here provides us with a new principle of unity, a new distinction between ostensible and implicit meaning, and a new version of what the poem is really rather than nominally about. In an earlier essay, Frye put the matter bluntly: "Poetry demands, as Milton saw

[6] I have cited the original, extended form of this essay in *PMLA,* LXIV (1949), 183–188.

it, that the elements of his theme should be assimilated to their archetypes. . . . Hence the poem will not be about King, but about his archetype, Adonis, the dying and rising god, called Lycidas in Milton's poem." [7]

II

It will not do to say, as one is tempted to say, that these five versions of *Lycidas* really give us the same poem, in diversely selected aspects and details. The versions differ not in selection or emphasis, but in essentials. Each strikes for the heart of the poem; each claims to have discovered the key element, or structural principle, which has controlled the choice, order, and interrelations of the parts, and which establishes for the reader the meaning, unity, and value of the whole. Nor will it help put Humpty Dumpty together again to carry out the proposal we sometimes hear, to combine all these critical modes into a single criticism which has the virtues of each and the deficiency of none. To provide a coherent reading, a critical procedure must itself be coherent; it cannot be divided against itself in its first principles. A syncretic criticism is invertebrate, and will yield not an integral poem, but a ragout.

When there is such radical and many-sided disagreement about the real but nonliteral and esoteric meaning of the poem, the best hope of remedy, I think, lies in going back to Milton's text and reading it with a dogged literalness, except when there is clear evidence that some part of it is to be read allegorically or symbolically. This is what I propose, very briefly, to attempt. In a way, this puts me in a favorable position. A drawback in writing as a new critic is that it would be embarrassing to come out with an old reading; while I can plead that I have deliberately set out to labor the obvious, and can take comfort from the number of earlier critiques with which I find myself in agreement.

Looked at in this way, *Lycidas* turns out to be in some sense— although in some cases a very loose sense—about Edward King, about Milton, about water, about the problem of being a poet in an inimical world; and it is undoubtedly about at least one God (Christ) who died to be reborn. But it is about none of these in the central way that it is about certain other things that,

[7] "Levels of Meaning in Literature," *Kenyon Review,* XII (1950), 258.

to the literal-minded reader, constitute the essential poem Milton chose to write.

First, it is about—in the sense that it presents as the poetic datum, Milton's elected fiction—a nameless shepherd, sitting from morn to evening in a rural setting and hymning the death of a fellow poet-pastor, who is not Edward King but, specifically, Lycidas. The reason all our interpreters except Ransom treat the stated elegist rather casually, if at all, is that they tend to take as premise that a poem is an object made of words, or "a structure of meanings." So indeed it is. But as a starting point for criticism, it would be more inclusive and suggestive to say that a poem is made of *speech*, because the term "speech" entails a particular speaker. In *Lycidas* the speaker is an unnamed rustic singer whose speech refers to a state of affairs, describes the appearance and quotes the statements of other speakers, including Phoebus, Camus, and St. Peter, expresses his own thoughts and changing mood, and conveys, by immediate implication, something of his own character. The poem is therefore clearly a dramatic lyric, with a setting, an occasion, a chief character, and several subordinate characters (who may, however, be regarded as representing the speaker's own thoughts, objectified for dramatic purposes as standard personae of the pastoral ritual).

Tillyard is surely right, as against Ransom (and earlier, Dr. Johnson), in finding deep feeling in the poem, but he confronts us with the spurious alternative that the feeling must be either about King or about Milton himself. The feeling is occasioned by the death of Lycidas and the thoughts plausibly evoked by that event; and it is experienced and expressed not by Milton, but by a singer Milton is at considerable pains to identify as someone other than himself. Precisely what Milton himself thought and felt during the many hours—probably days—in which he labored over *Lycidas*, despite Tillyard's assurance, is beyond all but the most tenuous conjecture; although it is safe to say that, among other things, he was thinking how he might put together the best possible pastoral elegy. But we know precisely what the uncouth swain thought and felt, because the expression of his thoughts and feelings constitutes the poem, from the bold opening, "Yet once more, O ye Laurels . . . ," up to, but not including, the closing eight lines, when the author takes over as omniscient narrator: "*Thus* sang the uncouth Swain. . . ."

Readers of the poem at its first appearance knew that it was one of thirteen *Obsequies to the Memorie of Mr. Edward King*, and undoubtedly some also knew that the J.M. who signed the last obsequy was John Milton, whose circumstances and relations to King bore some resemblance to those presented in the poem. Such knowledge, however, does not displace but adds a particular historical reference to the two chief persons of the literal poem. *Lycidas* is not simply "about" King; it is a public ceremonial on the occasion of King's death, and the decorum of such a performance requires that the individual be not only lamented but also honored. And how could King be honored more greatly than to be made an instance of the type of poet-priest, identified by the traditional name "Lycidas," and to be lamented by a typical pastoral singer—in Ransom's phrase, a "qualified spokesman" for the public performance of a ritual elegy—whose single voice is resonant with echoes of poets through the ages mourning other poets untimely cut off? My insistence here may seem to be much ado about trivia, and, provided we are ready to fill out the details when pertinent, it can be a harmless critical shorthand to say that it is Milton who sings a lament for Edward King. But entirely to disregard these elementary circumstances may be the beginning of critical arrogance, which can end in our substituting our own poem for the one Milton chose to write.

The pastoral singer sets out, then, both to lament and to celebrate Lycidas. But consideration of this particular death raises in his mind a general question about the pointless contingencies of life, with its constant threat that fate may slit the thin-spun thread of any dedicated mortal prior to fulfillment and so render profitless his self-denial. This doubt, it should be noted, is not an ulterior "theme" beneath the ostensible surface of the poem. It is, explicitly, a topic in the thought of the lyric speaker, a stage in his soliloquy, which the speaker's continued meditation, guided by the comments of other imagined characters, goes on to resolve. This turn away from Lycidas to the circumstance of those who have survived him is not insincere, nor does it constitute a digression or an indecorously personal intrusion. It is entirely natural and appropriate; just as (to borrow a parallel from J. M. French) it is altogether fitting and proper for Lincoln, in the course of the *Gettysburg Address*, to turn from "these honored dead" to concern for "us the living." [8] After all, the doubts and fears of the lyric speaker concern the insecurity of his own life only in so far as he, like Lycidas, is a member of the genus Poet, and concern the class of poets only in so far as they share the universal human condition.

While initially, then, we may say that the presented subject of *Lycidas* is a pastoral singer memorializing the death of a dedicated shepherd poet-and-priest, we must go on to say that— in a second and important sense of "subject" as the dynamic center, or controlling principle, of a poem—its subject is a question about the seeming profitlessness of the dedicated life and the seeming deficiency of divine justice raised by that shocking death in the mind of the lyric speaker. That the rise, evolution, and resolution of the troubled thought of the elegist is the key to the structure of *Lycidas*, Milton made as emphatic as he could. He forced it on our attention by the startling device of ending the elegy, in a passage set off as a stanza in ottava rima, not with Lycidas, but with the elegist himself as, reassured, he faces his own destiny with confidence. But there is no occasion for Lycidas to feel slighted by this dereliction, for has he not been left in heaven, entertained and comforted by a chorus of saints, and given an office equivalent to St. Michael's, as guardian of the western shore?

III

If this, in barest outline, is the subject and the structural principle of the poem, what are we to make of the thematic imagery which, in the alternative interpretation by Brooks and Hardy, motivate and control its development?

Lycidas indeed, as these critics point out, incorporates many water and sheep-and-shepherd images; it also has song-and-singer images, flower images, stellar images, wide-ranging geographical images, even a surprising number of eye, ear, and mouth images. The usual strategy of the imagist critic is to pull out a selection of such items and to set them up in an order which is largely independent of who utters them, on what occasion, and for what dramatic purpose. Freed from the controls

[8] See J. M. French, "The Digressions in Milton's *Lycidas*," *Studies in Philology*, L (1953), 486.

imposed by their specific verbal and dramatic contexts, the selected images readily send out shoots and tendrils of significance,
which can be twined into a symbolic pattern—and if the critic
is sensitive, learned, and adroit, often a very interesting pattern.
The danger is, that the pattern may be largely an artifact of
the implicit scheme governing the critical analysis.

From our elected point of view, the images in *Lycidas* constitute elements in the speech—some of it literal and some figurative, allegoric, or symbolic—which serve primarily to express
the perceptions, thoughts, and feelings of the lyric speaker.
These images constitute for the reader a sensuous texture, and
they set up among themselves, as Brooks and Hardy point out,
various ambiguities, contrasts, and harmonies. But in *Lycidas*,
the procession of images is less determining that determined. If
they steer the meditation of the speaker, it is only in so far as
they cooperate in doing so with more authoritative principles:
with the inherited formulas of the elegiac ritual, and with these
formulas as they in turn (in Milton's inventive use of pastoral
conventions) are subtly subordinated to the evolving meditation
of the lyric speaker himself. In effect, then, the imagery does not
displace, but corroborates the process of feelingful thought in
the mind of a specified character. This, it seems to me, is the
way Milton wrote *Lycidas;* there is no valid evidence, in or out
of the poem, that he constructed it—as T. S. Eliot might have
done—out of a set of ownerless symbols which he endowed with
an implicit dynamism and set to acting out a thematic plot.

For the mythic and archetypal interpretation of *Lycidas*, as
it happens, there is a more plausible basis in Milton's ideas and
characteristic procedures. As a Christian humanist of the Renaissance, Milton was eager to save the phenomena of classical
culture, and thus shared with the modern archetypist an interest in synthesizing the ancient and modern, the primitive and
civilized, pagan fable and Christian dogma, into an all-encom-
passing whole. And Milton knew, from divers ancient and Renaissance mythographers, about the parallel to the death and
resurrection of Christ in ancient fables and fertility cults—
about what in *Paradise Lost* he called the "reviv'd Adonis"
(IX, 440), and the "annual wound" of Thammuz, identified
with Adonis by the Syrian damsels who lamented his fate "in
amorous ditties all a Summer's day" (I, 446–452). But these

facts are not adequate to validate a reading of *Lycidas* as a poem which is really about Adonis, or any other pagan fertility god. In *Lycidas* Milton makes no allusion whatever to Adonis, and he refers to Orpheus only to voice despair that even the Muse his mother was helpless to prevent his hideous death. In his references to these fables in *Paradise Lost,* Milton specifies that the story of the Garden of revived Adonis is "feign'd," lists Thammuz-Adonis among the "Devils [adored] for Deities," and describes the mother of Orpheus as "an empty dream" (VII, 39). For though a humanist, Milton is a Christian humanist, to whom revelation is not one more echo of archetypal myths but the archetype itself, the one Truth, which had been either corrupted or distortedly foreshadowed, "prefigured," in various pagan deities and fables. There is a world of difference between Milton's assumption that there is only one religion and Blake's archetypal assertion that "All Religions are One."

By conflating Christian and non-Christian story into equivalent variations on a single rebirth pattern, the tendency of an archetypal reading is to cancel dramatic structure by flattening the poem out, or even—in the extreme but common view that we get closer to the archetype as we move back along the scale toward the vegetational cycle itself—by turning the poem inside out. For if we regard the rebirth theme as having been revealed in the opening passage on the unwithering laurel, myrtle, and ivy, and as merely reiterated in later passages on Orpheus, on water, on sanguine flowers, and in the allusion to Christ and the risen Lycidas, then the denouement of the poem lies in its exordium and its movement is not a progress but an eddy.

The movement of *Lycidas,* on the contrary, is patently from despair through a series of insights to triumphant joy. We can put it this way: read literally, the elegy proper opens with the statement "Lycidas is dead, dead ere his prime"; it concludes with the flatly opposing statement "Lycidas your sorrow is *not* dead." Everything that intervenes has been planned to constitute a plausible sequence of thoughts and insights that will finally convert a logical contradiction into a lyric reversal by the anagnorisis, the discovery, that for a worthy Christian poet-priest a seeming defeat by death is actually an immortal triumph.

Milton achieves this reversal by a gradual shift from the natural, pastoral, and pagan viewpoint to the viewpoint of Christian revelation and its promise of another world, the Kingdom of Heaven. He carefully marks for us the stages of this ascent by what, to contemporary readers, was the conspicuous device of grading the levels of his style. For as Milton said in the treatise *Of Education,* issued seven years after *Lycidas,* decorum (including "the fitted stile of lofty, mean, or lowly" to the height of the matter) "is the grand master peece to observe." The problem of stylistic decorum had been particularly debated in connection with the pastoral, which had troubled Renaissance theorists by the duplicity of its stylistic requirements, since it typically dealt with high matters under the lowly guise of a conversation between two uncouth swains. Milton's comment on the fitter style probably was an echo of Puttenham's statement that "decencie," or "decorum"—the just proportioning of the "high, meane, and base stile"—is "the chiefe praise of any writer"; and Puttenham had also pointed out that, though the normal level of pastoral was the "base and humble stile," the form was often used "under the vaile of homely persons and in rude speeches to insinuate and glaunce at greater matters." [9]

Accordingly Milton's singer opens the poem with a style higher than the pastoral norm: "Begin, and somewhat loudly sweep the string" is what he bids the muses, echoing the *"Sicelides Musae, paulo maiora canamus"* with which Virgil had elevated the pitch of his Fourth, or "Messianic," Eclogue. (Puttenham had remarked concerning this pastoral that, because of its lofty subject, "Virgill used a somewhat swelling stile" and that under the circumstances, "this was decent." [10]) The initial level of *Lycidas* suffices for the early pastoral and pagan sections on sympathizing nature, the nymphs, and the death of Orpheus. But this last reference evokes the despairing thought: what boots the ascetic life for those who, like Lycidas, stake everything on a treacherous future? The immediate comfort is vouchsafed the

[9] George Puttenham, *The Arte of English Poesie* (1589), in George G. Smith, ed., *Elizabethan Critical Essays* (New York, 1904), II, pp. 155, 27, 40.

[10] *Ibid.,* p. 156. In his Epistle and gloss to Spenser's *Shepheardes Calender,* one of the chief models for *Lycidas,* E. K. had also emphasized the question of stylistic decorum in the pastoral. He observed of the October Eclogue, which concerns poetry, that the style is properly "more loftye than the rest" and that at its inspired close Spenser's "verse groweth so big, that it seemeth he hath forgot the meanenesse of shepheards state and stile." (Ernest De Selincourt, ed., *Edmund Spenser: Minor Poems* [New York, 1910], pp. 101, 104.)

singer in a thought in which the highest pagan ethics comes closest to the Christian: the distinction between mere earthly reputation and the meed of true fame awarded by a divine and infallible judge. The concept is only tangentially Christian, however, for the deities named in this passage, Phoebus and Jove, are pagan ones. Nevertheless "that strain," the singer observes, "was of a higher mood," and he therefore readdresses himself to Arethuse and Mincius, waters associated with the classical pastoralists, as a transition back to the initial key: "But now my *Oat* proceeds. . . ."

The next modulation comes when St. Peter raises by implication the even more searching question why a faithful shepherd is taken early, while the corrupt ones prosper. He himself gives the obscurely terrifying answer: the two-handed engine stands ready to smite at the door; infallible justice dispenses punishment as well as rewards. This time the "dread voice" has been not merely of "a higher mood," but of an entirely different ontological and stylistic order, for it has "shrunk" the pastoral stream and frightened away the "Sicilian Muse" altogether. It is not only that the voice has been raised in the harsh rhetoric of anger, but that it belongs to a pastor, and expresses a matter, alien to the world of pagan pastoral. A Christian subject is here for the first time explicit. The appearance and speech of Peter, although brought in, as Milton said in his subtitle, "by occasion," is far from a digression. It turns out, indeed, to be nothing less than the climax and turning point of the lyric meditation, for without it the resolution, inadequately grounded, would seem to have been contrived through Christ as a patent *Deus ex machina*. The speech of Peter has in fact closely paraphrased Christ's own pastoral parable (John 9:39–41; 10:1–18), addressed to the Pharisees, in which He too had denounced those who remain blind to the truth, who climb into the sheepfold, and who abandon their sheep to the marauding wolf, and had then identified Himself as the Good Shepherd who lays down His life for His sheep—but only, He adds, "that I might take it again." Once Christ, the shepherd who died to be born again, is paralleled to the dead shepherd Lycidas, though by allusion only, the resolution of the elegy is assured—especially since Peter, the Pilot of the Galilean Lake, is the very Apostle who had been taught by Christ, through faith and force of example, to walk on the water

in which he would otherwise have drowned (Matthew 14:25–31).
The elegiac singer, however, is momentarily occupied with the
specific references rather than the Scriptural overtones of Peter's
comment, with the result that the resolution, so skillfully planted
in his evolving thought, is delayed until he has tried to interpose
a little ease by strewing imaginary flowers on Lycidas' imagined
hearse. But this evasion only brings home the horror of the
actual condition of the lost and weltering corpse. By extraordi-
nary dramatic management, it is at this point of profoundest
depression that the thought of Lycidas' body sinking to "the
bottom of the monstrous world" releases the full implication of
St. Peter's speech, and we make the leap from nature to revelation, in the great lyric peripety:

> Weep no more, woful Shepherds weep no more,
> For *Lycidas* your sorrow is not dead,
> Sunk though he be beneath the watry floar . . .
> So *Lycidas,* sunk low, but mounted high,
> Through the dear might of him that walk'd the waves. . . .

This consolation is total, where the two earlier ones were par-
tial. For one thing, we now move from the strict judgment of
merit and demerit to the God who rewards us beyond the requirements of justice by the free gift of a life eternal. Also, the
elegist has had the earlier promises of reward and retribution
by hearsay from Apollo and Peter, but now, in a passage
thronged with echoes from the Book of Revelation and soaring,
accordantly, into an assured sublimity of style, he has his own
imaginative revelation, so that he, like St. John in that Book,
might say: "And I saw a new heaven and a new earth." His
vision is of Lycidas having lost his life to find a better life in a
felicity without tears; in which even that last infirmity of noble
mind, the desire for fame, has been purged "in the blest Kingdoms meek of joy and love," the earthly inclination to Amaryllis
and Neaera has been sublimated into the "unexpressive nuptial
Song" of the marriage of the Lamb, and the pastoral properties
of grove, stream, and song serve only to shadow forth a Kingdom outside of space and beyond the vicissitude of the seasons.
But the meditation of the lyric singer, as I have said, is ultimately
concerned with the dead as they affect the living; so, by way of
the Genius of the shore, we redescend to the stylistic level of

plain utterance and conclude with the solitary piper at evening, facing with restored confidence the contingencies of a world in which the set and rise of the material sun are only the emblematic promise of another life.

IV

We are all aware by now of a considerable irony: I undertook to resolve the five types of *Lycidas* into one, and instead have added a sixth. But of course, that is all a critic can do. A critique does not give us the poem, but only a description of the poem. Whatever the ontological status of *Lycidas* as an object-in-itself, there are many possible descriptions of *Lycidas*—as many, in fact, as there are diverse critical premises and procedures which can be applied to the text.

In the bewildering proliferation of assumptions and procedures that characterizes the present age, we need a safeguard against confusion, and a safeguard as well against the sceptical temptation to throw all criticism overboard as a waste of time. I would suggest that we regard any critique of a poem as a persuasive description; that is, as an attempt, under the guise of statements of fact, to persuade the reader to look at a poem in a particular way. Thus when a critic says, with assurance, "A poem means *X*," consider him to say: "Try reading it as though it meant *X*." When he says, "*Lycidas* is really about Milton himself," quietly translate: "I recommend that you entertain the hypothesis that *Lycidas* is about Milton, and see how it applies." From this point of view, the best interpretation of *Lycidas*—we can say, if we like to use that philosophical idiom, the reading which approximates most closely to *Lycidas* as an object-in-itself—is the one among the interpretations at present available which provides the best fit to all the parts of the poem in their actual order, emphases, and emotional effects, and which is in addition consistent with itself and with what we know of Milton's literary and intellectual inheritance and his characteristic poetic procedures.[11]

The persuasive description of *Lycidas* which I have sketched must be judged by the degree to which it satisfies these criteria

[11] See R. S. Crane's analysis of critical interpretations as hypotheses for investigating the structures of poems, *The Languages of Criticism and the Structure of Poetry* (Toronto, 1953), pp. 164–183.

of correspondence and coherence. To be sure it has a serious handicap, when measured against the startling discoveries in recent years of what *Lycidas* is really about. It is singularly unexciting to be told at this date that *Lycidas* is really what it seems— a dramatic presentation of a traditional pastoral singer uttering a ritual lament and raising in its course questions about untimely death and God's providence which are resolved by the recognition that God's Kingdom is not of this world. But surely this is the great commonplace in terms of which Milton, as a thoroughly Christian poet, inevitably thought. We cannot expect his innovations, on this crucial issue, to be doctrinal; the novelty (and it is entirely sufficient to make this an immense feat of lyric invention) consists in the way that the pastoral conventions and Christian concepts are newly realized, reconciled, and dramatized in the minute particulars of this unique and splendid poem.

I would not be understood to claim that the alternative readings of *Lycidas* I have described are illegitimate, or their discoveries unrewarding. They freshen our sense of old and familiar poems, and they force readers into novel points of vantage that yield interesting insights, of which some hold good for other critical viewpoints as well. I am as susceptible as most readers to the charm of suddenly being brought to see a solidly dramatic lyric flattened into an ornate texture of thematic images, or to the thrill of the archetypal revelation whereby, as Jane Harrison described it, behind the "bright splendors" of "great things in literature" one sees moving "darker and older shapes." But in our fascination with the ultra-violet and infra-red discoveries made possible by modern speculative instruments, we must take care not to overlook the middle of the poetic spectrum. The necessary, though not sufficient condition for a competent reader of poetry remains what it has always been—a keen eye for the obvious.

The Text of *Lycidas*

The sources for the text of *Lycidas* are four: (1) the manuscript of the poem, now at Trinity College, Cambridge, carrying the cancelled superscription "Novemb: 1637" (for the most significant corrections on this manuscript, see *supra,* pp. 10–11); (2) the first published text, set in italic type, in the memorial volume *Justa Edovardo King,* 1638; (3) the second published text in *Poems of Mr. John Milton,* 1645; and (4) the third published text in *Poems upon Several Occasions,* 1673. In collation, the 1645 text emerged as the most reliable of the three versions. As can be seen from the following list, the earlier edition (1638) has by far the greatest number of variants, all of which were corrected by Milton in 1645; while the later edition (1673) is merely a reproduction of the 1645 text with a few misprints. The present edition, therefore, reproduces the 1645 text, though in six cases (ll. 63, 82, 94, 163, 178, and 183) obvious misprints and errors in punctuation have dictated the adoption of readings from the text either of 1638 or 1673, or both.

In collating the three texts, the italic type of the 1638 edition has been ignored. Variants in capitalization are not shown.

Headnote: *MS contains only the first sentence; no headnote in 1638.*

1	1638	and once more,]		6	1638	deare]
2	1638	never-sere,]		7	1638, 1673	Compells]
	1673	never sear,]		8	1638, 1673	prime,]
3	1638	come]		9	1638	(Young Lycidas!)]
4	1638	rude]			1638	peere.]
5	1638	yeare.]		12	1638	biere]

13	1638	wind]
14	1638	some]
15	1638	well]
16	1638	spring;]
17	1638, 1673	somewhat]
	1638	string:]
18	1638	deniall]
	1638	excuse.]
19	1638, 1673	some]
21	1638	passes, turn]
22	1638	shroud.]
24	1673	flock;]
	1638	rill;]
25	1638	*does not indent*
26	1638	glimmering]
27	1638	a-field]
30	1638	Oft till the ev'n-starre bright]
	1673	bright,]
31	1638	burnisht]
32	1638	rurall]
	1638	mute]
33	1638	oaten flute:]
34	1638	Satyres]
	1638	cloven heel]
36	1638	Dametas]
	1673	Damætas]
	1638	heare]
37	1638	oh]
	1638	gone,]
38	1638	gone,]
39	1638	shepherds,]
	1638	cares]
40	1638	wild]
	1638	oregrown,]
42	1638	willows]
	1638	hasil-copses green]
43	1638	seen]
47	1638	flowers]
	1638	wardrobe]
48	1638	white-thorn blowes;]
49	1638	losse]
	1638	eare.]

50	1638	*does not indent*
	1638	Nimphs,]
51	1638	ore]
	1638	your lord Lycidas?]
53	1638	the old Bards]
	1638, 1673	*Druids,*]
	1638	lie,]
54	1638	shaggie]
56	1638	Ah]
57	1638	been]
	1638	done?]
59	1673	her self]
	1638	sonne?]
60	1638	universall]
61	1638	rore]
63	1645	*Letbian*]
64	1638	*does not indent*
	1673	Alass!]
65	1673	To end]
66	1638	stridly]
	1638	thanklesse]
	1673	thankless]
	1638	Muse?]
67	1638	done as others do,]
69	1638	Hid in]
	1638	Neera's]
70	1638	spurre]
	1638	raise,]
71	1638	infirmitie]
73	1638	guerdon where]
75	1638	Furie]
76	1638	thin-spun]
	1638	life;]
77	1638	Phebus]
	1638	eares.]
78	1638	growes]
	1638	mortall]
79	1638	glistring]
80	1638	lies;]
81	1638	lives, and spreads]
	1638	eyes]
82	1638	perfect witnesse]
	1645	all judging]

	1638	Jove:]
85	1638	*does not indent*
	1638	Oh]
86	1673	vocal]
	1638	reeds;]
87	1638	mood.]
90	1638	Neptunes plea.]
91	1638	felon]
93	1638	wings,]
94	1638	blowes]
	1638	Promontorie:]
	1645	Promontory,]
95	1638	storie;]
97	1638	stray'd;]
98	1638	aire]
	1673	Air]
	1638	brine]
99	1638	play'd:]
100	1673	fatal]
	1638	bark,]
103	1638	*does not indent*
	1638	Chamus (reverend sire)]
104	1638	hairie,]
106	1638	wo;]
107	1673	Ah;]
110	1638	massie]
	1638	metalls]
112	1638	mitred]
113	1638, 1673	thee, young swain,]
114	1638	Enough]
	1638	sake]
115	1638	intrude]
	1638	climbe]
116	1638	reckoning]
118	1673	guest;]
120	1638	sheephook,]
	1638	else]
123	1638	list]
	1638	flashie]
128	1638	grimme wolf]
129	1638	devoures]
	1638	**little**]

130	1638	doore,]
131	1638	and smites]
132	1638	Return,]
	1638	past]
133	1638	return,]
135	1638, 1673	Bells,]
	1638	flowrets]
136	1638	low,]
	1638	mild]
	1638	use]
137	1638	winds]
138	1638	starre]
139	1638	enammell'd]
140	1638	turf]
141	1638	vernall flowers.]
142	1638	primerose]
	1638	dies,]
145	1638	violet,]
146	1638	well-attir'd woodbine,]
147	1638, 1673	head,]
149	1673	*Amarantus*]
153	1638	surmise;]
154	1638	whil'st]
	1638	shores]
155	1638	farre]
	1638, 1673	hurl'd,]
156	1673	Hebrides]
157	1638	the humming tide]
159	1638	vowes deni'd,]
163	1645, 1673	ruth.]
164	1638	haplesse]
165	1638	wofull shepherds, weep no more;]
167	1638	floore:]
168	1638	day-starre]
170	1638	ore]
171	1638	skie:]
172	1638	high]
173	1638, 1673, and some copies of 1645	waves;]
175	1638	oazie locks]
176	1638	And heares]
	1673	nuptial]

1638   song;]

177   *This entire line, present in MS, is omitted in 1638; restored in 1645.*

178   *This line is indented one letter in 1645, 1673.*

    1645   *him*]

    1638   above]

179   1638   troups,]

    1638   societies,]

182   1638   Now, Lycidas,]

183   1645   Hence forth]

    1638   shore]

185   1638   perillous]

    1638   floud.]

186   1638   oaks]

187   1638   gray;]

190   1638   sunne]

192   1638   blew,]

193   1638   woods]

Signature in 1638:   J.M.]

appendix two

An Annotated Reading List

Abbreviations

AJP	*American Journal of Philology*
ELH	*Journal of English Literary History*
HLQ	*Huntington Library Quarterly*
JEGP	*Journal of English and Germanic Philology*
JHI	*Journal of the History of Ideas*
MLN	*Modern Language Notes*
MLR	*Modern Language Review*
MP	*Modern Philology*
N&Q	*Notes and Queries*
PMLA	*Publications of the Modern Language Association*
PQ	*Philological Quarterly*
RES	*Review of English Studies*
SP	*Studies in Philology*
TLS	(London) *Times Literary Supplement*
UTQ	*University of Toronto Quarterly*

THE TEXT OF *LYCIDAS*

Facsimile of the Manuscript of Milton's Minor Poems, ed. William A. Wright (Cambridge, 1899), pp. 28–32. Facsimile of the manuscript of *Lycidas.*

Justa Edovardo King, ed. Ernest C. Mossner, The Facsimile Text Society: Publication No. 45 (New York, 1939), pp. 20–25. Facsimile of the first published version of *Lycidas* (1638).

Poems of Mr. John Milton, ed. Cleanth Brooks and John E. Hardy

(New York, 1951), pp. 50–55. The text of the second published version of *Lycidas* (1645).

John Milton's Complete Poetical Works Reproduced in Photographic Facsimile, ed. Harris F. Fletcher (Urbana, Ill., 1943), I, pp. 52–56, 185–189, 347–352, and 434–443. Facsimile of the manuscript and of the first three published versions of *Lycidas* (1638, 1645, 1673).

Coffin, Charles M. (ed.), *The Major Poets: English and American* (New York, 1954), pp. 155–161. The text, with notes.

Darbishire, Helen (ed.), *The Poetical Works of John Milton* (Oxford, 1955), II, 165–170. The text of *Lycidas,* in what is doubtless the best modern edition of Milton's poems.

Fletcher, Harris F. (ed.), *The Complete Poetical Works of John Milton* (Boston, 1941), pp. 113–120. The text, with notes.

Hanford, James H. (ed.), *The Poems of John Milton,* 2d ed. (New York, 1953), pp. 139–151. The text, with notes.

Hughes, Merritt Y. (ed.), *John Milton: Complete Poems and Major Prose* (New York, 1957), pp. 116–125. The text, with comprehensive notes.

Masson, David (ed.), *The Poetical Works of John Milton* (London, 1874; 2d ed., 1890), I, pp. 187–201. The text, with notes.

Patterson, Frank A. (ed.), *The Works of John Milton* (New York, 1931), I, pp. 76–83, 459–474. The text, with notes.

Todd, Henry J. (ed.), *The Poetical Works of John Milton* (London, 1801; 2d enlarged ed., 1809), VI, pp. 3–62. The text, with notes.

Verity, Arthur W. (ed.), *Milton's Ode on the Morning of Christ's Nativity, L'Allegro, Il Penseroso, and Lycidas* (London, 1891; often reprinted thereafter), pp. 119–167. The notes on the text.

ON THE TRADITION

Austin, W. B., "Milton's *Lycidas* and Two Latin Elegies by Giles Fletcher, the Elder," *SP,* XLIV (1947), 41–55. The influence of Fletcher's *Adonis* and *Elegia* on Milton.

Bailey, John C. (ed.), *English Elegies* (London and New York, 1900). An anthology.

Chambers, Sir Edmund, "The English Pastoral," in *Sir Thomas Wyatt and Some Collected Studies* (London, 1933), pp. 146–180. A comprehensive survey.

Cory, Herbert E., "The Golden Age of the Spenserian Pastoral," *PMLA,* XXV (1910), 241–267. The influence of Spenser's *Shepheardes Calender* on the English pastoral, from 1579 to c. 1700.

Godolphin, F. R. B., "Milton, *Lycidas,* and Propertius, *Elegies,* III, 7 [*On the Drowning of Paetus*]," *MLN,* XLIX (1934), 162–166.

Greg, Walter W., *Pastoral Poetry and Pastoral Drama* (London, 1906). The best work on the historical development of European pastoralism.

Hall, H. M., *Idylls of Fishermen* (New York, 1914). A study of piscatory eclogues, especially Sannazaro's and Phineas Fletcher's.

Hamilton, H. F., "The Sources of Milton's *Lycidas,*" *Sewanee Review,* XVII (1909), 235–240. The influence of the *canzone* on Milton; more fully studied by F. T. Prince, *supra,* pp. 153 ff.

Harrison, Thomas P., Jr. (ed.), *The Pastoral Elegy,* with English translations by Harry J. Leon (Austin, Tex., 1939). A convenient anthology containing all the poems discussed by Professor Hanford (*supra,* pp. 27–55), as well as the best English pastoral elegies since *Lycidas* (Shelley's *Adonais,* Arnold's *Thyrsis*); with one of the finest brief surveys of the tradition (pp. 1–24). For other studies by Professor Harrison, see especially "Spenser and the Earlier Pastoral Elegy," *Texas Studies in English,* XIII (1933), 36–53; "Spenser, Ronsard, and Bion," *MLN,* XLIX (1934), 139–145; and "The Latin Pastorals of Milton and Castiglione," *PMLA,* L (1935), 480–493.

Hughes, Merritt Y., "Spenser and the Greek Pastoral Triad," *SP,* XX (1923), 184–215. The influence of Theocritus, Bion, and Moschus on *The Shepheardes Calender,* as tempered by Renaissance pastoralism.

Hughes, Merritt Y., *Virgil and Spenser,* University of California Publications in English, II (1929), Part I, "The Pastorals."

Lang, Andrew, "Introduction," *Theocritus, Bion and Moschus* (London, 1880), pp. xi–xliii.

Lee, Sir Sidney, *The French Renaissance in England* (New York, 1910). Including an account of the literary relationship between Marot and the English pastoralists.

Montgomery, Walter A., "The *Epitaphium Damonis* in the Stream of the Classical Lament," in N. M. Caffee and T. A. Kirby, *Studies for William A. Read* (Baton Rouge, La., 1940), pp. 207–220. A superficial treatment of the literary sources of Milton's Latin elegy.

Mustard, Wilfred P., "Later Echoes of the Greek Bucolic Poets," *AJP,* XXX (1909), 245–283. A perceptive study of the continuity of the tradition.

Norlin, George, "The Conventions of the Pastoral Elegy," *AJP,*

XXXII (1911), 294–312. A summary of the traditional conventions, with numerous illustrative quotations.

Rand, E. K., *The Magical Art of Virgil* (Cambridge, Mass., 1931), Chs. III–V. A study of the Eclogues.

Renwick, W. L. (ed.), *The Shepheardes Calender* (London, 1930). The best edition of Spenser's eclogues, with an adequate commentary.

Sandys, Sir John, "The Literary Sources of Milton's *Lycidas*," *Transactions of the Royal Society of Literature*, 2d Series, XXXII (1914), 233–264. A collection of the poem's allusions and references.

Shackford, Martha H., "A Definition of the Pastoral Idyll," *PMLA*, XIX (1904), 583–592.

Weitzmann, Francis W., "Notes on the Elizabethan *Elegie*," *PMLA*, L (1935), 435–443.

ON THE POEM

The most curious aspect of the commentaries on *Lycidas* is the enormous number of articles and brief notes on the "two-handed engine" (l. 130). Research has yielded parallels in the writings of such diverse figures as Gregory the Great, Dante, John of Salisbury, Savonarola, Du Bartas, Jehan Gerard, Phineas Fletcher, Donne, Thomas Adams, and Robert Burton; while the riddle itself has been variously interpreted as the two Houses of Parliament, or liberty as wielded by them; the temporal and spiritual authority of the Court of High Commission; the destructive power of the imminent civil war; "Puritan zeal" in general; the combined forces of England and Scotland, or of France and Spain; the Catholic Church; the pastoral staff; the keys of Heaven and Hell given to St. Peter; the lock on St. Peter's door; St. Peter's sword (Matt. 26:51, John 18:10); the "sharp two-edged sword" of the Johannine vision (Rev. 1:16, 2:12); the sword of Divine Justice (Ezekiel 21:9–17), particularly as wielded by Michael "with huge two-handed sway" (*Paradise Lost*, VI, 251); the axe in general, or, specifically, the axe that was "laid unto the root of the trees" (Matt. 3:10, Luke 3:9); the rod of Christ's anger; the Word of God; the Son of God; the scythe of Time; Man "in his dual capacity of labour and prayer"; the sheep-hook; the iron flail of Talus (*Faerie Queene*, V, i, 12; etc.); the temple of Janus; and so on and so forth. Readers of *Lycidas*, curious enough to look further into the matter, are

referred to the conjectures of the various editors of Milton as well
as to the comments contained in the following articles and notes:

E. C. Baldwin, *MLN,* XXXIII (1918), 211–215; Lowell W. Coo-
lidge, *PQ,* XXIX (1950), 444–445; Donald C. Dorian, *PMLA,*
XLV (1930), 204–215; J. Milton French, *MLN,* LXVIII (1953),
229–231; E. S. Fussell, *N&Q,* CXCIII (1948), 338–339; William
J. Grace, *SP,* LII (1955), 583–589; Leon Howard, *HLQ,* XV
(1952), 173–184; R. E. Hughes, *N&Q,* II (1955), 58–59; Maurice
Hussey, *N&Q,* CXCII (1948), 503; Maurice Kelley, *N&Q,*
CLXXXI (1941), 273; Edward S. LeComte, *SP,* XLVII (1950),
589–606, and XLIX (1952), 548–550; George G. Loane, *N&Q,*
CLXXXI (1941), 320; Kenneth McKenzie, *Italica,* XX (1943),
121–126; Esmond L. Marilla, *PMLA,* LXVII (1952), 1181–84;
Charles G. Osgood, *RES,* I (1925), 339–341; Harry F. Robins,
RES, V (1954), 25–26; R. J. Schoeck, *N&Q,* II (1955), 235–237;
Donald A. Stauffer, *MLR,* XXXI (1936), 57–60; John M. Stead-
man, *N&Q,* III (1956), 249–250; Thomas B. Stroup, *N&Q,* VI
(1959), 366–367; Marian H. Studley, *English Journal,* coll. edn.,
XXVI (1937), 148–151; E. M. W. Tillyard, *Milton* (London,
1930), App. F; Mindele C. Treip, *N&Q,* VI (1959), 364–366;
W. Arthur Turner, *JEGP,* XLIX (1950), 562–565; George W.
Whiting, *Milton and this Pendant World* (Austin, Tex., 1958),
pp. 29–58; and numerous contributions in the *Athenaeum* (June 30,
1900, p. 815, by H. L.; April 14, 1906, pp. 451–52, by W. H. Ward;
April 28, 1906, p. 515, by M.D.; and May 5, 1906, p. 547, by G. H.
Powell) and particularly in *TLS* (June 16, 1927, p. 424, by G. M.
Harper; July 28, 1927, p. 520, by N. W. Hill; November 22, 1928,
pp. 909–910, by K. N. Colville; December 6, 1928, p. 965, by
Nowell Smith; April 11, 1929, pp. 295–296, by A. H. T. Clarke;
April 25, 1929, p. 338, by G. M. Trevelyan; June 12, 1930, p. 496,
by C. W. Brodribb; April 25, 1936, p. 356, by Heinrich Mutsch-
mann; August 29, 1936, p. 697, by A. F. Pollard; June 5, 1943, p.
271, by C. W. Brodribb; June 12, 1943, p. 283, by K. C. Tomlin-
son and W. R. Dunstan; June 19, 1943, p. 295, by K. A. Esdaile;
and July 3, 1943, p. 319, by H. Beckett).

For other studies of *Lycidas* primarily and the *Epitaphium Damonis* incidentally, the following studies may be consulted:

Adams, Henry H., "The Development of the Flower Passage in
  Lycidas," *MLN,* LXV (1950), 468–472. Milton revised ll. 142–
  150 in order to depart from Shakespeare's parallel passage (*The
  Winter's Tale,* IV, iv, 113–132) and to reinforce the funeral idea.
Adams, Robert M., *Ikon: John Milton and the Modern Critics*
  (Ithaca, N.Y., 1955), pp. 160–162. A caveat against the exces-
  sive scholarship that threatens to drown *Lycidas* in a sea of un-
  important details.

Allen, Don Cameron, "The Translation of the Myth: The Epicedia and *Lycidas*," in *The Harmonious Vision* (Baltimore, 1954), pp. 41–70. A comprehensive study of *Lycidas* in the light of various traditional concepts and ideas. See further "Milton's Alpheus," *MLN*, LXXI (1956), 172–173, on "the possible anagogical implications" of Milton's allusion.

Banks, Theodore H., "A Source for *Lycidas,* 154–158," *MLN*, LXII (1947), 39–40. The source was, probably, Shakespeare's *Pericles*, III, i, 57–65.

Barker, Arthur, "The Pattern of Milton's *Nativity Ode*," *UTQ*, X (1941), 171–172. Brief but important comments on *Lycidas*, calling attention to the poem's organization; for a quotation from this essay, see *supra*, p. 126.

Battestin, Martin C., "John Crowe Ransom and *Lycidas*: A Reappraisal," *College English*, XVII (1956), 223–228. A severe criticism of "A Poem Nearly Anonymous," *supra*, pp. 64–81.

Berkeley, David S., "The Revision of the Orpheus Passage in *Lycidas*," *N&Q*, V (1958), 335–336. The possible reasons for the revision of ll. 58–61.

Brett, R. L., "Milton's *Lycidas*," in *Reason and Imagination* (London, 1960), pp. 21–50. A superficial survey of Milton's relation to Christian humanism, concluding that *Lycidas* is concerned with "the battle between the reason and the senses; between humanism and Puritanism; between the Renaissance and the Reformation conceptions of poetry."

Brooks, E. L., "*Lycidas* and Bible Pastoral," *N&Q*, III (1956), 67–68. On the similarities between Peter's speech (ll. 113–131) and Ezekiel 34.

Bush, Douglas, *English Literature in the Earlier Seventeenth Century* (Oxford, 1945), pp. 366–368. Observations on *Lycidas*, which can be supplemented with Professor Bush's discussions of Milton in *Mythology and the Renaissance Tradition in English Poetry* (Minneapolis, 1932), Ch. XIV, and *The Renaissance and English Humanism* (Toronto, 1939), Ch. IV.

Coffman, George R., "The Parable of the Good Shepherd, *De Contemptu Mundi,* and *Lycidas*: Excerpts from a Chapter on Literary History and Culture," *ELH*, III (1936), 101–113. The persistence of the Johannine parable (John 10:1–28) among preachers, reformers, and artists.

Cowper, William, *Correspondence,* ed. Thomas Wright (London, 1904), I, 164–165. The letter to the Rev. William Unwin, October 31, 1779, on Johnson's observations on *Lycidas;* partly quoted in the Preface, *supra*.

De Beer, E. S., "Milton's Old Damætas," *N&Q*, CXCIV (1949),

336–337. Doubts whether this refers to a particular person. Cf. M. H. Nicolson, *infra*.

Diekhoff, John S., "Milton's Prosody in the Poems of the Trinity Manuscript," *PMLA*, LIV (1939), 177–183. The effect of Milton's revisions on the prosody of *Lycidas*. Cf. the same author's "Critical Activity of the Poetic Mind: John Milton," *PMLA*, LV (1940), 748–772.

Finney, Gretchen, "A Musical Background for *Lycidas*," *HLQ*, XV (1952), 325–350. Compares *Lycidas* with seventeenth-century Italian musical drama.

Fox, Robert C., "Milton's *Lycidas*, 192–193," *Explicator*, IX (1951), No. 54. A reminder that the blue in the shepherd's mantle (l. 192) is the traditional symbol of hope (cf. Spenser's Speranza, *Faerie Queene*, I, x, 14).

Fraser, G. S., "Approaches to *Lycidas*," in *The Living Milton*, ed. by Frank Kermode (London, 1960), pp. 32–54. "Random reflections" on the poem's art and emotional impact. Largely a refutation of Robert Graves, *infra*.

French, J. Milton, "The Digressions in Milton's *Lycidas*," *SP*, L (1953), 485–490. Lines 64–84 and 113–131 are "probably the core of the poem."

Friedland, Louis S., "Milton's *Lycidas* and Spenser's *Ruines of Time*," *MLN*, XXVII (1912), 246–250. Spenser's elaboration of themes later used in *Lycidas*.

Graves, Robert, "The Ghost of Milton," *The Common Asphodel* (London, 1949), esp. pp. 321–325. Violently opposed to Milton ("a monster and a renegade"), the author concludes that *Lycidas* is "a poem strangled by art."

Hanford, James H., "The Youth of Milton: An Interpretation of his Early Literary Development," in *Studies in Shakespeare, Milton, and Donne*, University of Michigan Publications: Language and Literature, I (1925), 89–163. One of the finest older essays still of considerable value.

Hardy, John Edward, "Reconsiderations: I. *Lycidas*," *Kenyon Review*, VII (1945), 99–113. The "blueprint" for the essay printed *supra*, pp. 136–152.

Knight, G. Wilson, "The Frozen Labyrinth: An Essay on Milton," in *The Burning Oracle* (London, 1939), p. 70. Typical of the attacks against the unity of *Lycidas* ("it is an accumulation of magnificent fragments").

LeComte, Edward S., *Yet Once More: Verbal and Psychological Pattern in Milton* (New York, 1953), pp. 24–26. Milton's "technical delight" in combining various forms of verbal repetition charges *Lycidas* with emotion.

Lloyd, Michael, "Justa Edovardo King," *N&Q,* V (1958), 432–434. Examines the possibility that the memorial volume on King was intended as "a unified work within a flexible comprehensive design."

Lynskey, Winifred, "A Critic in Action: Mr. Ransom," *College English,* V (1944), 242–243. An emotional reaction to "A Poem Nearly Anonymous," *supra,* pp. 64–81.

Mabbott, Thomas O., "Milton's *Lycidas,* lines 164 and 183–185," *Explicator,* V (1947), No. 26. The lines refer to Palaemon (cf. *supra,* p. 187n).

Machen, Arthur, *The Hill of Dreams* (New York, 1923), pp. 137–138. A novelist's attempt to account for the "magic" of *Lycidas:* despite its "touches of greasy Puritanism," the poem is "probably the most perfect piece of pure literature in existence; because every word and phrase and line [are] sonorous, ringing and echoing with music."

McKenzie, Kenneth, "Echoes of Dante in Milton's *Lycidas,*" *Italica,* XX (1943), 121–126. Relates *Lycidas,* ll. 108–131, to *Paradiso,* XXIX, 70–126. Cf. P. Toynbee, *infra.*

Marks, Emerson R., "Milton's *Lycidas,*" *Explicator,* IX (1951), No. 44. On Milton's distinction between water as killer and water as nourisher of life.

Mayerson, Caroline W., "The Orpheus Image in *Lycidas,*" *PMLA,* LXIV (1949), 189–207. An interesting study of Renaissance interpretations of the Orpheus legend (ll. 58–63).

Nicolson, Marjorie H., "Milton's 'Old Damoetas,'" *MLN,* XLI (1926), 293–300. Identifies "old Damoetas" with Joseph Mead (suggested by others: William Chappell, Robert Gell). Cf. E. S. de Beer, *supra.*

Ogden, H. V. S., "The Principles of Variety and Contrast in Seventeenth Century Aesthetics, and Milton's Poetry," *JHI,* X (1949), 159–182. A consideration of *Lycidas* as "a disciplined interweaving of contrasting passages into a unified whole."

Oman, Sir Charles, "Of Poor Mr. King, John Milton, and Certain Friends," *Cornhill Magazine,* CLVI (1937), 577–587. On "the companions of *Lycidas*" in the memorial volume of 1638.

Oras, Ants, "Milton's Early Rhyme Schemes and the Structure of *Lycidas,*" *MP,* LII (1954), 12–22. An excellent study of Milton's "mastery in making rhyme express mood and matter with force and precision."

Rand, E. K., "Milton in Rustication," *SP,* XIX (1922), 109–135. Possibly the finest appreciation of Milton's Latin poems, including the *Epitaphium Damonis.*

Rinehart, Keith, "A Note on the First Fourteen Lines of Milton's

Lycidas," *N&Q,* CXCVIII (1953), 103. "It seems probable that Milton deliberately approximated the sonnet form as if to express by breaking somewhat from that metre and rigid rhyme scheme, evidence of the fact that he is 'forcing' himself poetically."

Ross, Malcolm M., "Milton and the Protestant Aesthetic: The Early Poems," in *Poetry and Dogma* (New Brunswick, N.J., 1954), pp. 201–204. Milton's peculiar use of Christian symbolism makes *Lycidas* "a thoroughly Protestant achievement."

Ruskin, John, *Sesame and Lilies,* I, 20–24 (London, 1951), pp. 41–48. Observations on *Lycidas,* ll. 108–129, of which the most famous is perhaps the comment on "blind mouths" (l. 119): "A 'Bishop' means 'a person who sees.' A 'Pastor' means 'a person who feeds.' The most unbishoply character a man can have is therefore to be blind. The most unpastoral is, instead of feeding, to want to be fed,—to be a Mouth." (For an exception to this interpretation, see John A. Himes, *MLN,* XXXV [1920], 441.)

Saintsbury, George, "Milton and the Grand Style," in *Milton Memorial Lectures* (London, 1909), pp. 83–107; reprinted in *Collected Essays and Papers* (London, 1923), III, pp. 175–196. An attempt to define "the grand style," largely concerned with *Lycidas.*

Saunders, J. W., "Milton, Diomede and Amaryllis," *ELH,* XXII 1955), 254–286. With *Lycidas* (ll. 64–69) as a starting point, the author studies the relationship of the poet to his audience.

Scholderer, V., *TLS,* June 28, 1947, p. 323. Suggests that *Lycidas* was written in a single day. This untenable theory, attacked by Richard Bell and Parry Michael in *TLS,* July 12, 1947, p. 351, was further defended in *TLS,* July 26, 1947, p. 379; mercifully, however, the issue was thereafter permitted to die.

Steadman, John M., "St. Peter and Ecclesiastical Satire," *N&Q,* V (1958), 141–142. Milton's use of St. Peter has a precedent in a fifteenth-century Italian play.

Stroup, Thomas B., *"Lycidas* **and the Marinell Story,"** in *SAMLA Studies in Milton,* ed. J. M. Patrick (Gainesville, Fla., 1953), pp. 100–113. The poem's "intellectual frame of reference" illustrated by its echoes of *The Faerie Queene,* esp. III, iv.

Sypher, Wylie, "The Metaphysicals and the Baroque," *Partisan Review,* XI (1944), 3–17. Discusses, with illustrative quotations from *Lycidas,* Milton's place in the mannerist tradition that includes Caravaggio, El Greco, Rubens, Rembrandt, Michelangelo, Bernini, Wren, *et al.*

Thompson, W. Lawrence, "The Source of the Flower Passage in *Lycidas,*" *N&Q,* CXCVII (1952), 97–99. In lines 142–150, Milton was indebted to Ben Johnson's masque *Pan's Anniversary*. Cf. H. H. Adams, *supra*.

Tillyard, E. M. W., *The Miltonic Setting* (London, 1938), pp. 35–42; and *Poetry Direct and Oblique*, rev. ed. (London, 1945), pp. 81–84. An extension of the comments made *supra*, pp. 58 ff.

Toynbee, Paget, *Dante in English Literature* (New York, 1909), I, pp. 123–124. Relates *Lycidas*, ll. 108–131, to *Paradiso*, XXVII, 19 ff. Cf. K. McKenzie, *supra*.

Waddell, Helen (trans.), *Lament for Damon* (privately printed, 1943). In a note prefixed to her translation, Miss Waddell answers principally Dr. Johnson's charge that there is "little grief" in *Lycidas*.

Wagenknecht, Edward, "Milton in *Lycidas*," *College English*, VII (1946), 393–397. The poem is concerned with the problem of evil "in one of its most acute forms."

Wallerstein, Ruth, "Rhetoric in the English Renaissance: Two Elegies," *English Institute Essays 1948* (New York, 1949), pp. 153–178. A study of *Lycidas* and Donne's *Elegie on ... Prince Henry* in the light of the contemporary theory of rhetoric; greatly expanded in the perceptive *Studies in Seventeenth-century Poetic* (Madison, Wis., 1950), Part I, "The Laureate Hearse: The Funeral Elegy and Seventeenth-century Aesthetic," including a reconsideration of *Lycidas* and a discussion of the memorial tributes to Edward King by John Cleveland and Joseph Beaumont (pp. 96–114).

Whiting, George W., *Milton's Literary Milieu* (Chapel Hill, N.C., 1939), pp. 101–107. The geographical references in *Lycidas* indicate Milton's "particularly close" familiarity with the maps and explanatory comments of Ortelius and Camden.

Woodhouse, A. S. P., *Milton the Poet* (Toronto and Vancouver, 1955), pp. 9–10. Brief but perceptive comments, arguing that the complex pattern of *Lycidas* is based on "the dynamic of the Christian monody, the transition from mourning to consolation effected by the conception of immortality," and that fundamentally "Milton's mind travels from the particular in the death of Edward King to the general enigma [of the promising youthful life prematurely cut off] and back again to the particular, this time in his own career, subject as it must be to the hazards of time and fortune." See further the same author's "Milton's Pastoral Monodies," in M. E. White (ed.), *Studies in Honour of Gilbert Norwood* (Toronto, 1952), pp. 261–278, a consideration of the way the tradition became "a vehicle for Milton's profoundest emotions and an instrument, not indeed for solving, but for transcending his problems."